D0396407

Skin in the Game

*How Putting Yourself First
Today Will Revolutionize
Health Care Tomorrow*

John Hammergren
with Phil Harkins

WILEY
John Wiley & Sons, Inc.

Copyright © 2008 by John Hammergren and Phil Harkins. All rights reserved.

Published by John Wiley & Sons, Inc., Hoboken, New Jersey.
Published simultaneously in Canada.

No part of this publication may be reproduced, stored in a retrieval system, or transmitted in any form or by any means, electronic, mechanical, photocopying, recording, scanning, or otherwise, except as permitted under Section 107 or 108 of the 1976 United States Copyright Act, without either the prior written permission of the Publisher, or authorization through payment of the appropriate per-copy fee to the Copyright Clearance Center, Inc., 222 Rosewood Drive, Danvers, MA 01923, (978) 750–8400, fax (978) 646–8600, or on the web at www.copyright.com. Requests to the Publisher for permission should be addressed to the Permissions Department, John Wiley & Sons, Inc., 111 River Street, Hoboken, NJ 07030, (201) 748–6011, fax (201) 748–6008, or online at http://www.wiley.com/go/permissions.

Limit of Liability/Disclaimer of Warranty: While the publisher and authors have used their best efforts in preparing this book, they make no representations or warranties with respect to the accuracy or completeness of the contents of this book and specifically disclaim any implied warranties of merchantability or fitness for a particular purpose. No warranty may be created or extended by sales representatives or written sales materials. The advice and strategies contained herein may not be suitable for your situation. You should consult with a professional where appropriate. Neither the publisher nor authors shall be liable for any loss of profit or any other commercial damages, including but not limited to special, incidental, consequential, or other damages.

For general information on our other products and services or for technical support, please contact our Customer Care Department within the United States at (800) 762–2974, outside the United States at (317) 572–3993 or fax (317) 572–4002.

Wiley also publishes its books in a variety of electronic formats. Some content that appears in print may not be available in electronic books. For more information about Wiley products, visit our web site at www.wiley.com.

ISBN 978–0–470–26278–8

Printed in the United States of America
10 9 8 7 6 5 4 3 2 1

Contents

Foreword   v

Acknowledgments   ix

Introduction A Thousand Miles of Health Care
              and the Last Two Feet   1

Chapter 1   Unmanaged Care   7

Chapter 2   From Tree Bark and Roots to Bar Codes
              and Robots   23

Chapter 3   Why We Go to the Hospital Today and Why
              We Will Go There Less Often in the Future   47

Chapter 4   The Doctor Will See You Now   83

Chapter 5   Accounting for Care   113

Chapter 6   How Technology Is Putting the Patient
              at the Center of Care   143

Chapter 7   The Blueprint for Change   161

Appendix   Resources, Web Sites, Tips, and Guidelines
              for Educating Yourself   187

Notes   209

References   211

Index   217

Foreword

In 1988, I founded Linkage, Inc., a company with the primary
objective to improve organizations worldwide through the devel
opment of strong leaders and leadership teams. Since then, we
have partnered with companies worldwide from virtually every industry and have concluded from our studies that it is effective leadership
that transforms organizations, and in some cases even industries.
Further, we have learned that radical change doesn't happen through
evolution. It is leaders who blaze the trail forward to real change by
taking charge and putting skin in the game. From early on, Linkage,
Inc. has held close ties to the health care industry, and I consider myself
lucky to have interacted with and served some of the finest hospitals,
providers, insurers, universities, and distributors from all over the world.
It has been amazing to observe the great care, the advances in medicine, and the totally dedicated leaders who take on the challenges of
delivering health care to now more than a quarter of a billion people
in the United States.

It was almost 10 years ago that I first became acquainted with
McKesson Corporation, a health care services company with over $100
billion in sales and an international company with a grand vision to

facilitate an American health care revolution. Over the past decade, I have become familiar with the leadership and rich 175-year history of the company, largely through my close working relationship with John Hammergren, McKesson's CEO.

Several years ago John and I discussed his views on the state of American health care, and what needed to change to avert the looming collapse of the system as we know it today. I was struck with his clear thinking regarding what was in store for our nation's future and his strong leadership around the steps we should take to reinvent health care in this country.

John and I were both tired of hearing how bad health care was in the United States and even more suspicious of the quick solutions that seemed to end up with "Let's move to a government-run system." In fact, it had become our strong conviction that health care in America is not broken; it is stalled, stuck in place, and needs a big push to get it going again. I was so inspired by my discussions with John that I encouraged him to offer his message in a book and thereby inspire the health care debate in a larger way. I pledged my personal time and the considerable resources of my company to co-write this book with John.

Skin in the Game is the result of our efforts.

Throughout the chapters that follow, it will be John's voice and conviction that you hear telling the story of American health care, backed by the findings of an independent research team set up specifically for this project. Our study began close to home with the McKesson story, which is fascinating in its own right and provides a colorful backdrop for the chain of historic events that have helped shape our health care system over the past two centuries. Along the way, we examined all areas of what has come to be our health care industry and discovered a number of guiding principles, most notably a simple, overarching goal for which to strive: *accessible health care for all that is cost-effective, safe, reliable, and patient-centered, provided in a way that encourages improvement in quality and delivery and the quest for new medicines and best practice standards.*

This is what we all want. Yet this goal can be realized only with the help of strong leaders who have the conviction to see us through the dramatic changes that will reshape the country's health care system in the coming years. That's why we have called this book *Skin in the*

Game—because it's going to take the personal involvement and support of each and every one of us to get things going and keep them going in the desired direction.

Each of us will at some point in our lives be touched by the health care industry. My own story is typical. A dozen years ago, my wife of 30 years was taken from our family because of the onslaught of an aggressive leukemia. She received the best care available at the time during her long fight, yet I know that the treatment she received then is already considered ancient history today. In just a few short years we have witnessed incredible advances in treatments that have and will continue to grant us longer, healthier, and more fulfilling lives. I want to see this trend accelerate tenfold in the future because I don't want to see future generations of families go through the same painful loss I experienced. This book is a wake-up call for anyone not currently involved in this important national dialogue.

We did not write this book for the sake of publicity or for monetary gain. In fact, all of our proceeds from the book will go to charity. Our motive is to take advantage of a rare opportunity to share a solution-based point of view, one that will bring about continuous, measurable change that will noticeably improve our lives over the next few years.

Throughout this book, while telling the story of health care, we have made an effort to lay out the most important actions that citizens and leaders alike must undertake to actualize the aforementioned common goal. We must get the right people involved doing the right things, and we must outline and execute a plan of attack that gets us to the place where we ultimately want to be. These steps are universal and have been taken countless times in many other industries. Now is the time for us as a nation to take control of our health care industry, and the only way to do that is by getting personally involved—or, in other words, putting some skin in the game.

—Phil Harkins

Acknowledgments

There are customarily acknowledgments in books that recognize those who made contributions. This book has so many to acknowledge that it will not be possible to list all who provided input, ideas, perspective, and information along the way. There were medical care providers, academics, scholars, policy makers, thought leaders, and researchers—entire teams of very important contributors including:

Our Original Team

All good things begin with a powerful group who organize thinking and delineate clear paths to get work done. This began one weekend over 18 months ago when a core team gathered to discuss the scope of our thinking around health care. We believed that a clear message around the American health care system—an optimistic viewpoint that focuses on achievable solutions—was much needed. We concluded that the story of our health care system in itself is a rich and interesting part of the American culture, and that many of the answers we seek are embedded within this story. We knew it would require this task force to keep teams of researchers, writers, and organizers engaged and committed. Without this group there would not be a book.

We especially wish to thank Paul Kirincic who believed so deeply in the project and stayed committed—working side by side with the various teams and becoming a passionate champion for everyone involved. Paul, you were the true believer. Thank you for your ideas, hard work, and valuable input. You were the glue of our team.

At the meeting, Keith Hollihan, an accomplished author and master of historical prose, participated and offered immeasurable advice and perspective. He spearheaded the proposal and drafting of many of the exciting narrative stories. There would be no book of this quality without Keith.

B.G. Dilworth was a considerable force in grounding our team with clarity from which we were able to present our ideas to our publisher. He acted as consultant, guide, proofreader, and counsel throughout the entire process. Thank you for never giving up on us, and for your confidence and strength.

Our editor, Deb Englander, from John Wiley & Sons, believed in our concept, supported our efforts, and helped us through the rigorous publishing process.

Our research team proved to be an outstanding group and a firm link to the historical truths that define our clear message around health care. The complexity of the American health care system is world known. We knew it would take a special team of tireless warriors who would dig in and uncover the most prescient evidence to support the very principles of the book. From them we found notable stories that we believe enliven our collective message—stories like "The Abigail Story" and the account of the notable Dr. Codman who had the answer before our country was ever ready. To our team: so much thanks to Stacy Thayer, for a year of invaluable work, and to Justin Bourke, for nights, weekends, and non-stop effort on this project. And thanks as well to Jeff McCusker, whose resourcefulness made an immeasurable impact for the team.

Those Inside of McKesson

The McKesson executive team's ideas and thoughts have guided the content of this book from the very beginning: Jeff Campbell, Paul Kirincic, Paul Julian, Marc Owen, Pam Pure, Laureen Seeger, Randy

Spratt, Patrick Blake, John Figueroa, Duncan James, Domenic Pilla, Nigel Rees, Emad Rizk, Sunny Sanyal, and Brian Tyler.

There were a number of additional dedicated individuals from McKesson who deserve heartfelt appreciation for their time and professional advice: Billie Waldo, R.N., Giovanni Collela, M.D., Jackie Mitus, M.D., Mary Beth Navarra, Michael Fillion, Michael Myers, Paul Work, Sandeep Wadhwa, M.D., Tim Canning, Tim Caver, and Tom Leonard.

And we acknowledge the more than 30,000 employees of McKesson, as they enter the company's 175th year in business and place their own mark on health care.

Those Outside of McKesson

Special thanks to the board members, especially Dr. David Lawrence, who provided invaluable information, a wealth of input on the front end, and then went beyond expectations and helped enormously to shape the final writing though his careful reading, edits, and critical review of the text.

And to the hospital administrators and health care representatives who not only contributed through their sage input and advice, but contribute every day by serving as an unshakable example of the best aspects of the American health care system.

These core providers, administrators, managers, and policymakers took the time to share their solutions and gave us help in piecing together our message: Brian Day, M.D., Debra Gibson D.TCM, L.Ac, Colleen Brophy, M.D., William Stead, M.D., Darrell Kirch, M.D., Philip Alexakos, Jeffrey Brickman, Joseph Perras, M.D., Laine Dilworth, Phillip Rodgers, M.D., Robert Perras, D.C., Stephen Alexakos, Jayne Morrissey, Mike Halter, John Lloyd, Edward Schottland, and Nahum Vishniavsky, M.D.

Finally, thanks to those that read and edited materials and drafts, and challenged us with their sound advice and unwavering commitment to quality: Diane Cierpial, Wendy Hammergren, Ellen Rosenberg, and Kate Rohrbach.

Introduction

A Thousand Miles of Health Care and the Last Two Feet

Where I grew up in small-town Minnesota, we had convenient, local, personal health care. The family doctor, the local hospital, and the pharmacist on Main Street were all connected. They all knew each other, and they all knew me. Health care was not perfect. Human error was a major part of the gamble. Medical practice lacked today's medical science. We didn't know as much about prevention and wellness in those days. If you needed special treatment, you were looking at big out-of-pocket expenses, and probably travel and extended time away from home, since the advanced facilities and surgeons were almost exclusively housed in major cities. Living to age 65 in decent shape was considered a pretty good life, and if you got seriously sick or were chronically ill, things were grim.

I saw a lot of the apparatus of health care, firsthand and from the bottom up, as a young teenager. My father was a traveling medical supply salesman. He fostered connections with hospitals, doctors, and pharmacists all over the state, and in the summers I would sometimes

1

join him on business trips, waiting in doctors' offices while he spoke with physicians, going out to dinner with him and his customers in the evenings. There wasn't much in the way of technology then—I still remember janitors resharpening hypodermic needles in the backs of storerooms—but there was tremendous connection. My father's customers were friends. Doctors and pharmacists ordered supplies that they needed for the care of their friends and neighbors. Human caring—the most prominent reason why people get into health care in the first place—was front and center.

Probably the most formative event in my life was the death of my father when I was 16. He was misdiagnosed with a gastrointestinal disorder, and died from cancer 12 months later. It was not an easy death, and not an easy life for my mother and me after he was gone. But my father was well cared for while he was ill. When my mother passed away a few short years ago, the experience of her sickness and death seemed less intimate, more impersonal, and more clinical than my father's passing. Perhaps I was just older and hardened to what I had witnessed over the years. For many of us, this kind of feeling reinforces the impression that technology and sophistication don't always mean better care, even though they can and should. The caregivers seldom know us outside the care setting, and we see them infrequently. They are rushed and seem less connected to us as patients than they used to be and certainly less than we believe they should be.

When I traveled with my father on his sales trips, I never imagined that I would end up with a career in health care, but that's how it worked out. I held management and executive positions in a number of prominent health care companies before joining McKesson Corporation in 1996, where I'm now president and CEO. I have had the privilege of a lifetime watching health care from an insider's business perspective. My vantage point at McKesson gives me a unique overview of the entire industry.

In the grand scheme, our health care system is a wonder of the world, a scientific marvel, one of the most incredible accomplishments of any civilization. But if you're sick and need care, it doesn't matter how far health care has come in its evolutionary history; you just worry about the last two feet—the distance between you and your doctor as you sit and discuss your condition and how best to treat it.

In this book, we're going to tell you the story of our health care system, where it came from and where it's going. You may not believe it, but all of the things you dread most about visiting the doctor or hospital these days—lengthy waits, bureaucratic paperwork, hurried examinations, and the inevitable insurance hassles (if you're lucky enough to have insurance)— will soon be a thing of the past. We are on the verge of a health care revolution in terms of cost, quality of care, and customer service. You'll know those changes have arrived when your doctor, along with every other member of your personal health care team, is connected and informed about you and your health, and you feel cared for and cared about instead of that they couldn't care less. In the near future, the health care system that right now seems so sprawling and impersonal will be centered on you.

The driving force behind that shift will be the market, and you will need to put skin in the game in order to assure yourself the best care today and the best opportunities for care in the future. Patients, as customers, will have the incentive to choose their care providers based on information about value—meaning cost, quality, and convenience. Physicians, hospitals, and insurers will compete for your health care business by offering better service and constant innovation. The government, with its swelling ranks of retired baby boomers threatening to bankrupt Medicare, will be motivated to let the market do what it does best while enabling access for all. Those changes are coming. You can prepare for them by understanding how our health care system is evolving and what your role will be. This book will give you the tactics and the mind-set to become an informed consumer in control of your own health-related decisions once and for all.

Is our system still the best in the world? I believe it is, despite the problems that need to be overcome. But it isn't where we currently stand that is important; it is where we are headed. The worry with any complex system facing evolving challenges is regression. If we do nothing, if we maintain the status quo and stifle innovations in service and technology, then we actually move backwards. The debate over the direction of health care in this country has incited passionate arguments from all sides. Many options are being put forward, but however we choose to change and grow, I believe we should all strive to achieve a system in which:

- **Everyone** gets the care they need, when they need it.
- **Patients** are positioned at the center of their own care decisions, informed and empowered to make choices based on quality, convenience, and cost.

- **Care providers** coordinate referrals, tests, appointments, treatments, follow-ups, and payments seamlessly.
- **Errors**, waste, and long waits are eliminated.
- **Innovations** in diagnosis, treatment, and delivery are constantly being made and quickly spread, creating new standards of best practice that benefit everyone.

Sounds great, you say; now, how much will it cost? The historical solution to overhauling health care has been to throw more money at our problems while also, ironically, attempting to contain costs. Health care already eats up 15.3 percent of our gross domestic product (GDP) at \$2.2 trillion a year, and that number is projected to reach \$4 trillion by 2016. We all want the best health care money can buy, but who can afford it? In that dilemma the arguments start and the sense of hopelessness about the future returns.

As you will learn in this book, the five points we have listed describe the health care system that is on the way, not in the distant future but in the next five to 10 years. While such a claim may seem revolutionary, if not overly idealistic, it actually represents the logical next step in the evolution of our health care system. Powered by the spreading adoption of existing information technology and the general shift toward market economics, our health care system is undergoing a transformation that will make the inefficient, error-prone, wasteful, impersonal, uncoordinated care we get now a thing of the past.

The gaps in health care—those many voids in quality and efficiency—are being filled in and connected. A new era of medical care is just over the horizon.

This book will show you in real-world terms that our health care crisis is a solvable business problem already being tackled on numerous fronts. I make no grand claims about the simplicity or ease of the task. The health care industry is not a single corporate entity that a Jack Welch type of business leader can sweep in and fix. It's complicated, messy, confusing, and sometimes contradictory. Despite the scale of megahospital systems, giant pharmaceutical companies, billion-dollar insurance providers, and multilayered government bureaucracy, our health care system is still essentially a fragmented cottage industry, localized, low-tech in communication infrastructure, tradition-bound, and unaligned.

Two things are happening to shift the old paradigm. First, the high-tech productivity and quality boom experienced by other industries is finally catching up to health care, making a fully digital and integrated system possible for the first time. Most people, even many industry insiders, are unaware of the advances that are being made, or how they are transforming the concept and delivery of care. Second, health care is undergoing a consumer revolution. Hospitals and clinics are seeing some of their business jump to retail outlets in pharmacies, shopping malls, and even airports, and the best care is becoming that which is provided by the appropriate source at the appropriate time at the best quality and cost. As a result of this new digital freedom and retail choices, health care is becoming increasingly accessible, and patients (also now commonly known as consumers) are being offered more control than ever before over their health care decisions about where, when, and from whom to seek advice and treatment.

The net effect is that health care is becoming higher quality and more personal, so much so that we believe we are approaching a new golden age of health care. That phrase would usually bring with it a sense of nostalgia—a yearning for a time when health care was not about long waits, malpractice suits, and aggravating paperwork. However, having researched the history of health care for the writing of this book, I now know that there really wasn't a time when everything was better than it is today, and I'm certain that we've never lived in an era when we had even close to the level of medical expertise and care options we have now.

Chapter 1

Unmanaged Care

Many people consider our health care crisis to be a social or even moral problem requiring more money, expanded coverage, and extensive reform to resolve. Some are calling for a socialized, not-for-profit, government-run or single-payer system, though the majority recognizes that American tradition and society are not amenable to a system that is too centralized or restrictive of choice or entrepreneurial efforts.

What's becoming better understood is that our health care crisis is fundamentally a business problem. The system is overstrained and is breaking down due to outdated information technology (IT); poor application of the basic principles of market economics; overall inefficiency in terms of work flow, care delivery, and the spreading of best practices; a lack of transparency around quality and cost; and blocked access to making informed consumer choices.

Don't get me wrong: I'm not assigning blame for any of these built-in flaws. They are a result of the way our health care system has developed into a set of parallel cottage industries that until recently have never had a

7

real chance of being integrated into a seamless, efficient industry. Doctors, hospitals, insurers, suppliers, and the government have all run their shops separately and distinctly from each other, so that literally one part of the system cannot talk to another in any trustworthy, efficient, error-free way.

At the patient level, our system's problems become compounded, creating so much doubt, stress, and aggravation that many people elect not to seek out health care until an easily treatable condition lands them in the emergency room instead.

If you're healthy and your family members are healthy, you probably don't think about the health care system much. But if you or a family member is receiving treatment, whether because of an injury, an illness, or even a happy occasion like the birth of a child, you think about the system all the time. I imagine you feel immense gratitude for some of the very caring and competent strangers who are looking after you and great frustration over so many of the other aspects of getting treatment. There are the long waits and endless paperwork, the necessity of telling your story or the details of your condition or treatment over and over again, the impersonal processing of what feels intensely personal to you, the redundancy of tests, the challenge of getting clear information, the costs of treatment and medicine, the fears about side effects and mistakes, the difficulty of coordinating insurance coverage, not to mention your concerns about whether you are getting the right care in the best hospital by a doctor, nurse, or technician who knows his or her stuff.

Take a simple doctor's visit. No matter how busy you are or how far in advance you schedule the visit, you wait 45 minutes or more to see the nurse and doctor. When you're in the examination room, your doctor has less than 12 minutes of quality time to spend with you because he or she is in a rush to see the next patient. A good portion of those 12 minutes is spent figuring out your medical history. After your diagnosis, you get your prescription on a piece of paper. You then physically carry it to the pharmacist and wait around for it to be filled, blissful in your ignorance that there are 140 million illegible prescriptions every year.

The economics of the entire interaction are a complete mystery to you. Your doctor's visit will cost you a co-pay fee up front, if you have insurance, but you won't know what the examination really cost until you get the bill months later. If you have insurance, you probably don't bother to check that statement, but if you do, the numbers and codes are almost impossible to unravel, and you would get little comfort knowing how much confusion is rampant behind the scenes in those back offices. The doctor charges one thing, the insurance company pays something else, and chances are it takes three exchanges back and forth before the final claim is settled, and you are lucky if you do not receive calls or notices drawing you into the dispute. Small wonder. There are 1.5 trillion claims each year, and a full 30 percent of those claims have errors, while 15 percent get lost. Twenty-five percent of claims are still paper-based, and it costs $20 to $25 to manually process them.

Consider how strange this would be if it were applied to any other economic transaction. Imagine you go to Macy's to buy a tie or blouse. You want to pay for the item, but the price isn't marked. You ask the salesperson, who says, "Sorry, we have to mail you the bill." You insist you want to pay right now, and the salesperson's manager says, "We just can't do it that way. The price is different for different people, and we don't know what your credit card company or bank will allow us to charge you." Four to eight weeks later you get the bill, but you have no idea if you've been charged the right price. Take the metaphor further: Suppose when you go shopping at Macy's, you can't choose to buy a more expensive blouse or tie even if you want to, and you can't shop at Wal-Mart or Bloomingdale's down the street even if they're having a sale. In the same way, you can't pay a doctor to spend more time with you. You can't check the doctor's record of quality and service to make an informed choice. You can't determine which treatments or prescription drugs your payer reimburses in advance of your doctor's recommendation. What's more, you have no skin in the game—no economic motivation or incentive to take a stand for your own health—and neither does anyone else involved in the transaction.

In terms of consumer frustration, health care ranks with the airline industry. Like airports today, emergency rooms and physician clinics are all about delays and inconvenience. It takes an average of three hours and 43 minutes to get treatment at an emergency room. It takes an average of 55 days to schedule an appointment with your primary care physician. But while airlines have a remarkable record of getting us safely to our destination, the health care industry is not so impressive. Deaths from medical errors alone amount to 100,000 per year, and that number doesn't even include the one million or so injuries that do not lead to death.

Think about that. A hundred thousand deaths is the equivalent of a 747 airplane falling from the sky every single day, killing everyone on board.

If that were happening in the airline industry, every plane would be grounded until we fixed the problem. In fact, in the airline industry, safety standards and operating procedures are strictly adhered to, regardless of carrier. Every catastrophic accident gets thoroughly reviewed, and any technical or engineering faults are corrected industry-wide. In health care, this is not the case.

Despite all the frustrations inherent in flying today, there are areas where its customer service, such as it is, actually outshines health care. Competition and efficiencies have driven the cost of a flight down to levels that encourage ever-increasing numbers of travelers. You can shop and buy tickets online, which gives you access to the information necessary to be an educated consumer and makes it easier and more convenient to book a flight. At the airport, self-check-in kiosks have streamlined the ticketing process. And you don't need to seek out the best airline with the most famous pilot to know that you're going to be safe. Your plane is operated by a well-trained team using sophisticated controls and systems while following strict protocols of operation to ensure that quality and safety are 100 percent every single time.

In comparison, the health care industry is inconvenient, inefficient, price regulated, fraught with errors, and wildly varied in terms of quality of outcomes.

When it comes to health care decisions, you are not provided access to important information and you have less power than the government or your insurance provider to make your own decisions. You can't go online to choose your doctors based on quality and cost data, or even book your appointments or hospital stays. You don't have self-service kiosks to check in, confirm your appointment, or obtain a prescription. And we still rely on the hospital emergency room as the last resort center of care even when other options might be more efficient and practical. Imagine forcing every traveler in the United States to take a plane even when a train, boat, bus, or car might be more sensible and effective— that's what happens in health care every single day.

Quality of care is another area where most people don't know the extent of the problems we're facing. While we've made tremendous progress in advancing the science of diagnosis and treatment, we've done a poor job ensuring that all health care providers are in possession of the latest protocols and best practices. How do you know that your physician or hospital will be able to offer you top quality care? It's practically a random walk. In fact, whether you see a doctor in a clinic, obtain scheduled surgery, or are rushed to the emergency room in a crisis, you have only a 55 percent chance of receiving the best recommended care, which means getting scientifically appropriate, evidence-based medical treatment. Looking at six killers—heart disease, cancer, stroke, chronic obstructive pulmonary disease, diabetes, and Alzheimer's disease—which together consume 25 percent of our health care dollars, the *New York Times* found that "the medical system has been unable to turn proven remedies into everyday care."[1] Of the million people who have heart attacks every year in this country, half of them die. Moreover, "half the people who need to be treated to prevent heart attacks are not treated and half who are treated are treated inadequately. Patients go home with the wrong drugs or the wrong doses or misimpressions about the importance of taking their medications." With everything we know about heart disease, we could drastically reduce the impact of heart attacks now, but because of the fragmented and nonstandardized nature of the health care system, 500,000 people die every year.

Thirty percent of our health care dollars are spent on treatments that do not improve our health or are completely redundant. If you look at quality across the country, between hospitals, doctors, and clinics, the variations are simply staggering. Yet we provide no information to help patients, as health care consumers, to seek out the best doctors, hospitals, and treatments—in part because there is resistance to providing that information and in part because we don't have enough standards in place to process the data. From doctor to doctor and illness to illness, medicine remains as much art or craft as science. The mystique of the physician is such that we view our doctors as heroes, working on their own to dispense the right care based on years of accumulated wisdom. In no other industry do we leave implementation of best practices to an individual practitioner. Airline pilots don't fly by feel or individual instinct. They manage to fly us safely the same way each day as an integral part of an overall flight system designed to function flawlessly time after time.

Today, the average 65-year-old spends four times as much on health care as the average 40-year-old. Why? Naturally, our health issues pile up as we get older, but the system isn't designed or aligned to give us the preventive focus to keep our health care costs down over a lifetime. Private insurers have no incentive to worry about our health condition post-65, even as the number of people over 65 in this country will double in the next 30 years and Medicare is projected to go bankrupt by 2017.

Meanwhile, because treatment is not coordinated between care providers and insurers, chronic conditions are more costly than they should be. We now have 100 million people with chronic conditions in this country, and we can expect that number to reach 134 million by 2020.[2] Chronic illnesses are expensive because they are long-term, requiring prolonged medication periods and many visits to doctors or hospitals. Our health care system, however, is set up to deal most efficiently with acute illnesses during one-off visits. We provide little support or incentive for the chronically ill to manage their conditions more effectively so they can avoid more expensive treatments and emergency room visits later. This is not because we don't care, but because our health care providers are only just now organizing into teams that coordinate care seamlessly from emergency room to clinic to outpatient facility and pharmacy.

Compounding all these problems is a growing labor shortage. We are losing primary care doctors, nurses, geriatricians, and pharmacists at an alarming rate. By 2020, it is estimated that we will have shortages of between 85,000 to 96,000 primary care physicians, one million nurses, 36,000 geriatricians, and 157,000 pharmacists. Even foreign-born medical students, attracted to the excellence of our medical schools, are going back home to practice—and so are the foreign-born nurses we've come to rely on so much. Some of these clinicians are drawn to the increasing number of choices outside the United States, including fully accredited hospitals that operate like five-star hotels. In addition, many American care providers are leaving their professions because the intellectual and emotional satisfaction has diminished since they entered their practices. As reimbursements for service become capped and the stress and paperwork pile up, the rewards are simply no longer worth it.

It's not just patients who are frustrated by the situation we find ourselves in. Care providers, who deal with the problems every single day, are sick of it, too.

Choices for Tomorrow

Those are the obstacles, and they cannot be simply brushed aside with the wave of a policy maker's pen. Indeed, they are the focus of much of the dialogue about health care in the media and among politicians today. But there are also changes happening that will alter the equation for the better—changes that we all need to encourage and support.

To say that health care is behind the times in terms of technology is a laughable understatement. I'm talking about a system in which, at present, the fax machine is a more commonly relied upon communication tool than e-mail. I can receive a BlackBerry message from a colleague climbing a mountaintop, yet I still show up at a doctor's office to learn that my hospital test results have not yet arrived weeks after they should have.

Every other industry in this country, from financial services to automotive manufacturing, has become automated in the past 20 years. But not health care. Across the board, information technology, business process improvements, six sigma, and total quality management strategies have helped sluggish U.S. industries become more productive by making goods and services cheaper, more accessible, more reliable, and of better quality. Think of Wal-Mart. Its satellite ordering system cuts prices to the bone. Or take your local bank. Every single day, anywhere in the world, you can access your money and account balance at the touch of a fingertip. Remember a time when you had to visit a teller whenever you needed to make a deposit or withdrawal, and you carried your checkbook around as an extension of your wallet? Vaguely, I'm sure, and yet it has been only 10 or 15 years since those service innovations took place.

In the same way, going forward, our health care information will be available any time, anywhere, through web-based portals. Using secure information systems, any hospital, specialist, nurse practitioner, or pharmacist who needs to view your records will touch a screen and see everything he or she needs to know. You'll make appointments online, and your clinic will get approval from your insurance provider in advance and send the electronic bill along instantly after the visit. Your prescriptions will be sent to the pharmacist electronically as well, ready for you when you arrive at the pharmacy. This means no more lining up to drop off prescriptions at the pharmacy or, perhaps more stressful, no more begging your doctor's staff to phone in your prescription when you're in a hurry.

You'll be able to communicate with your physician by e-mail if you have follow-up questions about your most recent visit. Your physician, in turn, will be able to view your latest test results or that 3-D magnetic resonance imaging (MRI) on the computer at his office or the one at home that sits on her kitchen counter. She'll do rounds at the hospital with a handheld device that allows her to tap into the latest medical research instantly, consult the best practice protocol, and order treatment then and there. The drugs that you need will be dispensed by robots, and the dosages will be checked by bar-code scanners before they're administered. Every prescription, every patient, every tool, every care provider, and every test result in the hospital will be tracked and monitored through radio-frequency identification (RFID) tags—tiny, advanced transponder tags that use radio waves to identify people or objects.

If you haven't experienced a hospital stay recently, you can't imagine how radical these changes will feel. Some people, fearing change, say we shouldn't automate the processes of health care because we will lose the human touch. I believe that the human touch can only be reclaimed by relying on automation. There's nothing inherent in information technology that restricts or impedes relationships—in fact, IT can build and improve relationships. Ask your daughter, who made a dozen friends at her new college before she even set foot on campus, because she'd met them on Facebook. Her initial interactions may have been only virtual, but they provided instant access to information that might have taken several in-person meetings to reveal. Similarly, doctors are demanding ways of interacting electronically with patients, other care providers, and data banks because it's easier, it's more productive, and it frees up time each day that can then be spent more and more with patients.

Technology allows us to rid the health care system of errors, paperwork, and inefficiencies. In return, it allows care providers to focus more on you. Imagine the nurse who has 30 percent more time for holding a patient's hand or talking with a loved one about treatment because his paperwork has been automated. Imagine the doctor who avoids needless tests because she has diagnosed and treated you accurately the first time; the extra hours currently wasted filing claims for reimbursement can now be spent on keeping her skills and knowledge up to date. Imagine the primary care physician who feels fulfilled and engaged with his work because he is connected with his patients and their care plans over the long term, not just in isolated, hurried visits.

The savings and benefits that come from upgrading our health care system are enormous and already being felt. Roughly 20 percent of the $2.2 trillion we spend annually on health care goes to paperwork and red tape. Improvements in information technology infrastructure, such as the McKesson Revenue Cycle Solution, have already begun to fill in the white space in this area, eliminating the inefficiencies and freeing up money and time that can be spent on better care. Another 25 to 30 percent of our $2.2 trillion goes to wasted care in the form of preventable errors, incorrect diagnoses, redundant treatment, unnecessary infections, and extra time spent in the hospital. Team-based medicine, bar-code prescription scanning, evidence-based medicine—all of these are systems and innovations that are being put into place to eliminate such waste so we can reapply that money as well. These will be discussed further later in the book.

Everyone into the Pool

Currently, the average health care customer experience is dismal. Instead of feeling supported and guided by a benevolent system, it's more likely that you feel shunted aside like an irrelevant spare part while the great machine of health care grinds on by. The majority of health care workers care deeply about patients, but to the patient lost in the bureaucratic maze, the incidents of quality care are few and far between. As a patient you have little power to influence the care you get. Access to information is a problem for all involved: You are poorly informed about your condition and your choices, and your care providers are poorly informed about you. In the future, however, you will find yourself in a very different position: at the center of decisions, well informed and highly connected, serviced by an industry that is actively looking after your needs.

One of the most important customer-related problems we have today is access to care. As you will read in Chapter 5, I am part of a group of business leaders who recognize that the United States needs universal health coverage, which is not to be confused with nationalized health care or any other kind of single-payer system. There are two compelling reasons for this. First, employer-based health care, implemented in the 1950s as a union concession for capped wages, has become a tremendous competitive burden on American corporations. Second, Americans not eligible for group plans have relatively few choices, because our current private insurance system doesn't adequately serve to spread risk, reduce costs, and encourage good health, since there are too many people not in the pool.

Forty-seven million people are uninsured in the United States today, because they cannot get insurance coverage through their employers and are unable or unwilling to purchase it for themselves. To get everyone from that group into the pool, consumers must have an incentive to buy health insurance with before-tax dollars, just as corporations do today; and the government must support those who can't otherwise afford health care by enabling them to buy coverage from private insurers. Insurers, in turn, must stop turning down customers because of preexisting conditions and be allowed to charge more to customers who engage in unhealthy behaviors.

As a tool for spreading risk, universal coverage only makes sense. After all, you can't drive a car in most places in this country without car insurance. People who have bad driving records pay more for their insurance than those with good records. Universally accessible insurance paves the way for more competition within the insurance industry. Insurance companies should be able to compete for your business no matter where you live; and you should be able to shop for the best deal and keep the insurance of your choice wherever you live for as long as you live.

Even once we've insured everyone, we're still left with two mutually exclusive insurance pools in the country: private insurance and government insurance. Millions more Americans are not in the private insurance pool because their health care is covered by Medicare or Medicaid. This has a couple of powerful effects on the health care marketplace. First, the government's reimbursement of medical goods and services provided under Medicare and Medicaid is consistently out of step with the actual market price. Today, for many physicians, 50 percent of their patient load is price-controlled by a single payer, Medicare or Medicaid, and the other half is subsidized by private health plans. If we adopt market-based pricing mechanisms across the board—including in the realm of Medicare and Medicaid—then we remove economic distortions that keep the system out of balance right now.

While Medicare has begun to experiment with some market-based price-setting approaches, there are many examples where the market has negotiated prices below government-set levels, and the government ends up paying too much. There are many other examples where the government has used its monopoly power to pay below cost, leaving the rest of us to make up the difference. This interference hampers the efficiency of the market and creates a dance of confusion in which health care providers anticipate and react to government edict at the expense of anticipating and reacting to actual customer demand. As a result, some desperately needed services, such as family medicine, go undersupplied, while services that are needed but widely available, like cardiology, remain stuck at artificially high prices instead of having to compete for customer dollars through the mechanisms of price, quality, and convenience. When the government artificially caps health care spending, it does not reduce the costs; it just shifts them around.

For instance, take pharmaceutical prices. According to a recent study, every dollar spent on beta blockers for patients with heart disease nets $38 in health care benefits; every dollar spent on statins to reduce high cholesterol returns $9 in health benefits. Those are terrific gains, improving lives and reducing costs, yet our regulatory and economic incentives actually impede even more progress. In 1988, for example, there were 25 companies selling vaccines in the United States, and the vaccine business was a model for innovation. Yet by 2001, largely due to lawsuits, there were only *four* vaccine businesses left. Thankfully, the government relaxed the legal chokehold on vaccine manufacturing in the wake of 9/11 and the national anthrax scare, so vaccine innovation has come alive again. We are now seeing new breakthroughs for cervical cancer, malaria, and more, through profit-making efforts led by companies like Merck in this newly rejuvenated market.

The private insurance industry, whether it wants to acknowledge this or not, has little incentive to see people live healthier lives beyond 65 when their customers automatically drop out of the employer-based system and enter the government-based system. Take an overly simplistic example: What insurance company would want to pay for a heart transplant three days before a customer would turn 65, at which time the government would foot the bill and the patient's revenue would be lost to the insurer? More to the point, what insurance company is motivated to develop a plan for treating chronic illnesses like Alzheimer's or heart disease when those conditions are not going to manifest and become expensive until after the patient has stopped being a customer? We need to better align economic interests with health and ethical interests if we're going to get better health care, and a major step toward doing that is to begin phasing out our two-tier worker/retiree insurance system with innovative cradle-to-grave insurance choices. We all need more skin in the game.

Today, when choosing doctors, you have no way of knowing whether they are the best at what they do, or among the worst. When you go to a hospital for knee surgery, how can you know whether that hospital does 1,000 knee replacements a year or 20? And whether the outcomes are predominantly excellent or consistently mediocre? You won't know ahead of time whether the hospital coordinates care among team members to ensure you get the best rehabilitation after the operation, or just drops off your chart in someone else's in-basket. You also don't know how much your treatment costs—and you couldn't care less, because someone else is paying for it.

Would you make any other consumer decision that way? We expend more time and effort buying a disposable good like a car than we do looking after an indispensable good like our health! Our current system restricts the choice, information, and incentives we need to be rational consumers.

In the near future, you, your insurance provider, and your primary care doctor will have access to high-quality information to help you make better choices. Think of it as a J.D. Power–like experience where the value of something is evident in terms of its price and quality. You will be able to consult a consumer-guide database that will detail a doctor's performance record or a hospital's quality measures. This database, whether offered by your insurance provider, the government, or some third party, will enable you to choose the cancer clinic that has a 95 percent survival rate for prostate cancer over the one that has an 85 percent survival rate. It will enable you to identify the orthopedic surgeon who does six flawless knee replacement surgeries a day over the one who does only six a month.

You'll know how much it all costs, and you'll be able to make your decision based on some personally assigned balance of cost, quality, and convenience. Imagine the kind of conversations you will have with your health providers then: "I appreciate you're the best surgeon, Dr. Smith, but Dr. Jones is nearly as good, costs me 30 percent less, and is available right away." Similarly, you'll be able to choose the clinic with same-day appointments over the one that makes you wait two months. You might go to the neighborhood hospital because it's closer, or you might go to the one on the other side of the city because it has zero staphylococcus infections, automated bar-code scanning for prescriptions, and best-practice protocols for its clinicians.

In response to this level of transparency and choice, care providers, insurance companies, and hospitals will begin to compete for your business like never before. We will see a surge in quality and service as a result, and a steady reduction of overall costs as industry players struggle to be the low-cost provider.

Cost doesn't matter to you now, but it will in the future. Today, most of us get our health insurance from our employers. Consequently, the market forces that have reshaped the rest of the economy are almost completely absent when it comes to making personal health care decisions. Most of us have a co-pay of $20 or less when we see a doctor. That doesn't provide much incentive to look for a better deal, or even take better care of our own health. We need a different approach, one where insurers, care providers, and consumers share responsibility for health-related choices. As patients, as consumers, we need more skin in the game.

Health savings accounts (HSAs) are one of the ways consumer incentives are changing. HSAs are high deductible plans that double or triple patients' financial responsibility for the care they receive. They are attractive to consumers because they represent significant tax savings. Those tax breaks are worth it on a societal level because they induce consumers to think about the price of care and the value of preventative measures and healthy behaviors. It's your money, after all, so it pays to take care of yourself. You may not have heard of HSAs before, or you may have dubious feelings about them, but HSAs are being adopted five times faster than 401(k)s were after they were initially introduced in 1979. They'll be a major component of our financial considerations, and an investment in our own healthy future.

Coupled with those kinds of incentives, costs are becoming more transparent. Soon, we'll be able to clearly see the costs of our care and our own financial responsibility—what we have to pay—on a computer screen or in an easy-to-read e-mail before we even get treated. When we get to the hospital, we'll stand before an ATM-like kiosk and swipe our health card to electronically check in, while also automatically paying our co-pay or balance. When we check out, the co-pay will immediately be deducted from our health savings account, and there will be no bill to pay. That's the kind of transaction simplicity we get now at the pharmacy counter when we pick up a prescription. What's more, it's a means of aligning payment systems, reducing inefficiencies, and sharing information by allowing payers and providers to have more visibility into costs, patient populations, and treatment plans.

Health care is rapidly becoming a retail experience. You may not have noticed it yet, but we've reached the cusp of this monumental shift. And the signs of that transformation—e-mails from the family doctor, shorter waiting times in waiting rooms, less crowded emergency rooms— will become apparent to you soon.

Quality, Service, and You

Some people today, even some inside the health care system, say that a nationalized health care system would be better. In fact, however, it would make our situation much worse. I've touched on some of the reasons already—the distortions in the market, the way capping prices only shifts costs, the way transparency and competition increases quality—but you'll read all of that in more detail in the chapters to follow.

In fact, we don't have a health care *system,* per se. We have a remarkably disconnected set of silos in which doctors, hospitals, insurers, and suppliers operate independently and sometimes at odds with each other, and the patient is left out in the cold.

As a nation, we have the greatest medical and research institutions in the world. Our scientists and practitioners push the most significant advances. Our pharmaceutical companies are the best innovators. Our biotech companies drive understanding of the essence of human life. That's why the United States doesn't have just one great hospital or drug company, but hundreds. That's why we're always at the cutting edge of human knowledge.

But we can do so much better. The quandary surrounding our health care system is that while it is medically advanced, the quality of care we receive is dismally low, coupled with costs that are still prohibitively high. According to a study done by the World Health Organization, the United States, while ranking first in the world in health care spending, ranks only 37th in overall performance. No other innovative industry in the world has succeeded in the long term by being high in cost and low in quality. Instead, the natural progression of a successful industry is to increase reliability and quality while driving cost out of the system by constantly improving operations.

How will you know when the health care industry has finally entered the twenty-first century? When error rates at hospitals are close to zero. When doctors and nurses use evidence-based protocols in your treatment. When you can decide how much to spend on treatment, and you have the information and the opportunity to determine the best value. When your primary care physician is in charge of your extended care team, operating as your command central. When all members of the medical community—nurses, doctors, pharmacists, and specialists—work together seamlessly on your behalf. When their combined efforts are tracked, measured, and reported on, and the insurance reimbursements awarded to them are based on performance. When you see that hospitals, pharmacies, and doctors are working harder in all aspects to make sure you are an informed consumer who has trust and confidence in the services they offer and the prices they charge.

In the chapters that follow, I am going to tell you the story of our health care system. I will give you an appreciation for how far we have traveled in the past hundred years, explanations for why we are in the midst of a crisis now, and a picture of the great strides we are making that have already begun to turn things around. I will help prepare you for the change that is coming, and help you better navigate the system we have today. While many decry this period in health care as the worst of times, 10 years from now I think we are going to look back and see it as the dawn of an astounding new era.

Chapter 2

From Tree Bark
and Roots to Bar
Codes and Robots

I'm hands-on. I like to roll up my sleeves and see how things work. So in 1996, shortly after joining McKesson Corporation as president of the Health Systems division, I took a field trip to our state-of-the-art distribution center in Sacramento, California. There I learned that our distribution centers around the country received product from 3,000 manufacturers and fulfilled orders from 25,000 pharmacies daily. To understand how all that product was actually moved, I spent a few hours that day working as a picker, the warehouse worker assigned to pull a pharmacy's order from the shelf and forward it to the shipping department. The floor supervisor outfitted me with an apron, a tote box, and a special wristband with an infrared scanner used to read bar codes. The names of drugs are complicated and often remarkably similar to one another, so the bar-code system ensures accuracy when pulling drugs from the shelf and increases the pickers' speed when they're on the warehouse floor. When my first pharmacy order came in, I received an itemized list through the computer on my arm; then I walked down the long warehouse aisles to locate the various products with my scanner. I picked each item and put it in the pocket of my apron until I had collected the entire order; then I transferred the items to the tote box and sent it along the conveyor line, where they were scanned again and loaded into the right truck to be shipped to the pharmacy that had placed the order.

I was proud of myself and impressed by the bar-code-driven system. Then I noticed that I'd forgotten to take some of the items out of my apron and put them in the tote box! The entire warehouse was shut down until my errant tote box could be located and my mistake corrected. It was a relatively simple human error, but luckily our system was able to correct it without putting any patients at risk. The floor supervisor demoted me back to head office, and I was happy to hang up my apron and infrared scanner and get back to my desk.

Everyone knows the health care industry is complicated, but when you consider the immensity of detail and the number of moving parts, the mind begins to reel. If my mistake had not been caught, a pharmacy at a hospital somewhere might have run out of a medicine that could save someone's life. Think about it: One small error by a warehouse worker could be directly responsible for someone's death! My company, McKesson, sometimes thinks of itself as one of the so-called plumbers of the industry, working behind the scenes to maintain operations and make sure mistakes like that can't happen. Yet within our business alone, we connect more than 3,000 manufacturers, 25,000 pharmacies, 35,000 physician practices, and 20,000 health care facilities, all serving over 100 million patients every day. We bottle medicines, move pallets, track inventory, stock shelves, dispense pills, automate refills, check dosages, process claims, guide diagnoses, monitor vital signs, and counsel patients. We're one of those out-of-sight organizations working the infrastructure of the world's most complex and decentralized industry.

After my less than perfect day as a picker, I wanted to see how things worked at the other end of the supply chain. So a few months later I spent a day in a hospital pharmacy. What I saw was shocking: how little the system of dispensing medicine in hospitals had changed since the

1900s, despite the great increase in the number of drugs and volume of orders, and the technological advances made on the distribution side. The pharmacy was deep in the basement of the hospital, poorly lit and cramped. The shelves were lined with little cardboard boxes with small blue and white labels. The drugs themselves were identified only by their scientific names, many of which were confusingly similar. Every order was filled painstakingly by hand. The pharmacy technician looked at the doctor's handwritten prescription, picked the medicine from the shelf, counted it, and put it in little packages to go upstairs. Before sending it on its way, the on-duty pharmacist had to check each order again by hand. Then, on the hospital floor, the nurse used handwritten charts to figure out which drugs went to which patient, painstakingly sorting the many packages by hand before sending them off to patient rooms to be administered. Had I not seen it with my own eyes, I wouldn't have believed it. There were no fail-safes in place to ensure that those drugs were being taken at the right time and in the right way. There was no system in place to determine whether the patient was taking any other drugs that might cause an adverse reaction. In the entire process, there wasn't a bar code to be seen, so that anywhere along the way a mistake could easily be made and no one would be the wiser until a patient fell ill or died from receiving the wrong medicine or the wrong dosage of the right medicine.

Medical errors hadn't yet become the big news story they are today, but it was easy for even an outsider to see that the system was susceptible to error. I'm not an innovator myself—I'm more about business execution—but I recognized at the time that hospital pharmacies needed reliable automation to put an end to the preventable deaths and injuries caused daily by medication error. Why couldn't the bar coding not stop at our distribution centers, but rather continue until the medicine reached the patient? With the proper equipment in place, drugs could be scanned when they were received by the hospital pharmacy, then scanned by the pharmacist when filling the order, and scanned again by the nurse when reading the chart, who in turn could scan the bar-coded wristband on the patient before administering the dosage. Moreover, all of this data could be sent back to a central computer system to double-check that each dose was being administered in precisely the right way and that there was no possibility of an adverse cross-reaction between drugs. It was so obvious, I couldn't believe it wasn't already in use.

Today, a few short years later, that's the way things are done in some hospitals. Robotic systems receive and sort medicines in the hospital pharmacy, thereby freeing up the pharmacist's valuable time from the need to double count pills. The bar-code system mechanizes the entire process, electronically connecting the doctor's computerized prescription pad to the pharmacist and back to the nurse administering the dosage and the patient receiving the medicine. Unfortunately, not every hospital pharmacy or drugstore has upgraded, but where such systems are in place, medication errors have been reduced by 80 to 90 percent. McKesson's own system generates a half million alerts of potentially adverse effects every week. Those range from very simple alerts that probably wouldn't harm a patient, such as medication being administered sooner or later than prescribed, to much more serious errors such as the wrong patient being treated or the wrong drug being used. Knowing that all those errors have been prevented by technology makes me feel better. Knowing that most hospitals do not have such systems in place makes it clear we have a lot of work still to do.

This is the kind of system upgrade the entire health care system needs to undergo. As previously noted, the various components of health care—doctors and other care providers, drug manufacturers and pharmacists, hospitals and clinics, and private and public reimbursement plans—have evolved more as separate cottage industries than as an integrated system. Despite the enormity of the services provided, the scientific advances, and the dollars involved, we still rely on a fragmented industry to care for us, one that operates much the same way as it did 50 or even a 100 years ago. The paperwork, the mistakes, the enormous waste of money, the long lines, and the interindustry disconnections are all outputs of an antiquated system that is finally beginning to be modernized.

Early Days in the Drug Business

To understand the health care system we have today and where that system is headed in the future, we need to be aware of its beginnings. On the surface, our current system—with its high-tech hospitals and laboratories, its multibillion-dollar corporations, and its highly trained care providers—bears little resemblance to the days when patent medicine was delivered by peddlers in covered wagons, and doctors worked out of the backs of drugstores. But if we follow the development of medical care over the past two centuries, we can better understand how our health care system has evolved, and how, in a good way, it is coming full circle in terms of access to treatment and the relationship between patient and care provider.

So where does American health come from? The place I'd like to begin is with the rise of health care delivery, the backbone of our modern health care system. Popular myths notwithstanding, not all medicine was snake oil, and not all those who dispensed medicine were hucksters in our country's early days. A parallel field of legitimate medical treatment functioned quietly alongside the more boisterous sham practitioners who went from town to town and often did more harm than good selling their tonics and potions. Until the Revolutionary War in 1776, most drugs were imported from Europe ready-made. Once the British navy interrupted regular cross-Atlantic shipments to the colonies, American druggists began to make their own drugs using botanicals like roots, tree bark, or herbs, or chemicals sold by local wholesalers.

Botanicals

I have before me a circular addressed to drug-gatherers by one of our principal Western dealers in indigenous drugs, from which I extract the following:

"Most medicinal roots are perennial (that is, the roots continue more than two years, whether the leaves continue or not), and should be gathered any time between maturity or decay of the leaves or flowers, in the summer or fall, and the vegetating of the succeeding spring. Biennial roots, or those that live but two years (like burdock and yellow dock), should be collected of the growth of one year—any time between September and the time they commence running up to seed in the following spring.

"Barks should be gathered as soon after they will peel in the spring as possible, and all the moss carefully removed. It is

(continued)

Botanicals *(continued)*

usually best to fell the tree and remove the moss while the bark is on the tree.

"Leaves and herbs should be collected just before they mature, and before they begin to fade; the stems and stalks rejected, as when dry they are a hard woody substance, nearly inert.

"Flowers when they first open; and

"Seeds just before they are quite ripe, as they, like leaves and flowers, ripen after being gathered.

"Roots should be thoroughly cleansed from dirt and foreign substances, and if large, like Indian turnip, &c., sliced.

"All the above articles should be dried; the sooner the better. For the first few days it is best to expose them to the sun and air, avoiding any dew or dampness; then spread around on floor and shelves, watching them to see that they do not heat by being piled too thick, till nearly dry. Most roots require from three to six weeks to dry sufficiently to be safe.

"For shipping, it is best to pack them hard in coffee-sacks or large gunnies and burlaps; the next best is good flour barrels."

These circulars appear to be distributed with great circumspection among herb-gatherers and country stores throughout the Southern and Western States, and in all probability serve as a guide to the gatherers. The few gatherers with whom I have been able to converse personally, proved very slow to give information, but from their conversation I judge that they preserve their collections on the general principles above specified.

From the article "Indigenous Drugs," by C. Lewis Diehl, *American Journal of Pharmacy,* Vol. XLIII, 1871.

As science advanced and the drug business became more professionalized, an apparatus of knowledge and education came into existence. In 1820, the first United States pharmacopoeia was published, a reference book listing descriptions of drugs and directions for creating compounds. In 1821, the first U.S. pharmacy college was established in Philadelphia.

William Procter Jr., the father of modern pharmacy, taught there, and some of the alumni were a who's who of later pharmaceutical giants. In 1823, a second pharmacy school was established in Boston, and then a third, in 1829, in New York.

By the 1830s, there were approximately 200 professional drugstores in New York City, serving a population of 220,000 people. Bulk drugs came in sacks. Some compounds needed to be ground by hand with pestle and mortar. Many drugs were dispensed as powders wrapped in carefully folded paper, while others were dissolved in liquids. Pills, ointments, tinctures, and popular remedies like sodium bicarbonate were made in the store. To seal a bottle or vial of medicine, a piece of wet cork was squeezed on a cork press, then inserted into the glass opening. To make a pill, powdered medicine was given a doughy consistency, cut into little pieces, and dusted with licorice powder. There was no running water, so fresh supplies had to be fetched at nearby pumps. Besides running the store and preparing medicine for sale, druggists also provided services like bleeding and leeching. Doctors often bought their medicine from the drugstore or even worked out of the back room, caring for patients.

The drug distribution business arose to meet the demand for medicine. In 1833, John McKesson and Charles Olcott opened a small wholesale drug and chemical shop at 145 Maiden Lane in New York City. The two partners launched their business by buying out the stock and lease of a wholesaler who had decided to retire. Both men were already experienced druggists. McKesson had been working since he was 14 for a chemist and a well-established wholesale and retail drug business. Olcott had been trained as an apothecary—the precursor of today's pharmacist, who also typically worked as a chemist and provided medical advice and even occasional surgery and midwifery.

Maiden Lane was the heart of Manhattan's wholesale district, and the street was quite lively. The Olcott, McKesson store was just a few blocks from the waterfront at the East River. With the opening of the Erie Canal in 1825, New York City had established itself as the primary center for commerce and trade in the United States, superseding other vital port cities like Philadelphia, Baltimore, and even New Orleans. The East River waterfront was a booming seaport as a result. The docks were

A Little Side-Talk with the "Freshmen" in Pharmacy
The situation of a boy just entered on duty at a dispensing store
is not to be envied. The calls for his service are numerous and
frequently beyond his appreciation, so as to make him feel that
he is as yet almost powerless to perform his duties from his ignorance of the material with which he has to deal. Besides the
mechanical operations, which require dexterity and nimbleness,
and which at first are performed with a bungling slowness, he is
constantly at fault in finding the locality of drugs, when called by
name, or the implements required by a dispenser on whom he is
waiting. . . . His duties, besides the cruder ones of opening, sweeping and dusting the shop, making fires, etc., embrace, in a thorough establishment, the use of the contusing mortar and pestle
and the handmill in preparing drugs for percolation and infu-
sion, the washing of mortars and graduated measures, the cleansing of spatulas and other implements used for ointments, the
washing of new and old bottles, the replacing of bottles, etc.,
used at the counter, cutting labels, making paste, filling shop bottles and drawers from the storehouse and the cellar, the filling,
corking, sealing and labelling of bottles of liquid and other preparations, wrapping packages and folding powders, making and
using filters, the management of gas heat in making syrups, infu-
sions, plasters, etc., and in conducting evaporation and distilla-
tion, the stirring of liquids for extracts, the making of pill masses
and the rolling of pills, garbling and cutting drugs, and many
other engagements, too numerous to mention here.

Editorial by William Procter Jr., *American Journal of Pharmacy,* Vol. XLIII, 1871.

lined with tall schooners and steamships. Merchants and agents bought
and sold goods, while laborers crowded the streets with barrels and wagons, loading and unloading cargo.

At the time, there were dozens of small wholesale firms in New York
City serving the increasing number of professional drugstores. The competition among firms led to a lot of jostling, and a successful firm often

bought out its smaller rivals to grow its stock and market share. By 1835, Olcott, McKesson & Co. had managed to purchase one of the oldest and most respected drug wholesale businesses in New York. By 1842, the firm had purchased a new building at 127 Maiden Lane, large enough to handle its business expansion. By 1843, Olcott, McKesson & Co., with two more acquisitions under its belt, had become well established in the New York business community. It also had a new partner. Ten years earlier, the firm had run an employment ad to find some help. A young man named Daniel Robbins walked nearly 75 miles from Poughkeepsie, New York, along the Hudson River to apply for the job. Brought on as an apprentice, he started attending the College of Pharmacy of the City and County of New York (he was to become the first president of the alumni association in later years). Robbins was named a partner in the Olcott, McKesson firm in 1841. When a fire destroyed its New York warehouse in July 1850, the company immediately restocked itself, rebuilt the warehouse, and changed its name to Olcott, McKesson & Robbins. In 1853, after Olcott's death, the firm's name was shortened to McKesson & Robbins.

While snake oil salesmen like Doc Rockefeller were plying their wares across the country, firms like McKesson & Robbins were expanding their business, too. Travel was becoming easier, and the patterns of trade were shifting. Instead of waiting for peddlers to visit their towns, buyers who represented druggists often went to trade centers on the water route along the Erie Canal and the Great Lakes a few times a year. There, they would be met by greeters who represented the wholesale firms. In order to have sufficient inventory of drugs and other goods on hand, wholesalers began to build warehouses and ship products in larger quantities.

In 1855, McKesson & Robbins moved a few blocks north into what was then considered uptown Manhattan to occupy 100,000 square feet of space at a new headquarters at 91–93 Fulton Street. The expansive complex, which would become grandly known as "The White House," included parts of four nearby buildings for storage and even a generator plant. The firm also became one of the first wholesale drug businesses to establish its own laboratory, using the top two floors of the main building for its manufacturing division. Soon, McKesson & Robbins was producing its own pills, tablets, and extracts, and distributing them in an ever-widening market. It also expanded its business line to include a range of fancier goods, such as sea sponges, essential oils, exotic tinctures, perfume extracts, and mineral waters. From its headquarters in New York, the McKesson & Robbins–labeled products were distributed across America and around the world. Through its buying and selling agents in London, Liverpool, Paris, Berlin, Hamburg, Milan, and Amsterdam, the firm began selling products with local labels in Central and South America, as well as China, Japan, South Africa, Australia, and New Zealand. In one new gold mining community in the Montana territory, two men who went into the drugstore business sent a bag of gold powder worth $20,000 to the McKesson & Robbins office with the instructions to "Send us complete stock."

From Bulk Sacks to Gelatin Pills

McKesson & Robbins developed its own laboratory because drug use was changing. In the past, doctors and druggists dispensed "heroic" doses of a single drug in order to treat a patient's illness. A new theory suggested that repeated and regular applications of smaller uniform doses provided a more effective treatment. This required greater standardization in terms of the size of the dose and the content and quality of the drug. For professional druggists, the new way of packaging of drugs made it increasingly economical and efficient to order ready-made pills from drug wholesalers or manufacturers rather than to produce them in-house.

From 1861 to 1865, the American Civil War had a major impact on health care and the drug manufacturing and distribution business. During the course of the war, 620,000 Union and Confederate soldiers died. More than half of those men were killed not on the battlefield but by other causes, mainly disease and infection; 1.2 million men suffered from malaria, 140,000 from typhoid fever, 130,000 from measles and pneumonia, and 180,000 from syphilis and gonorrhea. Diseases spread rapidly in the crowded camps, where personal hygiene and nutrition were poor, and water and sewage ran together. Surgeons operating in field hospitals near the battle lines treated the wounded with no understanding of germ theory or infection. Antibiotics had not yet been discovered, and unsterilized hands, instruments, and gauze went from wound to wound and soldier to soldier with devastating results.

Medicine became an aspect of the waging of war. Confederate doctors relied heavily on tree bark, roots, and botanicals to treat their wounded and sick, and the Confederate Army raided and blockaded large and vulnerable shipments of medicine from the North. The Union Army, however, organized itself to produce and distribute medicine on a more industrial scale. As the fighting began, it updated its Medical Supply Table to clarify which drugs should be distributed to the surgeons in the field. Strychnine, magnesium sulfate, opium, quinine, chloroform, ether, gauze, and medicinal whiskey were among the many required products. Drugs were produced at military laboratories in New York City and Philadelphia, collected by the Medical Purveyor of the Army at main depots in those cities, and distributed to subdepots closer to the fighting. A military wagon was designed to transport those medical supplies, and medical knapsacks were dispensed to each medical officer in the battlefield. These knapsacks were carefully packed with a set variety of medicines and supplies, arranged in handy locations for ready access, and weighed between 18 and 20 pounds.

U.S. Army Medicine Pannier Put Up by Edward R. Squibb, MD, Brooklyn, New York

The Pannier should always be kept top up and handled with care. It should be carefully protected from the sun and rain because either heat or moisture will cause many of the pills to flatten and run together, whilst if the pills be dried so hard as to protect them against such contingencies they are liable to pass through the alimentary canal without dissolving and therefore without effect.

The Pannier should always be kept locked when not in use and the key in the possession of the medical officer or hospital steward.

The bottles should always be kept in the places indicated in the diagram and when taken out by the aid of the diagram should be carefully identified by the label or by the number, if the label be lost or defaced, to prevent mistakes from bottles getting misplaced.

The Whiskey when kept in tinned iron vessels for some time is liable to be blackened by a chemical reaction between the acids of the whiskey and the iron. This discoloration is not hurtful.

The military drug laboratories could not meet all the Union Army's needs, however, and even private drug manufacturing concerns got more business than they could handle. As the war went on, medicine was bought and sold like commodities on an open exchange, the prices subject to market manipulation and speculation. In an effort to ensure high quality and low price, select suppliers were chosen. In New York City, the preferred supplier was the Squibb Works. Dr. Edward Squibb had been instrumental in establishing the Army's state-of-the-art research laboratory in Brooklyn in 1858, and was a lifelong crusader for drug quality. (Over a century later, in 1989, Dr. Squibb's company would merge with Bristol-Myers—founded in Clinton, New York, in 1887—to form what was then the world's second-largest pharmaceutical enterprise.) In Philadelphia, the Union Army's main supplier was John Wyeth, the pharmacist who had invented the tablet press and thereby helped standardize the dispensing of medicinal doses. Wyeth's firm became American Home Products in 1926, makers of Preparation H, among other famous brands.

The Civil War was a boon to drug manufacturing in general and helped bring those firms to new scale. Charles Pfizer, a chemist from Germany, had founded his laboratory in Brooklyn in 1848, but by 1868 business was so good he was able to move his administrative headquarters to Manhattan at Maiden Lane where Olcott, McKesson had once operated. Colonel Eli Lilly, a pharmacist who organized the 18th Indiana Light Artillery Battery and served during the Civil War, launched his laboratory in 1876. McKesson & Robbins' renown as a drug manufacturer was enhanced in 1870 when the firm pioneered the development of the gelatin-coated pill. The covering preserved the medicine from deteriorating in the air, especially in humid or tropical climates, and the oval shape made the pills easier to swallow. Hundreds of different medicines were soon dispensed this way, and McKesson & Robbins won medals of merit in Vienna in 1873 and in Philadelphia in 1876 for its contribution to pharmaceutical science.

After the Civil War, there were so many firms producing drugs that profit margins shrank. Fly-by-night drug firms scrimped on quality and oversold on false promises. Increasingly, it made sense for some drug wholesalers to withdraw from the manufacturing side of the business and focus on distributing other companies' products. All in all, it was a difficult time for business, and trust needed to be reestablished among manufacturers, wholesalers, and the nation's 25,000 retail druggists. In March

1876, 62 drug wholesalers in 16 cities and 11 states formed the Western Wholesale Druggists' Association to "obliterate the feeling of distrust and jealousy that seems to exist" within the industry by adopting policies and regulations to provide better service. McKesson & Robbins joined the Association in 1880. The organization added over 20 more members within six years and became the National Wholesale Druggists' Association (NWDA) in 1883. Through the NWDA's reform efforts, prices became stabilized, credit arrangements were improved, and a regulated system of trade discounts became established between manufacturers and wholesalers.

A new breed of traveling salesman arose to serve the needs of those 25,000 pharmacies. NWDA studies had shown that expert salesmen, with the ability to discuss the varying merits of different drugs and preparations and even news of new regulations, were of great value to a druggist. As the drugstore became more specialized, a pharmacist's expertise in the latest medicines was his key selling point. The traveling salesman functioned as the retail druggist's reliable confidant, becoming a critical component of the drug distribution value chain that was forming nationwide.

The extensive network of new railway lines made the salesman's travel possible. In 1860, there were 31,000 miles of track. By 1910, there were 240,000 miles. Telegraph lines stretched along those tracks, shrinking distances, weaving the country more tightly together. No longer did customers travel to regional centers to meet with greeters and buy supplies from warehouses. Instead, the traveling salesman came to the customer. At the end of the nineteenth century, traveling drug salesmen lugged their trunks of products over thousands of miles a year, often following a single rail line from beginning to end, visiting at least a town per day, taking orders from customers and then going back to the train station that night to hand their notes off to the outgoing mail car attendant so that the sales could be processed and delivered as quickly as possible. Then, the next day, they'd be in the coach car of the first freight train of the morning, en route to another town down the line.

Despite the growing professionalization of the drug industry, the quality or effectiveness of drugs remained a troubling issue. Patent medicines didn't go away with the passing of men like Doc Rockefeller; instead, they became better packaged. Firms sprang up out of nowhere to hawk new treatments, creating florid names and fancy bottles, tins, or boxes to help sell their goods. It's no coincidence that the advertising industry rose in prominence at the same time. In 1905, a series of articles in *Collier's Weekly* described the patent medicine industry as "The Great American Fraud." According to author Samuel Hopkins Adams,

> Americans will spend this year some seventy-five millions of dollars in the purchase of patent medicines. In consideration of this sum, it will swallow huge quantities of alcohol, an appalling amount of opiates and narcotics, a wide assortment of varied drugs ranging from powerful and dangerous heart depressants to insidious liver stimulants; and, far in excess of all other ingredients, undiluted fraud. For fraud, exploited by the skillfullest of advertising bunco men, is the basis of the trade. Should the newspapers, the magazines and the medical journals refuse their pages to this class of advertisements, the patent medicine business in five years would be as scandalously historic as the South Sea Bubble, and the nation would be the richer not only in lives and money, but in drunkards and drug-fiends saved.

Motivated by muckraking writers like Adams and Upton Sinclair and by reform-minded medical professionals like Dr. Edward Squibb, the U.S. Congress passed the Pure Food and Drug Act in 1906. Patent medicines relied on secret recipes, and patients often self-medicated with little understanding of the actual properties or effects of the products they ingested. The Pure Food and Drug Act regulated the labeling of drug products and restricted false claims of efficacy or quality. In 1938, the act was updated and expanded to guard against cosmetics that could cause blindness or other physical harm and medicines that proclaimed miracle cures for diabetes or tuberculosis. Out of those acts came the Food and Drug Administration, the government agency that regulates the approval of new drugs today.

Economies of Scale

By the turn of the twentieth century, with the development of warehouses, the expansion of markets, the arrival of the traveling salesmen, and the adoption of regulations ensuring drug quality, the modern drug industry was taking shape.

The retail drug business was changing, too. Druggists worked long, hard hours, seven days a week, dispensing medicine, serving customers, and treating illnesses. The stores themselves were carefully constructed environments of health and community. Drugs were dispensed from the back, where the various powders and pills were kept in labeled drawers. In the front of the store, there were tall, polished wood cabinets with sliding glass doors, and decorative glass pharmacy globes filled with blue, green, or red liquid. To bring in customers, a drugstore stocked general goods, candy, and sundries like postcards and soap. But the dominant feature of the store was usually the soda fountain. Seventy-five percent of drugstores had one. Elaborate and expensive, soda fountains were adorned with shiny metal spouts and spigots, dark wood handles, and marble countertops. Coffee, desserts, light meals, and, of course, ice cream sodas were among the typical offerings that made a corner drug-store an appealing place to visit.

Most drugstores were family-owned businesses. One of the first pharmacies in the country was founded in Greencastle, Pennsylvania, in 1825 when John Quincy Adams was president. Carl's Drug Store stayed in the Carl family until 1974, and remains an independently operated pharmacy today. In Spring Valley, Illinois, Thompson Drugs was estab-lished in 1885, and a member of the Thompson family has served as the store pharmacist ever since.

Other independent pharmacies, however, began to expand and fran-chise their businesses in the early 1900s. In 1893, Charles R. Walgreen Sr. was an apprentice druggist at a highly respected drugstore in Chicago. That year, there were 1,500 drug stores in operation. Walgreen took note of the best service innovations he saw, and launched his own store in 1901. He made his aisles wider, put in brighter lighting, broadened his selection of merchandise, and put a premium on customer service. When a customer called in with an order, Walgreen ran the "two-minute drill." While he kept the customer on the phone with small talk, his assistant would fill the order and run it over to the customer's house before the call had ended, to the amusement of the surprised customer.

By 1910, Walgreen had two stores and began to serve hot meals at his soda fountains, a new innovation in the business. By 1919, he had opened his twentieth store and had a management team serving under him. In 1922, another soda fountain innovation rattled the industry: a scoop of vanilla ice cream was added to the traditional chocolate malted milk, and the milkshake was born. America became milkshake mad. The pace of growth exploded, and by 1929 there were 525 Walgreens stores across the country. Walgreen Co. started to advertise in print, and, in 1931, became the first drugstore chain in the country to advertise on the radio.

Walgreens' Recipe for Old-Fashioned Chocolate Malted Milk

1. Use a Frosted Malt Can
2. $1 \frac{1}{2}$ oz. Chocolate Syrup
3. 3 - #16 Dips of Vanilla Ice Cream
4. $5 \frac{1}{2}$ oz. of Cold Milk
5. Add Malt Powder (One Heaping Tablespoonful)
6. Place On Mixer Only Until Mixed – Do Not Over Mix
7. Use a Generous Portion of Whipped Topping In A #1808 – 10 oz. Glass
8. Pour Malted Milk in Glass Approximately $\frac{2}{3}$ Full
9. Serve Remainder Of Malted In A Shaker Along With The Glass To The Guest With Straws and Package of Fountain Treat Cookies

Source: www.walgreens.com/about/history/hist4.jsp.

A different path to expansion was taken by business innovator Louis Liggett. In 1902, Liggett convinced 40 independent drugstores to join a retail cooperative called United Drug Stores. The cooperative chain sold products under the Rexall brand, though many stores maintained their own names until the 1940s. At that point, Justin Dart, a Walgreen employee, consolidated the United Drug Stores under the Rexall name, and began a national advertising campaign on such syndicated radio programs as *Amos 'n' Andy*. By 1958, the company was the largest U.S. franchise with 11,000 stores, and showed no sign of slowing down. Then came the rise of discount chains like Thrift Drug and Eckerd Pharmacy, which changed the business model again.

During the rise of the franchise chains, McKesson & Robbins' specialized market remained the independent drugstore. The firm was in financial trouble, however. Profit margins for drug wholesalers were extremely low. A survey conducted by the National Wholesale Druggists' Association in 1922 showed that average net profit in the industry was less than 1 percent of sales. To gain new economies of scale, McKesson & Robbins partnered with a number of well-established drug wholesalers to create a system of franchised distribution agents selling McKesson & Robbins–labeled products exclusively. But in the mid-1920s, the family-owned business was sold.

The buyer was a man named Dr. F. Donald Coster, president of Girard & Co., a small drug manufacturing firm based in Mt. Vernon, New York. Although Coster secured the backing of a group of Connecticut bankers, he was a con artist who had lied about his background and even his name, and wanted to use the venerated firm in part as a cover-up for illegal activities. Nevertheless, for the next 13 years, Coster ran the majority of the business legitimately and even had great success with a strategy to develop a robust network of wholesale distributors across the country to serve the needs of independent drugstores.

In 1928, Coster consolidated his network of wholesale distributors and the manufacturing division under a single company, McKesson & Robbins, Inc. In one fell swoop, he had created a $100 million corporation. The innovative move was heralded in the industry as being good for every party concerned. Drug manufacturers immediately saw the advantage of being able to deal directly with one firm that had retail relationships all over the country and the marketing might and economy of scale to distribute product efficiently and reliably. Small druggists welcomed the development because they were being threatened by the growing national chains like Walgreens and Rexall. By 1929, there were more than 61,000 drugstores in the country selling nearly $2 billion in merchandise. Only 4,000 of the 61,000 drugstores were franchises, but those chains were generating three times as much revenue on average as independent drugstores were. Independent retailers were eager for the modern store management and service innovations that McKesson salesmen promised their businesses through McKesson's Plan of Service, and 15,000 independent drugstores signed on in short order.

A year later, the Great Crash led to the Great Depression. In the pharmacy business, the McKesson & Robbins consolidation was credited with lessening the economic strife. During the worst of those years, McKesson & Robbins helped retailers stay in business through generous credits. Prohibition ended in 1933. By 1936, net sales for McKesson & Robbins had reached $155 million, with 700 salesmen on the drug distribution side of the business and 400 selling liquor to stores, hotels, restaurants, and clubs. The past, however, eventually caught up with Dr. F. Donald Coster. He was blackmailed by old acquaintances who threatened to reveal his past, and was under investigation for the irregularities in his Canadian and crude drug operations. Coster's executive leadership of the company was suspended, and he committed suicide rather than face the shame of exposure.

Even a company of McKesson & Robbins' size and prominence could have dissolved, given the shock of the financial and personal scandal that erupted. But the firm's position in the drug business lent urgency to its rescue. As one of its Wall Street creditors put it, "McKesson is necessary to the function of distributing drugs in this country." In 1938, McKesson & Robbins was in trusteeship, under the leadership of an interim president until the company emerged from oversight into private management and solid footing. After the end of World War II, as the American economy ramped up, McKesson & Robbins needed to streamline its operations. Delivering product quickly and reliably at low cost was the key to business survival. A state-of-the-art warehouse was built in Houston in 1947 to improve processes. Checking, pricing, packing, and office jobs were simplified in order to increase productivity. In the following years, personnel numbers held steady while the company shipped even higher volumes of product.

By 1958, McKesson & Robbins had $600 million in annual sales, with over 100,000 customers. Twelve hundred McKesson & Robbins drug salespeople made 250 million calls on three out of every four drugstores in the country. One out of every five drugstores had been modernized by the company. Across the industry, pharmaceutical sales had increased by 400 percent compared to 10 years before, and new drugs were being introduced at a rate of 400 a year. Truly, by this point, the drug business had become big business in America.

Today, 90 percent of the drug wholesale business in the United States is delivered by three firms: AmerisourceBergen, Cardinal Health, and McKesson Corporation. Some people are quick to criticize large corporations today. But without economies of scale and incredibly efficient distribution capabilities, delivering medicine and medical supplies is too unprofitable to be a viable business; and without reliable distribution, our health care system would collapse in a day. Even with economies of scale, the drug distribution business edges by with a slim 1 to 2 percent operating margin. But with this comes a great imperative to constantly reinvent and revamp the approach in order to use the most current best practices. Not only that, but the nature of the business alone is such that even the slightest error carries a high price. Six sigma has already become an industry standard among the larger distributors, with many other new and inventive means of safety and accuracy well on the way.

Imagine millions of prescriptions delivered on time each day to 26,000 pharmacists, and all of those orders and bills processed through one system. With so many constituents relying on one behind-the-scenes process, it is in everyone's best interest to make the system work more efficiently, effectively, and transparently—and to keep improving it all the time.

In the overhaul of health care, we all have our role to play.

The Technological Leap

In many ways, over the course of the 1900s and even into the twenty-first century, the means by which drugs were delivered to drugstores and dispensed by pharmacists changed very little. In the past 20 years, though, technology has started to have an increasingly important impact. I think of 1988 as the dividing line. That's the year a hospital pharmacy at Southwest Texas Methodist Hospital in San Antonio discovered a way to dramatically cut response time in filling prescriptions. What great innovation led to such a stellar improvement? The fax machine.

It took only 140 years. The telephone had been common in pharmacies ever since Carl's Drug Store in Pennsylvania hooked one up in 1906—doctors were among the first to patch a call through. But the first fax patent had been issued in 1843, decades before the telephone or even Morse code. By the 1980s, it was finally making headway in corporate America as an important business communications tool. When the device was brought into the pharmacy business in 1988, it signaled a break point in the increasingly rapid technological changes to come.

Imagine how far we can bring health care now if we only bring it up to speed with the technological advances of the past 20 years. In 1988, we didn't have the Internet, e-mail, wireless communication, RFID labeling, or Global Positioning System (GPS) locators. Since then, we've revolutionized communication, supply chain management, data management, and work flow.

The problems haven't changed. Concerns about dispensing medicine are the same today as they were a hundred years ago. As William Procter wrote in 1871 in the *American Journal of Pharmacy*:

> How can the junior be sent with safety to fill bottles and drawers unless every receptacle is labeled correctly according to its contents? . . . Labels drop off, covers become displaced, and at times residues returned to the store-room are heedlessly thrown into the wrong barrel. . . . Only lately one of the best dispensers of Dublin caused the death of a prominent citizen by an error arising from sending an ignorant agent to the store-room to fill the carbonate of ammonia bottle—cyanide of potassium being substituted. Hence the importance of an intelligent and frequent supervision of these depositories to insure *order*, out of which comes safety and dispatch, and untold satisfaction.

But until recently there was little we could do to dramatically improve the situation. Today, robotic dispensing and bar codes on drugs and patients are examples of the way technology is bringing health care into the high-tech age. Computerized physician order entry systems allow the doctor to enter medication orders directly into a computer system, eliminating the need for prescription pads and illegible scrawls. Such systems can force doctors and pharmacists to account for other variables like a patient's weight or age, and the possibility of allergies and complications due to other drugs. Simple errors like confusing two drugs with similar names are quite common. Alerts make doctors and pharmacists stop and determine whether they really intend to prescribe what they are prescribing. In the past, we had no such fail-safes. But now, because of technology, we are ridding our system of errors, increasing efficiency, and lowering costs while also giving nurses, doctors, and pharmacists more time with patients.

In drugstores, for instance, new technological advances are about to radically change the role and practice of the pharmacist. Drugs have had an enormous impact on quality of life in the past 100 years. They are part of the reason why we have gone from an average life span of 47 years in 1900 to 77 today. Vitamins, introduced in the 1910s and 1920s, improved nutrition for the average person. Penicillin and other antibiotics, introduced in the 1940s, have saved millions of lives that otherwise would have been needlessly lost to infection, just as today targeted cancer drugs are involved in turning many forms of cancer into manageable chronic conditions. In the early 1900s, the pharmacist was our neighborhood counselor, a friendly confidant we could go to for advice and care when it would have been too inconvenient, expensive, or embarrassing to visit the doctor. Yet, for decades the pharmacist was discouraged from talking to patients about their prescriptions. The 1952 Code of Ethics for the American Pharmaceutical Association said that "the pharmacist does not discuss therapeutic effects or composition of a prescription with a patient. When such questions are asked, he suggests that the qualified practitioner (physician or dentist) is the proper person with whom such matters should be discussed."

Since 1965, when such guidelines were repealed, the pharmacist has been more free to talk to patients in theory, and yet the workload and the layout of the pharmacy hardly encourage such exchanges. There were over 3.2 billion prescriptions sold in the United States in 2003, and the number of pharmacy school graduates has declined. Like health care providers in general, most pharmacists go into the business because they want to use their knowledge and social skills to help patients. Unfortunately, pharmacists spend much of their time hidden in the back of the drugstore, filling prescriptions for impatient customers, serving as little more than overeducated pill counters.

In the near future, most of a pharmacist's mundane tasks will be automated or delegated to technicians. Inventory will be maintained by RFID-labeled systems that monitor stock and send in orders for what is needed. Prescriptions from the doctor will be sent directly to the pharmacy computer, eliminating irritating drop-off visits and waiting. Technicians or robots will dispense medicine. And patients will even receive their prescriptions in multidose blister packages tailored for their precise daily needs instead of a bag full of labeled bottles with vague or confusing dosage instructions.

All of this automation doesn't mean you will need your pharmacist less—it means you will talk to him or her even more. I see the pharmacist of the future as an essential hub of health care. Soon, you will go to your pharmacist for health care knowledge, and the pharmacist's primary role will be to manage the medication side of your treatment. The pharmacist will be part of your team of care providers, working much more closely with doctors and nurses to understand and provide whatever treatment or therapy you require. The pharmacist may even be the one who prescribes your medicine based on the diagnosis offered by the physician or a nurse-practitioner. Even today, pharmacists who are certified diabetes educators (CDEs) have proven the efficacy of such an approach. According to the American Diabetes Association, these professionals frequently provide diabetes patients with "education not only on medications, but also the overall disease state, nutrition, physical activity, decision-making skills, psychosocial adaptation, complication prevention, goal setting, barrier resolution, and cost issues." And by using the resources that are at our fingertips, we will be able to push ourselves further in this direction. In its future high-tech incarnation, the pharmacy will function a lot more like the pharmacy of the early 1900s.

Retail health care clinics are opening in pharmacies right now and will be everywhere in the next few years. CVS, Walgreens, Rite Aid, Brooks Eckerd, and Osco are all opening staffed clinics in their drugstores. Perhaps even more significant, mass merchants like Target and Wal-Mart are doing the same thing. The development is built around bringing service into the health care industry. Parents with children who have ear infections, workers who know they need antibiotics for a sore throat, even people with chronic conditions like diabetes that currently require multiple trips to the doctor or pharmacist—all will be able to do one-stop shopping at their local drugstore.

How does it work? Walking into the store without an appointment, you sign up at the kiosk, get a beeper, and take a seat or shop until your care provider is available, either a doctor or a nurse-practitioner who can provide a diagnosis and access a physician by computer or phone for further consultation, if needed. In addition to saving you time and trouble, this development also provides you with more bang for your health care dollar. A typical visit to a retail in-store clinic costs $25 to $65. A typical visit to a physician clinic costs about $110. A typical emergency room visit for an illness like strep throat costs over $300. Imagine these cost savings spread across millions of patients. Not surprisingly, major health insurance providers are typically eliminating co-pays for visits to retail clinics as a way of encouraging patients to access the system in more cost-effective ways.

There are those in the physician community who argue that health care provided in the pharmacy setting is a negative because of a dilution in quality of care. Some have genuine concerns, whereas others are worried about a drop in the volume of their own patients. Some states are responding as a result. But in the future, quality care will not be judged by whether you are able to see the most credentialed health care provider but by whether you receive the appropriate care through the appropriate source at the appropriate time. If your child has an ear infection, the most cost-effective and convenient way of obtaining antibiotics is through the local pharmacy. That means it's also the highest-quality health care, too.

Those are some small but critical examples of the ways health care delivery is evolving to improve quality, safety, and efficiency while reducing costs. Such changes may not seem revolutionary on their own, but they will collectively alter the health care landscape for the better. At each point, your relationship with your care providers will be intensified, made more meaningful, and brought closer to home. Throughout the overall care cycle, you will have better information, more options, and greater influence and control. In that sense, the future will resemble the past, except with all the tremendous benefits of modern science and technology as well.

Chapter 3

Why We Go to the Hospital Today and Why We Will Go There Less Often in the Future

O ne day, I walked into Duke University Medical Center in Durham, North Carolina. I was there to attend a series of business meetings, but the humanity of the place hit me hard. In a corridor off of the emergency room, I saw a family huddled together, quietly weeping. Like kissing at airports, grieving in hospitals does not draw obvious attention, and the family was unaware of anyone else around them. The source of grief was not evident, but it was impossible to be unaffected by their pain, and I walked on through the hospital finding it difficult to shake the feeling of despair and wondering how doctors and nurses handle it every day.

I checked the information board to confirm the floor and wing I needed to reach. The list of hospital departments included many—like biostatistics, bioinformatics, and neurobiology—that didn't even exist 10 years ago. As I approached the end of a hallway, the automatic doors swung open and I saw coming toward me a young and healthy-looking woman in a wheelchair pushed by an attendant. For a moment, I imagined her to be another sad case, another example of the kind of crisis or trauma that can bring us to hospitals, but then I saw what was really happening and couldn't help but smile. The young woman had a glow about her. Her husband followed, carrying a newborn in a blue wrap. He was in deep conversation with the baby, speaking Spanish in a soft tone, his finger making sure that the blanket was not covering the baby's mouth. I remembered the feeling of carrying my own daughters out of the hospital for the first time, and I gave the man a knowing smile as we passed.

Between the two encounters, the grieving family and the family experiencing the greatest of joys, I'd managed to see the full circle of life in under five minutes. Hospitals see it every day. If America is the great melting pot, the hospital might be the one place we all still come together as equals. Visit any big city hospital at any time of the day or night, and you will see people from all economic classes, cultures, religions, and languages, experiencing the full range of life's trials and blessings. The hospital is the central focus of our modern health care system, the place of ultimate reckoning, where the most advanced scientific knowledge and technology meet the vulnerability of patients in need of care. During a constant 24-hour cycle that includes countless episodes of grief, despair, joy, and relief, a hospital manages to function despite a complex and sometimes contradictory set of medical duties and responsibilities. At its chief entry point, the emergency room, it has all the bustle of an airport. In the way that it must bed, feed, and care for patients staying overnight, it rivals the busiest hotel and catering service while administering complicated medical procedures at all hours. In terms of its everyday technology and testing services, it functions like an advanced research lab on constant overload. Its operating budget, administrative complexity, talent management demands, community relations, and need for leadership make it as challenging to run as the most sophisticated global business. Where it is affiliated with a university, the hospital also serves as a top-flight educational institute, running programs to train and develop nurses, doctors, pharmacists, and technicians in every specialty under the sun.

Duke University Medical Center is exceptionally leading-edge both as a care facility and as a research institute. Like any city hospital, it handles the most everyday traumas, from heart attacks and car accidents to a construction worker's nail gun injury and a young soccer player's split lip. At the same time, in other parts of the hospital, it is researching pulmonary function and drug effectiveness, among many other concerns, pushing our progress and understanding of medical knowledge forward. As a level-one trauma center, Duke's surgeons and medical specialists are on call 24/7. Fifteen minutes after being admitted to Duke University Medical Center with a baffling disorder, you can receive the most advanced neurosurgery from one of the best surgical teams in the world.

Truly, we've come a long way in our medical knowledge and our ability to provide the best care. Yet, most hospitals in this country struggle with nearly crippling cost overloads and operational challenges while straining, like the Atlas of Greek myth, to keep the world of health care balanced on their shoulders. If it were possible to design a new health care system from scratch to suit our current and future needs, no one would deliberately re-create the system we have now. Hospitals, in particular, would be conceived in different ways to offer different kinds of service. But before we reimagine hospitals for the future, let's see how the modern hospital developed and the reasons why it has taken its current form and function.

Development of the Hospital

As early as 1658, a hospital was built in Manhattan, or New Amsterdam as it was then called, by the Dutch settlers. The West India Company, which controlled the New World colony, did not want to incur the expense of construction and operation, but a sanitary place was needed to provide for sick slaves and soldiers without family, so a small shelter was built to house these unfortunates when they fell ill. For everyone else in our nation's early history, however, health care took place in the home.

The first proper hospital, meaning one with facilities we would recognize today and staffed with educated doctors, would not appear in

America until a century later, the inspiration of Dr. Thomas Ball, a Quaker and a surgeon who had completed his medical study in England. Ball had visited the world-class and venerable facility in Paris, the Hôtel-Dieu, and wanted to bring its approach and sophistication to the colonies. Unfortunately, the General Assembly in Pennsylvania was no more eager to pay for a hospital for the sick poor than the West India Company had been a hundred years earlier.

Dr. Ball was persistent, however. He circulated the idea among leading figures in Pennsylvania, and finally enlisted a friend and visionary leader, Benjamin Franklin. Taking up the cause, Franklin appeared before the assembly and offered a challenge: If he and Ball could raise two thousand pounds in contributions toward the launching of the endeavor, the General Assembly would pledge to match that amount. The leader of the assembly accepted the challenge, not believing that Franklin had any hope of raising that kind of money. Only eight months later, Franklin visited the assembly again having accomplished his financial goal, and the assembly was forced to live up to its promise in turn.

The Pennsylvania Hospital was chartered and funded in 1751. The first patients were admitted on February 11, 1753. Over 250 years later, the Pennsylvania Hospital still stands as part of the Pennsylvania Health System. The hospital's mission, to "Take Care of Him and I will repay Thee," is inscribed on its seal and reminds us that hospitals were originally charitable poorhouses. Only three types of patients could be refused admission: those judged incurable lunatics, those with infectious distemper and communicable forms of mental derangement, and women with young children unless the children were taken care of elsewhere. Inside the hospital, patients were forced to follow strict rules of conduct. They had to comply exactly with the orders given by physicians and nurses, and were forbidden to talk when physicians were on the ward. They were to help nurses care for other patients if able, and they were to dress in bedclothes and refrain from perverse language and spitting on the floors.

To a large extent, our early hospitals were built to segregate the sick who could not afford care or whose families could not keep them, the victims of plague or other infectious diseases, and the occasional foreigner or sailor who became ill or injured far from home. People who checked into a hospital typically did not get better—more times than not they became even sicker and often died. If you were sick and needed treatment desperately, a hospital was the last place you would go if you had the means and the family resources to avoid it. With the concentration of disease, lack of sanitary conditions, poorly trained staff, and poorly designed facilities, it was no wonder people with resources avoided them.

Yet even the well-to-do didn't fare much better. For instance, when "Nabby" Adams, the daughter of John Adams, second president of the United States, developed breast cancer in 1811, she returned to her parents' home in Braintree, Massachusetts. In seeking out the best medical care of the time, Adams did not think of taking his married daughter to a hospital. Instead, he summoned a number of physicians who made house calls to examine the large tumor on Nabby's breast. They prescribed herbal remedies as a course of treatment for the disease. She seemed healthy otherwise, and they reasoned that the best approach was to "poison" the tumor to make it go away.

Nabby also sought the advice of her father's friend Dr. Benjamin Rush, writing him a letter and describing her condition. One of the signers of the Declaration of Independence, Rush was a doctor on staff at the Pennsylvania Hospital and a professor of medicine at the University of Pennsylvania. Although a very advanced thinker (he's considered the father of American psychiatry for his understanding of mental illness and alcoholism), Rush was also a man of his time who believed in bloodletting and patent medicines. Before President Thomas Jefferson sent Meriwether Lewis and William Clark off on their expedition across the continent, Rush gave Lewis a crash course in frontier medicine, teaching him about bloodletting and providing him with a medicinal kit that included opium, emetics to induce vomiting, and a large supply of "Dr. Rush's Bilious Pills," which were laxatives containing concentrated mercury that the men would come to name "Thunderclappers" for their effectiveness.

After reading Nabby's letter, Dr. Rush responded with more urgency than did her doctors in Boston. Internal medicines would not be enough; radical procedures were called for. According to Nabby's description, the tumor was movable, meaning it had not attached itself to the chest wall, so surgery performed without delay might save her life. Dr. John Warren was enlisted to perform the surgery. Dr. Warren had provided medical care to wounded soldiers during the Revolutionary War and would later become the founder of the Harvard Medical School in 1783. When he arrived at the Adams home, he brought several other surgeons and a medical kit that included a large fork, a wooden-handled razor, and a pile of compress bandages.

Nabby Adams wore a formal dress to her surgery. She lay down on a reclining chair, and was belted and strapped tight. Her dress was modestly lowered off her left shoulder. No anesthesia was available, nor any disinfectant, rubber gloves, or surgical masks. Dr. Warren stabbed the fork into her breast, lifted it up, and severed it with the razor. Upon examination, he discovered that the tumor was not self-contained but had spread to the lymph nodes under her arm. We can only imagine how painful and traumatizing it must have been for Nabby as Dr. Warren did his best to scrape and pull away the tendrils of cancer. The bleeding needed to be cauterized frequently by a hot piece of metal before the sutures were finally applied. All of this took place in the house, not a hospital, with some family members in the room, while others, unable to bear the ordeal, waited outside.

Luckily, Nabby Adams did not contract infection from the surgery—as she probably would have in a hospital—and her convalescence was smooth. Seven months later, she seemed well enough to return to her husband at their home in upstate New York. A few weeks later, however, her health quickly declined. The cancer, as cancer so often does, had returned, and this time it had spread throughout her body.

Wanting to die in her father's house, Nabby was brought back to Braintree. By this time, her physical appearance was transformed. She was thin, coughed often, and experienced terrible pain with the slightest movement. Her mother could hardly bear to be with her over the next few weeks, so the former president, John Adams, took the mother's traditional place. He tended to Nabby, cleaning and comforting her while providing painkillers that did nothing for the pain, until she finally passed away.

That experience was not unusual for many families of the time. Life and death occurred in the home. Sometimes that meant surgery was performed on kitchen tables, and children were born in master bedrooms. Hospitals were avoided at all costs due to the social stigma and the risk of infection and because the tools and treatments could be delivered by doctors as easily as the patients could be delivered to the hospital. The eminent Dr. Rush disparaged hospitals as sewers that wasted human lives, declaring, "They robbed the United States of more citizens than the sword.[1]"

Still, a protracted death or serious illness took over a house and left everyone in a state of misery and grief, unable to escape the smells and sounds, forced to break with normal routine and to do most of the cleaning and caring without outside help. As society became more industrialized and urbanized, the means to provide quality home care diminished. In agricultural or rural settings, there was often multigenerational family to rely on, so the load was shared among many, including older relatives no longer expected to work the fields. In cities, because of limited space and economic necessity, the nuclear family became the more common unit. Homes did not often have the extra room available to devote to a sick family member. What's more, wage earners could not easily take time away from work to provide care.

Over the next hundred years, at first slowly, and then at an explosive pace, hospitals began to appear on the scene and shifted the locus of care away from the home once and for all.

The Pennsylvania Hospital had been founded in 1752. The nation's second hospital, New York Hospital, was established in 1771 through a royal charter given by King George III of England. Like Pennsylvania Hospital, New York Hospital was also defined by its mission as a "Public Hospital for the Reception of the Poor Sick." The Revolutionary War delayed its opening until 1791, when New York Hospital was at first used to treat victims of the yellow fever epidemic. After that, many of its patients were military. In 1816, the hospital opened its own pharmacy, four years before the first publication of the United States Pharmacopoeia. Today, New York Hospital is merged with Presbyterian Hospital, as NewYork–Presbyterian.

The nation's third hospital, the Massachusetts General Hospital, was established in 1811. Former U.S. president John Adams led the first meeting of the MGH Corporation, and his son, John Quincy Adams, the future U.S. president, was also involved. One of the founding physicians was Dr. John Collins Warren, son of the surgeon who operated on Nabby Adams. Warren and his colleague, Dr. James Jackson, would launch the *New England Journal of Medicine* the following year, and Massachusetts General would be a critical driver of innovation in patient care over the next two centuries. In 1846, for example, Dr. Warren performed the first surgery where the patient had been administered ether, bringing anesthesia to the forefront of surgical practice and ending an era of almost unimaginable pain.

From 1861 to 1865, the American Civil War engaged the nation on the problem of health care like never before. Public hospitals were still considered places to be avoided, and military hospitals were even more primitive. Most were little more than log cabins capable of handling only a few patients at a time, a striking difference from the hospitals used in European military engagements like the then-recent Crimean War. In the United States, the vast numbers of wounded and sick in the Civil War would create an imperative for something incredibly different.

In 1861, a young surgeon, Dr. William Alexander Hammond, was commissioned to write a report about the state of the military's hospitals and the measures that could be taken to improve them. Dr. Hammond was appalled at the overcrowding, the bad smells, and the poor food. As a proponent of newly emerging standards of cleanliness and ventilation, he advocated for a change in hospital design, recommending the adoption of a pavilion plan in which well-ventilated wards with large windows branched out from a central hub, preferably in a grassy setting near trees and water. His plans called for five such hospitals to be built, each capable of holding 15,000 patients. In the end, only two smaller hospitals were constructed, and the beds' proximity to the overflowing privies did little to solve the problem of bad smells and the spread of disease.

In 1862, Dr. Hammond was appointed surgeon general of the Union Army. He was only 34 years old, and the Secretary of War, Edwin Stanton, did not support him, thinking him too young and inexperienced for the task. They quarreled on their first meeting and Hammond would never gain Stanton's backing. Nevertheless, Hammond proved to be a visionary leader. He immediately reorganized the medical department to be more efficient and centralized.[2] At the same time, he set out to build a massive military hospital that he hoped would become a model of modernity for the nation.

Local politicians across the Northern states lobbied hard for the hospital to be built in their districts. Hammond, indifferent to any political expediency, chose a site on a hill outside Philadelphia because he believed its beautiful terrain would be conducive to good health. Satterlee Hospital was a massive complex that covered four full acres with 28 pavilions and a two-story administration building. The largest military hospital in the world to that point, it cost over $200,000 to build (over $4.1 million today) and was, in many ways, a self-contained city, including barbershops, a pharmacy, a large library, and its own weekly newspaper. Patients were given 1,200 cubic feet of space each (compared to as little as 80 cubic feet in typical military hospitals), air flowed freely, laundry was clean, fresh water was pumped in from the nearby river, and a special latrine was built to provide more sanitary removal of sewage, albeit with mixed results. At the height of the war, there were nearly 4,000 beds in use. By 1864, the hospital had treated more than 12,000 patients and seen fewer than 300 deaths, which was a remarkable testament to success in achieving a relatively infection-free environment.

The war continued to generate astounding numbers of sick and wounded soldiers. The Satterlee model was the kick-start for a great boom in military hospital construction. Dr. Hammond maintained his focus on building hospitals that met his new standards. Construction guidelines covered the gamut of issues, from selecting the site to the size and configuration of the wards and the placement of ancillary services, offices, storage areas, chapels, and surgery rooms. By the end of the war, there were over 200 hospitals around the country containing 140,000 hospital beds.

Innovations associated with hospitals during the Civil War period were almost exclusively limited to the issues surrounding architectural design and construction. Little in the way of new technologies or new medical treatments emerged from all of the money and effort laid out to treat the millions of wounded and sick. For example, it wasn't until 1866 that Dr. Joseph Lister, a renowned English surgeon, first discovered that microorganisms were responsible for surgical infection and pioneered the process of antisepsis in the surgical operating room. Even that advance was made back at a civilian hospital, Massachusetts General. (The presiding surgeon was none other than the grandson of Dr. John Warren, who had performed surgery on Nabby Adams.)

Nor did the massive boom in military hospital construction have much of a lasting effect on the number and type of hospitals in the nation. When the war ended, the money for hospitals, as well as the apparatus driving supply, organization, and efficiency, dried up. Satterlee Hospital was shut down when the war ended, and its buildings were destroyed. Dr. William Hammond was not around to protest. He had been court-martialed in 1864 and removed as surgeon general, charged with purchasing a stock of cheap blankets on behalf of the medical department at inflated prices. The implication was that he had been involved in a kickback scheme. Hammond had created his share of enemies over the war years through his forceful leadership, starting with the Secretary of War himself, and the accusations against him were highly political. Although he was convicted of the charges, dismissed from the Army, and prohibited from taking government office ever again, his name would be cleared in 1879 in a retrial and his reputation somewhat exonerated.

Perhaps the most lasting impact of the focus on hospital construction during the Civil War was the idea that hospitals could be operated at a larger scale with systematic efficiency and cleanliness. Civil War hospitals like Satterlee showed how much could be accomplished to meet the needs of the sick and injured when the will and resources were made available. I can only imagine, too, that the vastly increased number of experienced physicians, nurses, ambulance operators, administrators, and supply clerks had an impact on health care when they returned to civilian ranks.

While the Civil War did not advance medical science to any great degree, a new civilian hospital soon would. Unlike the other early hospitals, which had been funded by legislative or royal charters, Johns Hopkins Hospital was created in 1873 through the single largest private endowment ever made when a Baltimore merchant bequeathed his sizable fortune. This largesse seemed to free the planners to accomplish something great. The hospital opened in 1889, and a medical school followed four years later. The Johns Hopkins University School of Medicine was revolutionary in the United States for being extremely well equipped and rigorous in its scientific teaching. As its medical school and hospital graduated the best-trained physicians of the day, the influence of Johns Hopkins spread throughout the country. Great medical schools and hospitals like Vanderbilt, Duke, Iowa, Rochester, and Washington University brought in Johns Hopkins graduates and emulated the Johns Hopkins approach. As we will see in the next chapter, American medicine never looked back.

According to a government survey, in 1873, when Hopkins made his philanthropic gift, there were only 178 civilian hospitals in the country (including mental institutions) with around 50,000 hospital beds. Unlike the prestigious Massachusetts General with its close connection to Harvard Medical School, few of the nation's hospitals had any relationships with medical schools. In the next few decades, however, everything changed. By 1909, there were 4,359 hospitals in the country (not including mental institutions or sanitariums) with over 400,000 beds.[3] By 1920, the number had increased to over 6,000 hospitals.[4] As the number of hospitals increased, the specializations of hospitals also became more varied. Some hospitals treated only women and children; others were founded to serve people from specific religious or cultural affiliations, like the Catholic or Jewish hospitals, or specific illness or treatment areas like ear, nose, and throat hospitals or maternity hospitals. There were even corporate hospitals, built for employees of the railroads and coal mining communities.

Before the Civil War, no one would have imagined the hospital becoming the central location for health care in the United States. As late as 1913, this was still the case. Only 13 percent of patients received treatment in hospitals; the rest went to pharmacies or to public health outposts for free outpatient treatment.[5] Nevertheless, the trend was proceeding in a clear direction. Hospitals were becoming a medical hub where doctors and patients met for their mutual convenience and because of the efficacy of treatment. The primary reasons for the shift were the change in the nature of the family structure and the growth in urban centers that accompanied industrialization, as well as the growing prominence of technology that could be found only at the hospital and the increasingly scientific practice of medicine. Because of the convergence of these forces, we stopped treating our sick and injured at home, and started bringing them to the hospital. The privacy of the family home was exchanged for the very public hospital ward, but this meant trained professionals were on hand at all hours. The chance of hospital-related infection went up, but so did the likelihood that the latest medical practice and technology were available. It was an imperfect trade-off but one that, on balance, greatly improved health care.

From the 1920s until our own day, remarkably little has changed. Hospitals have become more technologically and operationally sophisticated, but you would recognize and know your way around a hospital throughout the past century whether you were living in 1927, in 1967, or in 2007. You would also recognize the same problems and challenges, too.

The Complications Set In

From the 1920s, as hospitals became larger and more sophisticated, they also became less personal and more bureaucratic. While treatment of acute conditions and trauma energized hospital staff to draw on their best abilities, hospitals were accused of being neglectful in the treatment of chronically ill patients and the aged, whose care was presumably more mundane and less rewarding. As physicians became increasingly specialized, they seemed to fail to consider the patient as a whole human being. The quality of service and basic physical conditions within hospitals were also an issue. Even a hundred years ago, walls needed painting, hallways needed to be cleaned, food was bland and lacking in nutrition, and unpleasant odors filled the air. There were long waits for treatment, delays in getting results, lost records, poor communication, infection, and plenty of mistakes.

If you have ever felt shuffled along and forgotten in a hospital today, rest assured that you would have felt that way in the past. If you have ever needed to change a bedpan for a loved one because staff neglected the duty, or cleaned a sink because it had not been wiped in days, remind yourself that in the early years, nonpaying patients—who were most of us—cleaned floors, assisted less able patients, did laundry, and repaired sheets. If you've ever wondered whether those who have connections and wealth receive more attention and care than those who don't, you should know that in the early days, paying patients, meaning the wealthy, occupied private rooms and could have their butlers or servants at their bedsides. Indeed, even getting access to treatment was facilitated by a letter of recommendation by someone connected to a trustee or famous surgeon.

In 1911, after her 90-year-old father died at Massachusetts General, Joan Smith wrote a letter of complaint to the board in which she chastised the hospital staff for treating patients with disrespect, disdain, and arrogance. She cited incidents in which staff ignored cries for help, failed to supply information, and responded to questions with rudeness. The inefficiency, lack of nursing care, and bureaucratic delays made her regret deeply that her father's long life had ended in a hospital where he was so poorly treated.[6]

In a letter to the *New York Times* published April 10, 2007, a recent cardiac patient had this to say:

> To the Editor:
> Your article about heart disease scared me. You stressed the urgency of speed in obtaining immediate care.
> One morning a year ago, I woke up with chest pains. I was taken by my wife to the emergency room of a local hospital. Once there, I was asked by a receptionist to fill out a lengthy form one gets when becoming a new patient at a doctor's office. The receptionist then had to get all my insurance data. She even asked me if the month of February was a 2 or a 3 because she had to enter all these data into a computer.
> I was then asked to sit down and wait. After about 10 minutes, the emergency room doors swung open, and several doctors and nurses approached and put me in a wheelchair. They then raced me through the doors, placed me on another chair or bed, and attached me to various I.V. needles, gadgets, and instruments.
> All this struck me as humorous nonsense. Why were they in such a hurry when their admissions staff couldn't have cared less?
> Andrew Zwarun
> Austin, Texas, April 8, 2007

Finances and operational budgets, too, have always been a problem. As early as 1904, New York City faced a financial crisis with its hospitals that raised so much public outcry a call was made for more government and private funding. A study in 1905 showed that while basic hospital construction and operating costs had increased little since 1870, new technology and legal requirements had more than doubled the cost per bed from $1,200 to $4,400. In addition, hospitals needed more employees and more specialized doctors to keep up with the demands of acute care.[7] It didn't matter what model was used. Charity-funded hospitals and privately funded hospitals suffered the same problems: Budgets exceeded financial revenues, so cutbacks on service and staff were always a problem.

Getting patients to pay more was one solution, but hospitals were burdened by the difficulty of securing funding and the impossibility of turning away sick people who could not afford treatment. In the late 1800s, for instance, hospitals complained of being overrun by new immigrants or the poor who had nowhere else to turn, a familiar situation to those who complain that undocumented immigrant workers or families without health insurance overfill our hospital emergency rooms today.

Who is paying, how much care a patient should receive, and who controls the purse strings have always been challenges. In the 1800s, physicians volunteered to work at hospitals, receiving no pay or other form of remuneration and even supplying their own medicines, because of the prestige or credibility obtained by being associated with an institution. An important side effect of this approach was that physicians were not employees of hospitals, but freelancers, essentially independent in how they went about their work (i.e., how they treated the hospital's customers). As hospitals grew in stature and became more central to health care, some physicians were reluctant to send their patients to them for fear of losing those customers to the hospitals. But by the 1920s, as hospitals experienced an increasingly competitive marketplace, the balance of power swung again, with hospitals now needing outside physicians to feed their system with patients. Despite being freelance practitioners outside of the hospitals' operating control, physicians decided how their patients would be treated, even though those costs were borne by the hospital. Imagine running a business but having no budgetary control over how your managers make decisions. This put hospitals in an impossible situation and is still a source of conflict today.

Throughout the past 30 years, there were shifts in reimbursement that contributed to the fairly frequent use of health maintenance organizations (HMOs), particularly in the 1980s. However, HMOs are quickly going the way of the Edsel due to consumer backlash. The insurance companies that specialize in offering HMO plans are set back on their heels. Although such an approach has done little to make the hospital a budgetary paradise, it has frustrated physicians and patients no end. Physicians don't like being told what treatments they can and cannot prescribe. Patients don't like being told what physicians they can see and what treatments they can receive. When it comes to our health, no doctor or patient wants to think in terms of cost. It is easy to see how the reimbursement insurance companies agree to pay is ever more controversial. The reality is the insurance companies are in the business of limiting their risk—the amount of money they have to pay out. They reduce their exposure in four ways: (1) underwriting—limiting who they cover, (2) benefit design—trying to attract the healthiest customers, (3) coverage limits, and (4) preapproval of big ticket items. On the one side of the argument, insurance companies attempt to manage out waste and control risk. On the other side of the debate, restrictions on treatments and procedures can stifle innovation and negatively impact clinical results. How do we know what protocol or drug will be a vast improvement over the standard method if doctors and hospitals can't experiment? A reasonable balance is, and has always been, a struggle to maintain.

Today, hospitals are burdened by crippling costs. Take the emergency room. By law, every hospital in the United States must provide a minimum level of care to every person who arrives at an emergency room, regardless of the seriousness of the condition or the individual's ability to pay. In practice, this means that every emergency room patient is screened by a physician and no one is turned away. The American Medical Association estimates that every hospital provides upwards of $140,000 of uncompensated emergency care per physician annually. Most of us do not care about the money being spent, but we are frustrated by the staggering waits. Ninety-one percent of hospitals report overcrowding, 40 percent of them daily. Over the past five years, 70 percent of hospitals have found themselves in a situation where ambulance drivers had to be diverted to other hospitals because of this overcrowding.

Cost burdens arise for a variety of other reasons, too. Litigation has run rampant, and the costs of lawsuits are passed on to consumers directly in terms of higher charges, and indirectly in terms of more defensive medicine. Every year, 20 million unnecessary antibiotics prescriptions are given out, 7.5 million unnecessary medical or surgical procedures are performed, and 8.9 million unnecessary hospitalizations occur—much of this directly resulting from fear of litigation. Labor shortages are also raising costs. If we let more nurses and doctors into this country from abroad, we could staff our hospitals with lower-cost but highly skilled personnel. Waste and inefficiency are resource killers in today's hospitals. CEOs are caught in a double bind: suffering from poor efficiency as a result of outdated technology and techniques, but at the same time unable to invest in critical new technology because doing so affects the bottom line. I believe that in a highly regulated marketplace, there is simply little incentive for hospital CEOs to differentiate their organizations in a competitive sense, and we all suffer as a result. The investment in an upgrade of information technology systems would be a very strategic tactic to eliminate tremendous administrative and paperwork costs, but surprisingly few hospitals are willing to make such a capital expenditure. As health care services go global, however, and hospitals in other countries offer cheaper, better-quality service, hospitals in the United States that do not prepare for such competition will find themselves in bigger trouble than they are now.

Another persistent challenge for hospitals over the past hundred years and more has been the frequency of illness, injury, and death due to infection and error. Unnecessary injuries and death are not only tragic, but also expensive. Fever and infection that occurred from treatment in a hospital or health care service unit was first noticed in the mid-1800s. Awareness of it spread as the hospitals became more prominent and crowded fixtures on the health care landscape. In fact, the more sophisticated and famous a hospital was, the more frequent its incidents of mysterious fever.

Poor sanitary conditions were soon understood to be the primary culprit. Early figures like the famous Florence Nightingale preached the benefits of clean, well-ventilated facilities, contradicting the once-popular belief that mysterious infections and epidemics came from God. Surgeon General William Hammond was himself a major influence in improving the environment of hospitals through architectural design changes during the Civil War. And as science advanced, we came to understand the medical causes of infection better. For instance, for many years, pus and rotten flesh around a wound were seen as a sign that the body was healing by rejecting its bad tissue, rather than as an indication of rapidly progressing infection. As a result, physicians and nurses moved from patient to patient spreading infection without knowing it.

But even though antiseptic surgery practices improved in the 1900s, staph infections abound in hospitals today. According to a 2007 report from the Association for Professionals in Infection Control and Epidemiology (APIC), 1.2 million hospital patients get staph infections every year, 10 times more than was estimated in the last major study two years before. Of those who get infected, 48,000 to 119,000 patients die every year as a result.[8]

Altogether, the hospital system has always faced serious and complicated challenges, despite the best efforts of our brightest minds and most humane practitioners. Over the course of a century, numerous hospitals have fallen under public perceptions of impersonal service, low-quality care, shoddy facilities, cost overruns, overcrowding, poor information flow, and deaths and injuries from errors and mysterious infections. Today, these are characteristics that many hospitals are still trying to improve or eliminate.

Through the pioneering work of Dr. E. A. Codman a century ago, I hope to convince you that there is a way.

The End Results System

Ernest Codman, who lived from 1869 until 1940, was one of the Boston elite. He graduated from Harvard Medical School in 1895 and interned at Massachusetts General Hospital. A top surgeon at MGH, as well as a professor at Harvard Medical School, he also co-founded the American College of Surgeons (ACS), an organization that included such noted figures as George Crile, founder of the Cleveland Clinic, and Charles Mayo, founder of the Mayo Clinic. But despite his pedigree and station, Codman risked his professional reputation and gave up his affiliations in a zealous crusade for a simple idea. Codman believed that the quality of care a hospital provides should be measured objectively in terms of end results, and that such data should be made publicly available to provide physicians with standards for improvement and consumers with the information to make informed decisions. To many in the establishment of the time, his idea was far too radical and threatening to be adopted.

For centuries, surgery had been held in low regard by patients and doctors alike, and many surgeons were considered little more than butchers. By the early 1900s, however, with the rise of the great hospitals and their affiliations with the great medical schools, surgery had finally become a respected practice. Yet, in Codman's view, surgery was still not a science because it had done little to adopt standardized best practices, and hospitals were not doing enough to ensure that patients receive the best scientifically validated treatment known.

Dr. Codman described the end results idea as "the common-sense notion that every hospital should follow *every* patient it treats, long enough to determine whether or not the treatment has been successful, and then to inquire 'if not, why not?' with a view to preventing a similar failure in the future."[9] The technology for the system was a simple "end results card" assigned to each patient, which included data cells for descriptions of the patient's condition, the initial diagnosis, the course of treatment prescribed, the benefits and complications of the treatment, the diagnosis once the patient was discharged, and follow-up analysis for a number of years thereafter. In his own practice, Dr. Codman's end results cards included 141 deaths that occurred during his 15 years at Massachusetts General and another 337 cases after he left to practice surgery on his own. Codman did not limit his data to pro forma observations; he made qualitative judgments about the outcomes, particularly when the result was failure. He ruthlessly determined whether the fault was due to the skill of the surgeon, a lack of equipment, preventable errors, some behavior or attribute of the patient, or the disease itself.

As in our own time, many who worked in health care during Codman's day believed that health care results could not be measured, because there was too much variation between patients and conditions, and medical treatment involved more art than science. Codman disputed these notions in industrial terms by claiming that the only significant "product" of a hospital should be the results of the treatment provided there. He believed that high-quality results should be standardized so they can be reproduced in other settings, the way an industrialist would copy best practices in one factory and apply them to all others to achieve consistent low-priced production. In this way, Codman was promoting the link between science and management in order to measurably improve the overall quality of care.

Codman knew that in practice surgery led to constant experimentation based on particular conditions. But if those experiments were never recorded or collected, any innovations or process improvements benefited only the individual patient and physician and no one else. By focusing on results—and the means by which those results were achieved—a chief surgeon could assess the performance of staff physicians and reward them or coach them accordingly. Reaching further, Codman hoped to build an entire system for improving the efficiency and quality of care. Physicians would submit their end results cards to the American College of Surgeons or some other review body. Innovations would be surfaced quickly, evaluated effectively, and circulated to other hospitals. Those hospitals would then be responsible for monitoring and adopting the latest in best practices for the benefit of patients.

This notion had tremendous implications not only for the science of surgery but also for the business of running and marketing hospitals. For instance, as a hospital administrator, Codman was acutely aware of hospital costs. Efficiency for him meant eliminating unnecessary hospital visits, prolonged stays, and avoidable errors, because these cost money. In addition, Codman declared that assessing end results allowed a hospital administrator to further reduce costs by eliminating useless or less effective procedures. As Codman put it: "The prevention of waste and the judgment of the proportion which each item should take, in order to be sure of a product—the satisfied and relieved patient—is the essence of good hospital management. This idea . . . has never penetrated hospital managements. Their minds have been satisfied with treatment, not with the good results of treatment."[10]

Codman imagined that hospitals run efficiently—meaning those that obtained the best results with the least waste—would stand out in the marketplace and be rewarded accordingly. At the time, according to Codman, hospitals obscured performance results deliberately, and patients were in the dark about where to go for the best care. As Codman observed, "No one, be he rich or poor, knows whether he really has the services of a good surgeon . . . because [hospitals] do not find out which surgeons get the best results, and let the public know."[11] Codman urged hospitals to make their results public so that general practitioner physicians recommending treatment would know the best place to send their patients. Despite personal misgivings that rankings would become a form of crass advertising, he advocated for hospital and surgeon performance measures to be published in order to inform the marketplace.

In this way, Codman was the prophet of a more rational health care marketplace. He imagined a day when surgeons who were good at one particular procedure would concentrate on that and make it their specialty, thus earning top dollar for their repeatedly demonstrated skill. He also envisioned that hospitals would go the same route, and forcefully criticized the common practice of every hospital accepting every patient regardless of the aptitude or capability of the institution to treat that patient. Instead, if patients and prescribing physicians had sufficient information to make informed decisions, they would be rational actors and naturally choose the best hospital at the best price for a particular condition and avoid hospitals that performed poorly or charged more than the value of the procedure. Such competition would force hospitals to develop niche services, thus increasing the volume and quality of their work while lowering the price. Codman derided the fact that doctors' and hospitals' reputations and networks of relationships were the primary means by which they were able to charge fees, and instead envisioned a system in which the market rate for a surgeon's service would depend on his public record of performance. In a statement that still rings loudly today, he argued that the only thing that mattered to a patient was a surgeon's or a hospital's results, but such information was never made available. "Secrecy is the peculiar disease of efficiency," Codman stated, and publicity was the cure.[12]

Codman's belief that hospitals and physicians offer a product for sale in an imperfect marketplace is still a radical notion today. It is not surprising, therefore, that Codman experienced great difficulties in his lifetime. Like a bull in a china shop, his obsession with the end results approach wrecked many of his relationships.

To prove his theories, he resigned from Massachusetts General and opened a hospital of his own, moving his surgical practice from the vaunted halls of Mass General to a little house in a shabby part of the city where he had 12 beds for patients. It was a rash choice, but Codman believed he needed to be able to work outside the establishment to be free of the restrictions of stodgy trustees and less reform-minded colleagues. Why pay a high price for substandard work, he asked, when you can be guaranteed quality at a reasonable price? His hospital's motto was "A Hundred Dollar Hospital with a Hundred Dollar Surgeon," and he advertised a clear fixed fee for care. This put the onus on his surgeons to be as efficient and results-oriented as possible. No one was accustomed to thinking about health care and medical practice as a business. Nevertheless, Codman practiced what he preached. His hospital used the end results system faithfully, and he published and distributed the data to the public and the heads of major hospitals in the hope of winning converts.

But for all his brilliance, Codman's ideas never gained institutional support. His arrogance did not help matters. At a meeting of top surgeons and administrators to discuss the theme of hospital efficiency, Codman unveiled a cartoon he'd drawn that depicted the citizenry of

Boston as an ostrich with its head stuck in the sand, surrounded by greedy Harvard doctors and hospital administrators collecting a slew of golden eggs representing money paid for unnecessary surgical procedures. The point wasn't subtle and wasn't well received. No one liked being told they were taking advantage of an unwitting public.

Great events also got in the way. Codman blamed his failure to advance his ideas on the outbreak of World War I. The chaos of the war and the devastating flu epidemic that killed millions around the world made the implementation of any rational system difficult. Even so, he was able to organize an emergency hospital with an end results system in Halifax, Canada, after the explosion of a munitions cargo ship in Halifax Harbor in 1917 left thousands dead and injured. Still, by the time the war ended, Codman was broke and his hospital had been closed. For the rest of his career, he concentrated his considerable brilliance on an end results study of bone cancer. At the end of his life, Codman viewed that study as his one lasting legacy to the world.

It is my view, however, that the final chapter of Codman's legacy has not yet been written.

The Low-Cost, High-Quality Shift

Codman's approach to standardizing best practices can have an incredible impact on the quality of health care. A particularly strong example comes from the world of obstetrics.

Human birth, that most miraculous and yet natural of events, generally takes place in a hospital in this country. Although the procedure is so common it can seem routine, every parent knows that it is not. Much can happen during labor to create moments of uncertainty, anxiety, and real risk. If a crisis occurs, we soon appreciate the advances of medical science and may gain renewed awareness that for thousands of years, giving birth has been the most traumatic and life-threatening moment in a woman's life. Today, in the four million births that take place in the United States every year, the chances are excellent that everything will turn out right for both newborn and mother.

In fact, it didn't always look as though we would manage to achieve such progress. One of the greatest technological developments in obstetrics occurred in the 1600s with the invention of the forceps. Although considered primitive today, forceps saved many lives by allowing the doctor to pull a stuck baby out of the birth canal. Amazingly, their inventor and the early practitioners kept the technology secret for almost a hundred years because it gave them a competitive advantage. When knowledge about forceps finally spread in the mid-eighteenth century, they were soon a common tool for doctors.

By the 1930s, as antiseptics, blood transfusions, and labor-inducing drugs became available, more women began having their babies in hospitals. A 1933 study of maternal deaths, however, threw cold water on the idea of medical progress. The maternal death rate had not improved with the shift to hospital deliveries, and newborn deaths had actually increased. Moreover, two-thirds of all those deaths had been preventable. Despite access to the best medical technology, doctors did a worse job delivering babies in hospitals than midwifes did in the home.

The problem was that doctors did not always know what they were doing, and the reason was a lack of standardization. Over the following decades strict regulations were instituted, training regimens mandated, and precise steps in procedure established. Every time there was a maternal death, it was analyzed to see where things had gone wrong and how standards could be improved. By the 1950s, maternal deaths had fallen 90 percent. The newborn death rate had improved little, however, and was still a major concern until a simple metric changed everything.

The Apgar score was created in 1952 by Virginia Apgar, a brilliant doctor and anesthesiologist. Dr. Apgar was dismayed over the frequency with which unresponsive or blue infants were allowed to die untended. Her simple 10-point score assessed a newborn's condition on five aspects— Appearance (skin color), Pulse (heart rate), Grimace (responsiveness), Activity, and Respiration—and assigned points for how well the infant was doing in each category. Using the score, nurses and doctors could easily make an objective and clear assessment. What's more, they tended to work harder to raise the score to an acceptable level when it was low, and to try to generate better scores overall. During the 50 years that followed, tracking simple objectives and measures, the field of obstetrics managed the balance between constantly upgrading standards to improve reliability and continuing to innovate to improve care. Today, giving birth is extremely safe for mother and newborn.[13] In fact, recent studies show that newborn deaths in the United States are down to 6.3 per thousand births, while maternal deaths during childbirth are down to just one in every 10,000 live births!

I believe that quality should be measured in outcomes—lives saved or improved, procedures implemented successfully, errors reduced, and customer satisfaction raised. This spirit needs to be implemented in all aspects of health care and at all stages of the care cycle. In my view, the problems hospitals face are so persistent because hospitals have not adopted the operational quality and service standards common in a competitive business market. For many people—including physicians, patients, and policy makers—the idea of running a hospital and providing health care in general like a business is anathema. For some reason, we believe that the practice of medicine is more art and craft than it is business and science. But if we industrialize health care as if it were any other business, we can make it have lower cost and higher quality at the same time. Today, some pioneering health systems are making that exact shift with dramatic results.

Geisinger Health System in central Pennsylvania, for example, decided to overhaul its elective heart bypass surgery as a way of reducing its costs and providing higher-quality care. To do so, Geisinger's cardiac surgeons first came up with a checklist of 40 best-practice action items. Although Geisinger did not force surgeons to follow every item, the very existence of the list became a strong reminder of all the steps that needed to be taken before cardiac surgery. Now the culture of the hospital is to cancel an operation if any step has been forgotten.

In a move that would make Codman proud, Geisinger combined this thoroughness of approach with a fee structure for service that provides an incentive for quality outcomes. Geisinger charges insurers a flat fee for the surgery plus half the amount that would normally be charged for related care over a 90-day period following the surgery. In effect, this 90-day half-price charge functions as a guarantee of quality—you don't pay more if the hospital or surgeon makes a mistake, and they have an incentive to do it right the first time. In most hospitals, by way of contrast, an error or a poor outcome arising because of surgery requires extensive postoperative hospital care, which the hospital is able to charge to you or your health insurer. In other words, mistakes and low-quality treatment are, perversely, to the hospital's benefit since they generate more revenue. This is one major reason why the overall cost of health care continues to rise as quality declines—high cost often does equal low quality. In Geisinger's case, the hospital absorbs the costs if postoperative hospital care is necessary, and does better financially if surgery has a high-quality outcome and further care is not needed. Geisinger is trying to replicate this approach in other surgical areas such as hip replacement surgery and thereby expand its offerings to encourage health insurance systems to include its system in their offerings. Geisinger has even branded its service as ProvenCare. For a small health care system in the middle of Pennsylvania, this is a remarkably effective market-based approach to competing with the larger and more famous hospitals.[14]

Today, Codman's efforts at driving efficiency and improving quality and service have a great deal in common with the six sigma movement in business. Six sigma technology was developed more than 25 years ago by Motorola to improve product reliability. Engineers studying manufacturing production had determined that there were typically 66,000 errors for every million "opportunities" during the course of the production of a product or service. In other words, typical manufacturing processes were operating at a 6.6 percent error rate. Although this may seem like a small number, the ramifications in terms of product quality and customer satisfaction are enormous. What if 6 percent of the tires you manufacture are faulty and lead to highway deaths? Few businesses can stand such a high level of errors. By studying every stage of the production process, measuring outcomes, identifying and correcting errors, and installing innovations to improve performance, engineers hoped to almost halve error rates to 34,000 per million opportunities, with the goal of ultimately eliminating defects altogether.

Other companies, particularly in the manufacturing sector, adopted six sigma technology with great impact. When Jack Welch made six sigma practices a cultural fixture at General Electric, those who studied and followed his every move helped spread the approach to other industries and businesses. McKesson itself has adopted six sigma as the corporate standard, and with outstanding success.

Can six sigma be used in hospitals? I believe it must. We don't think about hospitals as manufacturing operations, but they are. Everything that happens to you in a hospital, from your trip through an emergency ward to your elective surgery, involves an established process with many steps. An error rate of 66,000 per million patient procedures seems like a reasonable number in theory until you consider the possibility that you or your child will have a 6 percent chance of receiving the wrong drug or being prepped improperly for surgery. As a consumer and a father, I want that defect rate to be as close to zero as possible.

It amazes me that we tolerate anything less than perfection in our hospitals when we don't tolerate it in other industries like toy or car manufacturing. Many practitioners and observers declare that health care has too many complex variables to be quantified, but as a patient, I would feel more confident knowing that the hospital has a thorough system in place for ensuring that all the steps involved in my treatment are taken. In fact, there are many areas in which a number of hospitals are implementing six sigma standards. These include reducing medication errors, reducing patient falls, reducing hospital-acquired infections, reducing administration errors, reducing lost MRI films, improving turn-around time for pharmacy orders, increasing operating room throughput, reducing emergency room errors, decreasing length of stay for stroke patients, and improving patient satisfaction. There is much more to be done. A number of other business standards can be copied exactly from other industries and thereby hasten the transformation of American health care. Other industries have utilized error-reducing methods, such as highly experienced production design and implementation managers who oversee entire processes. Such systems are considered standard in industries that have been successfully transformed. This is not the case with health care in the United States.

It is more common today for protocols and procedures to vary drastically not only between hospital systems but between physicians within hospital systems. We are very far from Codman's notion that performance innovations should be surfaced and spread across all hospitals to bring new standards of best practice to health care.

As is obvious from the list, six sigma targeted measures can be simple or complex, but they should be chosen for maximum impact. In that spirit, the Pittsburgh Regional Healthcare Initiative (PRHI) is trying to eliminate the most deadly and antibiotic-resistant form of staph infection—methicillin-resistant staphylococcus aureus (MRSA)—which can be found in every hospital in the United States. As I mentioned, staph infections kill 48,000 to 119,000 patients every year. So how do we stop this rampant killer? The basic tool is hand soap. Whereas 70 percent of nurses wash their hands before treating a patient, 70 percent of doctors don't. And yet we know that if hands aren't washed 100 percent of the time, staph infections cannot be eliminated. So how do we bring the defect rate to zero?

In order to understand how to do so, PRHI used the process engineering techniques common to companies like Toyota, the most successful organizations in the world at eliminating errors and improving quality. You might think that radical structural changes would be necessary to transform a hospital's ability to fight such an intractable problem, but this was not the case. Together with the doctors, nurses, and other staff, those studying the problem determined a number of extremely simple processes that could be instituted to make hand washing an unmissable step in any patient interaction.

These included making sanitizer dispensers available; using disposable gowns, masks, gloves, and equipment; cleaning the patient areas thoroughly; identifying infected patients, isolating them, and flagging their records for future admittance; and controlling antibiotics use.

None of this was groundbreaking or original on its own, but the trick was to make the process improvements stick. To do so, they analyzed where the breakdowns were occurring. Workers weren't using gloves 100 percent of the time because glove dispensers were often empty; the solution was to ensure glove dispensers were always stocked. Hand sanitizers were not always conveniently located; so sanitizers were placed everywhere they could possibly be needed. Nurses did not always wash their hands because their time was being wasted doing such menial tasks as looking for wheelchairs; so a new system was developed for the use of wheelchairs. In addition, to better deal with infected patients, their rooms were now clearly marked as hot zones with tape on the floor; all workers who entered those zones needed to be gowned, and all equipment such as stethoscopes used in the rooms had to stay there.

By implementing strict procedures surrounding all of these areas, PRHI has brought its staph infection rate to zero. The secret ingredients to its success were having the leadership to focus on a targeted problem, involving all the key stakeholders in coming up with workable solutions, and creating a system that supported the goal.

In Codman's universe, such a successful approach would be immediately adopted by every hospital in the country. In fact, PRHI uses Codman's end results model to share learning by linking patient outcomes data with care processes and distributing that information throughout its system. This has led to measurable improvements in quality and patient safety. Of course, the key word in all this is *measure*. PRHI's willingness to measure its performance forces it to analyze mistakes and spread improvement innovations. What gets measured and targeted gets improved.

Another story comes from the Dana-Farber Cancer Institute in Boston, Massachusetts. In 1994, in a tragic error, two cancer patients were administered extremely high doses of chemotherapy drugs. One woman died, and the other suffered permanent heart damage. The bad publicity from the event was very detrimental to Dana-Farber's reputation for safety, and strong measures were taken to institute a mistake-free culture. Today, Dana-Farber has a vigilant error-reporting system in place. Pharmacists are not allowed to fill handwritten or verbal prescriptions. Doctors must show the latest scientific results to pharmacists if they wish to prescribe dosages that are not standard. Nurses get the same instructions in the same way every time they administer a prescription. This system required a tremendous organizational commitment, cost approximately $11 million to implement, and involved extensive staff training and the hiring of doctor assistants to help mitigate the extra time and attention needed. Furthermore, Dana-Farber has been relentless about reporting and assessing all medical errors since 1994, no matter how trivial or noninjurious, in order to maintain its culture of error reduction. For the staff of Dana-Farber, the business case for such measures has been self-evident. Unfortunately, most hospitals in this country do not even track errors, let alone make attempts to learn from them. Tracking errors and learning from them is the kind of mind-set a six sigma culture can instill.

Changing Hospital Culture

The 1900s saw the rise of the corporation and a golden age of management and operational efficiency. From family-owned businesses, corporations sprang, then expanded, developed specialized divisions and units, and became complex global conglomerates. Focused on the market, they added or shed operations, products, or services as needed, had great incentive to innovate, and were able to control costs and improve quality as a means of competing for customers.

The American hospital, while it has become far more technologically sophisticated over the century, did not follow the same evolutionary path as the corporation. We all pay a steep price as a result—in terms of needless errors, infections, and injuries, substandard practices, and heavy costs. One-third of our health care dollars are spent at the hospital. Yet we are not achieving the low-cost, high-quality results of a typical industry. Instead, our hospitals are overburdened with patients, paperwork, and unnecessary expenses. While we have made tremendous progress in treating trauma, illness, and disease, the hospital is still a place that every health care consumer should avoid if possible because of the life-threatening risk of errors and infections and the poor quality of service.

If we want to fix our health care system, though, the hospital is the place to start. Hospitals will always be institutions that are difficult to lead and manage, because their business is crisis and they employ highly talented workers who can walk out the door at any moment. But hospitals or hospital systems that are run in an integrated fashion have a leg up in terms of producing high-quality, low-cost results. Systems such as St. Luke's, PRHI, the Mayo Clinic, and Covenant Health are able to upgrade, innovate, implement standards, integrate departments, and monitor patients better over the course of the entire care cycle than the stand-alone hospital operated by freelance physicians.

The first lesson of a successful system is that it's not about the doctor; it's about the system. This notion challenges the oftentimes typical belief that doctors and surgeons are unimpeachable demigods. It is all too common to see a system in which the solo heroic practitioner is given ownership over patients and becomes responsible for every decision concerning their well-being. This problem will be discussed more in the next chapter, but the concept as it applies to the organization is nothing new. Often the most successful businesses are those that recognize the value of the team and create an environment in which feedback and expression are encouraged. This is rarely the case in hospitals. But consider the fact that nurses, internists, technicians, and just about every professional in the hospital environment is extremely well trained and competent. To discourage the input of the team in favor of pride or competition is to limit valuable knowledge that can be learned from and put to future use. With many cases of medical error, it is not the individual practitioner's fault. Instead, the error can often be attributed to the fact that standard protocols are not in place, or that the medical team did not have the sway to hold the individual accountable for questionable decisions.

In some of the more advanced systems, protocols and processes can be implemented with confidence that they will be followed. As we saw through the hand-washing example, even simple measures can have significant impact, but if a physician feels no imperative to follow along, the protocol may as well not even exist. We see dramatic instances of this in top cancer hospitals or cardiovascular units where the treatment for the same disease or condition varies wildly from patient to patient because not all physicians in the hospital are following the latest and best protocols. In Codman's universe, standards would create a common base level of care, and innovations and improvements would be circulated, assessed, and adopted as new standards if proven worthy. But the statistics show that only slightly more than 50 percent of patients today receive the best scientifically based, medically appropriate care when they see a doctor. According to the RAND Corporation, 126,000 patients die every year as a result. We'll talk more about this in the next chapter when we discuss the idea of evidence-based medicine, but the reasons for the appalling statistics are because hospitals without strong systems do not monitor what their physicians are doing.

When physicians are not formally part of the hospital system as paid staff, it is difficult to get them to adopt new protocols, comply with new standards, follow new processes, or even use new technologies. The benefits of these can be amazing, however, and American hospitals need to move resolutely and speedily to a paperless electronic system. The shift will save immense amounts of time, which can be put toward better care. More important, though, a shift to a digital system will also save lives.

For example, in hospitals where the bar code and drug dispensary system I described in the previous chapter are in place, medication errors are eliminated. In addition, doctors are able to access blood tests, X-rays, MRIs, or CAT scans instantly when they are interacting with a patient, instead of hunting for those results, duplicating tests or paperwork, or simply delaying or making a mistake. As anyone who has been to the hospital recently knows, it is far more likely that many physicians will be examining you over the course of your treatment, not to mention the number of nurses, pharmacists, and technicians who play a part, too. Electronic systems keep everyone on the exact same page, allowing them to communicate as a team with one objective: taking care of you.

When hospitals go digital, the dream of better outpatient care can become a reality. No matter what condition brings you to a hospital, it is likely that most of the care you receive will be limited to that very short time before you are discharged. Follow-up treatment, where it exists, might amount to a phone call from a nurse's aide somewhere down the road. But with digital information systems we can track and monitor you remotely whenever needed. Very few patients actually follow the course of treatment or medication prescribed to them after their visit with their doctor. For example, in a test that was recently conducted on patients one month following discharge from a well-known cardiac rehabilitation facility, it was shown that none of the participants adhered to all three of the self-monitoring recommendations that were prescribed. But with a digital information system, a hospital or clinic can track patients to determine how they are progressing and why. Blood tests can be taken at home, and the data can be instantly transmitted to the doctor. The scale in your bathroom can monitor your weight and send that to the hospital. An e-mail message from the hospital can inform you when it is important for you to get a flu shot because you are at risk for a certain kind of pneumonia. The same e-mail message can allow you to schedule an appointment or a hospital stay.

Such capabilities are particularly helpful in the treatment of chronically ill patients. We are transitioning in this country from a health care system built to treat acute illnesses or traumas to one that will need to treat an aging and growing population of the chronically ill. Smoking and obesity-related illnesses alone cost $300 billion to $400 billion a year to treat. Much of that cost is borne by hospitals and their emergency rooms. We are projected to have eight million Alzheimer's patients in this country by 2025. A variety of serious chronic illnesses are threatening to cripple our hospital system and health care budget if we do not learn to treat them better on an ambulatory or outpatient basis. Digital technology, the kind that links patients, care providers, hospitals, clinics, labs, and pharmacies, is vital to reduce this load and give people lives that are as normal as possible, not enslaved to a hospital waiting room.

The Hospital in the Marketplace

I'm one of the lucky ones. I have a network of contacts and knowledgeable experts who know where to go for the best care for whatever specific illness or condition someone is confronting. Friends and colleagues ask me for such advice all the time, and I am happy to help. But my inside track comes from being the head of a large health care business with connections in every major health care institution or business in the country. Unfortunately, there's no system in place to provide necessary information about quality and expertise to the general public. If you have a serious or life-threatening illness, or a condition that can significantly impede your ability to enjoy life, you want the best treatment. But whether you go to the nearest hospital or to the top-recommended one, the chances of receiving scientifically appropriate care are at best a random walk.

In 2007, *Time* magazine asked physicians if they would go to their own hospital to receive treatment. I've asked that question to dozens of doctors and nurses myself. The answer is: It depends. As insiders, doctors and nurses are acutely aware of what procedures and treatments their hospital does well, and what their hospital does poorly. At one hospital, they might be happy to receive a stent to correct a heart valve; but they'd never dream of having a gallbladder removed there. As anyone who has tried to seek out the best heart surgeon or the best cancer specialist can tell you, such information is extremely difficult to uncover. It requires hard work and connections, and even then the choices are unclear.

The answer is not the individual doctor; we need to seek out the best hospital system. Top-performing hospitals have certain characteristics in common. They have a cohesive governance and leadership structure in place that is disciplined and inclusive—meaning that doctors, nurses, and administrators are united behind a commonly articulated mission of excellence. They have top leadership that focuses on continuous improvement by creating standards and guidelines; in other words, they systemize the health care process to focus on quality outputs the same way Toyota does in producing quality vehicles. They engage the entire leadership in strategic planning by creating an ongoing process to connect strategy to operational excellence, focusing on adopting internal lessons and external best practices into everyday routine. And they ensure the culture of the organization is focused and aligned around explicit objectives by monitoring, measuring, and taking steps to improve processes on a consistent basis, supported by putting ongoing training, development plans, and coaching and mentoring systems in place. This winning combination of vision, strategy, the pursuit of flawless execution, devotion to continuous improvement, and leadership is uncommon for sure, but not unheard-of in this country. St. Luke's Hospital, a recent recipient of the Malcolm Baldrige National Quality Award, is a great example. It uses a team approach to develop and apply clinical pathways or treatment protocols to guarantee quality treatment. Patient-focused care is emphasized through 12 Customer Contact Requirements, which are posted all around the premises. St. Luke's uses a Strategic Planning Process to improve strategy and leadership among employees. This incorporates assessments and improvement models to map out 90-day departmental action plans and ongoing individual development plans, which include leadership retreats, peer reviews, surveys, and standardized outcome measures.

But with the exception of the few examples we hear about through awards, how do we effectively know whether a hospital is applying such internal leadership and operational excellence standards? We need to look at outputs in terms of the quality of care. Although the measures did not go nearly far enough for Dr. Ernest Codman's liking, the American College of Surgeons did develop a set of minimum standards for hospitals in his lifetime. By 1918, the ACS was inspecting hospitals across the United States to determine if they met minimum standards. In 1951, the ACS was joined by the American College of Physicians, the American Hospital Association, the American Medical Association, and the Canadian Medical Association to create the commission that serves as the accreditation agency for all hospitals. Today, the Joint Committee—formerly the Joint Committee on Accreditation of Healthcare Organizations (JCAHO)—does unannounced surveys at hospitals around the country and works with the World Health Organization to standardize patient safety solutions. You can go to its web site at www.qualitycheck.org to view ratings and awards for hospitals in the specialties that interest you.

But such a rating system still doesn't go far enough. Codman's vision of hospitals operating in a more market-based environment will rescue our health care system by making efficiency—meaning high-quality, low-priced service—the standard for good care. As Codman understood, however, a market-based system requires complete transparency. Today, we can find out more about the vacuum cleaner we are about to buy than the cancer treatment we're about to receive. The digital age can change all this by collecting, updating, and distributing the information needed to make rational economic decisions. We need to be able to know which hospital has the least errors and the fewest incidents of staph infection. We need to know which hospital does the most hip replacement surgeries, how much it charges, and what the success rate is. Would you rather go to the hospital that does 10 cardiac stents a month or the one that does 10 a day? In a rational marketplace, patients and payers would gravitate to the providers that operate at low cost and achieve the best outcomes through high volume—thus rewarding them with more business.

Yes, there will be tumult when marketplace health care comes into existence. Some hospitals will close, others will thrive, and new ones will open with state-of-the-art processes, systems, and teams of professionals knowing how to improve outcomes and change the face of care. Hospitals that currently strive to be all things to all people may need to specialize in areas that differentiate them in order to succeed. We place a very high premium on convenience today. In rural communities or in big-city neighborhoods we allow hospitals to exist that underperform other hospitals simply because we want to avoid a community outcry. But if the customers of those hospitals knew that by driving an extra hour they would have a 20 percent better chance of higher-quality life after surgery, don't you think most people would make such a choice?

Whether or not we wish it to happen, the marketplace is coming to health care. Hospital systems like Geisinger and PRHI will be joining the Mayo Clinics, M.D. Andersons, Cleveland Clinics, and Dana-Farbers as standard-bearers in their particular specialties. In addition, medical tourism is becoming a very viable option. Today, heart surgery at the Apollo Hospital in India or Raffles in Singapore is becoming an increasingly attractive option for health care consumers with that need. Similarly, why pay $12,000 for elective dental surgery in Chicago when you can pay $1,500 for the same quality output at a clinic in Mexico City? As these options become more doable and widely known, and as health plans continue to throttle choice, consumers will do their voting with their wallets and their passports.

The genie is out of the bottle. The low-quality, high-cost conundrum is becoming widely understood in American politics. The demand for transparency is growing. I believe we're entering an age when we will not hold the medical profession in silent awe, but will be in a position to make demands for better quality. In the future, I think that the service and standards of the best-run businesses will be in place in hospitals across the United States. When we visit Disney World, we obtain a customer experience that is carefully manufactured. We're not allowed to see below the surface where the operational work takes place. We're not confronted by garbage, tired workers, and disorderly situations. We enjoy ourselves because we trust in their ability to deliver. Hospitals will learn to be like this, too.

We will use hospitals less often in the future. We will do a great deal of our medical business in nontraditional locations—the shopping mall, a kiosk at a place of work, at our home computer, or in the pharmacy—and we will go to the hospital only when necessary, for emergencies or scheduled treatments. Imagine yourself getting ready for a hip replacement operation. You've been equipped in advance with the tools necessary to take your blood and monitor your health. You get reminded by e-mail about your scheduled appointment for surgery. You show up mere hours in advance with your suitcase and check into your room, which has all the amenities and comfort of a fine hotel. When the time comes, your surgery takes place, and you have the comfort of knowing that the surgical team has performed this exact procedure many times, is using the latest scientifically proven protocols, and has a six sigma system in place to ensure that the procedure is error free. When the surgery is done, all of your follow-up care is tracked and monitored remotely. Everyone involved in caring for you has all the information they need at hand, and they are reminded automatically of the tests, follow-up visits, and therapy you require.

This is not a utopian vision; this is the market-based health care system that is on the way. In the future, health care organizations will provide us with all the information we need because they want our business. They will treat patients and their families as valued customers by making great efforts to improve the hospital experience on its surface levels—in terms of improved administration, faster through times, more time with the caregiver, and better physical surroundings—and by creating processes and procedures internally that eliminate errors and infections. We will know when that future has arrived when we feel in control, at the center of our own health care decisions.

Chapter 4

The Doctor Will
See You Now

Today, we have nostalgia for a time when doctors and nurses were truly care providers. In my youth, this role was exemplified by Dr. Marcus Welby on television. I think people responded to the depth of caring Dr. Welby showed his patients, treating the whole person, getting to know them at length, and worrying almost as much about their personal lives and families as their physical health. Before Marcus Welby, from the late 1930s well into the 1960s, there was Dr. Kildare, who showed a similar interest in the patient as a whole person. In the very first episode of the 1960s TV version, a young Dr. Kildare is told by the crusty senior physician, "Our job is to keep people alive, not to tell them how to live." Dr. Kildare ignored that advice, and his patients and the television audience were rewarded as a result.

Nowadays, a visit to the doctor's clinic or the emergency room can feel more like Kafka than Kildare. It takes months to get an appointment. You arrive at the physician's waiting room, and the first thing you do is fork over your co-pay and sign away your privacy. Then you sit for 45 minutes until the nurse ushers you inside and deposits you in a smaller waiting room. There, you sit for another 15 minutes before a different nurse appears and asks you a number of questions about your condition. Five minutes after that, the doctor shows up, harried and busy. He flips through your chart, consults the nurse's notes, asks many of the same questions, gives you a brief consultation, and issues a snap diagnosis with a prescription or a referral. Then you're done. The actual time spent with the doctor is 12 minutes tops, but you've been at the clinic for over an hour, and you leave feeling more like a widget on the assembly line than a whole person with concerns and a need for answers.

If you have a chronic condition, you struggle with this lack of connection on a daily basis. Beyond your primary care physician, you probably have up to 15 different professionals to deal with regularly, including specialists, technicians, nurse-practitioners, pharmacists, and possibly social workers. By necessity, you become the facilitator of your own health care. You carry around a file of notes and records because you know from experience that each link in the chain will be missing vital information and it is your responsibility to provide it. You also become an expert on your own condition because you keep up on the latest developments, treatments, and medicines, and you end up knowing more about yourself than some of the doctors and nurses in control of your fate. At an emergency room or during a scheduled hospital stay, the same circumstances are encountered, though compounded by the overcrowding, the urgency, or the disconnection between members of your health care team. All in all, even though you may be able to access the most technologically advanced treatment on the planet, the quality of care and the intimacy of care feel lacking.

Is that because health care providers don't care as much as they used to? Not a chance. In my experience, the men and women working in the health care trenches are just as frustrated as patients are. The problem is that we are operating with a broken business model. For example, in order to pay the bills on time, a primary care physician at a small clinic needs to maximize throughput. A cut in reimbursement means the doctor needs to increase patient volume just to hold his or her income steady. You feel that difference as a drop in the intimacy, duration, and quality of your time spent with the physician. Hospitals are bureaucratic and impersonal because they can't handle their loads. Overcrowding in the emergency room happens because there are 47 million people without health care coverage and many millions more with inadequate coverage or chronic conditions that rely on the hospital to be their de facto personal physician. Health care teams are poorly coordinated not because they have lousy social skills but because care providers aren't actually organized as teams and our health care industry's telecommunication capabilities are stuck somewhere between the early 1950s and the mid-1970s. On top of all that, care providers are overburdened because they're facing severe manpower shortages. We're training the same number of doctors in the United States that we trained in 1985, even though the population has nearly doubled and demand for health care is projected to increase by 50 percent between now and 2020. We also have a decreasing number of nurses who want to stay in the workforce.

On bad days, it's as hard for care providers as it is for patients to be positive about the vitals of our health care system. Yet the changes that are coming will go a long way toward alleviating the challenges we now face. In this chapter, I'll explain how patients and care providers will evolve in terms of expectations and roles, and why we may be seeing more of Marcus Welby in the future.

Evolution of the American Doctor

Near the end of his snake oil salesman days, John D. Rockefeller's father, known then by his alias, Dr. William Levingston, began traveling with a young huckster protégé named Charles Johnston. Old Doc Rockefeller dressed Johnston up as a Native American in war paint and feathers. Whenever they arrived at a new town, Rockefeller gathered customers by making a show of consulting the wise medicine man. Inevitably, the Indian's advice to the crowd was to buy more bottles of Doc Rockefeller's guaranteed cancer cure.

After a few years on the road, young Charles Johnston had had enough of that shady lifestyle and decided to become a real doctor. Although Doc Rockefeller was initially against the idea, he helped pay for Johnston's medical education. Over the course of his long and distinguished career as a credentialed physician, Johnston would rise to notable heights, eventually serving as the president of the College of Medicine and Surgery in Chicago. But until Doc Rockefeller's death 25 years later, Johnston feared that someone would dig up the dark secret of his past and brand him a quack.

Charles Johnston's transition from fake medicine man to president of an elite medical college hints at the lack of standards and established pathways in the medical field a hundred years ago. We think of physicians and surgeons today as having followed a strict regimen of education and training that produces their vaunted expertise. In fact, until the late 1920s, not only was medical training haphazard and shoddy, but the very principles of medicine and medical practice varied sharply from doctor to doctor and school to school. The development of education and practice standards came about only after a long and protracted battle between proponents of various approaches. The outcome of that battle still influences how medical care is provided today.

Dr. Benjamin Rush, whom we met in the preceding chapter when Nabby Adams wrote to him for medical advice, was considered the American Hippocrates for his great impact on early American medicine. Rush trained thousands of young doctors during his long career, and his strong opinions about the practice of medicine became the established standard for a hundred years. Rush was a great believer in heroic medicine. Updating the ancient Greek concept of the four humors, Rush declared that sickness was always due to some disturbance in the vascular system and every condition could be treated by bleeding, purging, or blistering the patient. As some recognized even then, Rush's doctoring did as much harm as good. But his unshakeable confidence comforted patients, and his eloquence and energy as a speaker and writer gave him many followers.

There was little formal training for doctors in the early decades of our country. Practicing physicians passed on advice or knowledge to any student willing to pay. In the 1820s, however, there was a boom in the creation of for-profit medical colleges. Many of those colleges are now forgotten, while others include notable medical schools at Harvard, Dartmouth, and the University of Pennsylvania. The curriculum was heavy on science (biology, chemistry, anatomy, etc.), but the lessons were virtually devoid of clinical training and scientific research. Education was primarily a business, and competition for students was so intense that there were few standards for entry or graduation. A graduation diploma was deemed to be the equivalent of a state-awarded license. Essentially, anyone who paid for the education was given the title of doctor.

It was during that boom in medical colleges, however, that Benjamin Rush's theories of heroic medicine went into decline and the principles of what was then considered traditional medicine blew apart. Few in the medical field were sure what good medical practice should actually entail, however, and a variety of nontraditional approaches gained popularity among practitioners, students, and patients. One prominent nontraditionalist was Samuel Thomson, a New Hampshire farmer and herbalist, who believed that the cause of all illness was cold, which could be remedied by restoring the body's natural heat through a variety of herbal remedies and emetics. Thomson was a major proponent of individual self-reliance and declared that physicians were utterly unnecessary for good health. He patented his own treatment ideas, and by 1840 had sold about 100,000 Thomsonian systems through sales agents throughout the country, claiming over three million converts. In defiance of traditional Western views, Thomsonian doctors began opening their own schools and competing directly with traditional doctors in the health care marketplace. In Cincinnati, they established one of the nation's largest medical schools.

Another group of nontraditionalist physicians, called the eclectics, maintained many traditional practices but denounced bloodletting and pushed herbal remedies. A stranger sect were the hydropaths, who avoided drugs or surgery in favor of ice, water, and steam to promote healing, while advocating rest, nutrition, and hygiene. The Christian Scientists, under Mary Baker Eddy, denied that disease even existed. Osteopathy emphasized muscular-skeletal alignment, mind-body harmony, and preventive care, while giving birth to the term *wellness*. Indeed, osteopathic medical schools exist today, and currently 6 percent of medical doctors in the United States are doctors of osteopathy (DOs). Even more prominent were the followers of Samuel Hahnemann, a German physician who never visited America. In Hahnemann's homeopathic school, illnesses were treated with infinitesimally small dosages of drugs that produced similar symptoms—an idea ("Like is cured by like") known as the first law of homeopathy that stood in strong contrast to Rush's heroic doses. Hahnemann also advocated a healthy lifestyle— fresh air, exercise, hygiene, and diet—as critical to good health. From 1825 until the start of the Civil War, homeopathy became the nation's most popular alternative approach to medicine. Many traditional doctors became homeopaths, and the field was supported by medical schools and journals and by wealthy and influential patrons. As late as 1921, President Warren G. Harding's personal White House physician was a homeopath.

In addition to these major sects, there were countless individual quacks and self-proclaimed experts adding to the confusion. The country was highly tolerant of individualism, even at the expense of standards and regulation. It was said that Benjamin Rush himself, one of the signers of the Declaration of Independence, had pushed for the right to medical freedom to be included in the U.S. Constitution alongside the right to religious freedom. In sympathy with such sentiments, and being lobbied hard by the homeopaths, many state legislatures began repealing medical licensing laws, allowing anyone of any medical philosophy to call himself a doctor. Traditional doctors responded to the threat to their authority by forming the American Medical Association (AMA) in 1847. At first, the AMA tried to establish admission and education standards to develop a more credentialed physician class, but those efforts were thwarted by the physician-owners of the many for-profit medical schools because such rules would reduce the number of paying students. The more consequential struggle for control over medical practice would take place during the American Civil War. By the start of the war, there were approximately 30,000 traditional physicians in the country, 2,500 homeopathic doctors, and thousands of garden-variety quacks. While soldiers fought and died on the battlefield, medical practitioners fought to determine what school of physicians would treat them.

Dr. William Hammond, who as surgeon general of the U.S. Army did so much to develop the nation's hospitals, took a strong stand on the application of medical standards. The states had medical boards to examine volunteer physicians, but they were disorganized and not systematic in their standards. Hammond declared that all regular army physicians would need to pass a federal medical board examination as well. The tests were strict and tough, involving a written component to determine literacy, an oral component to determine knowledge of basic science, and a clinical component to determine practical skill. Resistance was fierce. Doctors who failed were embarrassed. Some bribed the examiners to be passed. Meanwhile, Hammond's standards created a scarcity of field doctors, so his nemesis, Secretary of War Edwin Stanton, undermined his authority until Hammond lowered the qualifications required. Nevertheless, despite political pressure to reverse himself, Hammond maintained the ban on homeopathic physicians.

From the 1870s to the 1890s, states began requiring medical licenses again, and this time, standards were being raised. Johns Hopkins became the standard-bearer. Unlike the for-profit medical schools, Johns Hopkins medical college was blessed with a large endowment and was able to have particularly strict entry requirements. The leaders of the college, William Henry Welch, William Osler, William Halsted, and Howard Kelly, were famous pioneers of education and clinical practice who groomed a new generation of scientist-physicians. Welch had considered entry to medical school the easiest examination of his life, and he did a lot to change that experience for future doctors, demanding discipline and rigor through his lectures. Halsted was known as one of the world's finest teaching surgeons. He was also responsible for the invention of the surgical glove (but that was developed to protect the delicate hands of one of his favorite nurses, whom he later married, rather than to control the spread of germs). Kelly established gynecology as a medical specialty and became one of the pioneers of using radiation therapy for cancer treatment. Osler was considered the finest physician in the country, and his 1892 book, *Principles and Practices of Medicine*, became the medical field's most important text. His greatest contribution to medical education, however, was the establishment of the medical residency system in which apprentice doctors worked in hospitals under the tutelage of more experienced mentors, during a time when few medical students at other institutions ever touched a patient. Together these four men were monumental in establishing strict entry, curriculum, and graduation standards, while combining bedside teaching and laboratory research with traditional lectures over a four-year study period.

It was John D. Rockefeller's money that helped spread this best-practice approach to education around the country. Upon retiring from active business, Rockefeller had turned his attention to advancing scientific research, giving it an unprecedented push and setting the country on the course of innovation we still benefit from today. His first step was establishing the Rockefeller Institute for Medical Research, where his primary board adviser was William Henry Welch. Welch hired a doctor named Simon Flexner, his own protégé at Johns Hopkins, to be director of research. (Flexner had become interested in medicine while working as a youngster at his uncle's drugstore.) At the Rockefeller Institute, Flexner turned out to be a brilliant leader and manager. He identified great medical scientists, recruited them to the cause of research, and directed the teams that pioneered such innovations as organ transplants, blood transfusions, and serums to treat epidemic diseases like meningitis. Because of the success of the research institute, Rockefeller opened his wallet even wider and added a hospital. Under Flexner's direction, the hospital treated five specific diseases under study for free—polio, syphilis, heart disease, intestinal infantilism, and pneumonia. In this way, the Rockefeller Institute became the most renowned, best-equipped, and most talented medical enterprise in the world. In 1912, one of Flexner's researchers, Dr. Alexis Carrel, became the first American physician to be awarded the Nobel Prize in medicine.

The success of Rockefeller's institute and the passions of his key lieutenants had a critical impact on establishing medical orthodoxy in the twentieth century. Yet when it came to medicine, Rockefeller was a study in contrasts on a personal level. His father, as I've mentioned, was an outright quack and Rockefeller himself lived by strange self-taught principles of nutrition and health. His own physician and regular traveling companion was a homeopath ridiculed by renowned doctors for backward thinking. Ironically, one of Rockefeller's top philanthropic advisers, Frederick T. Gates, took it as a personal mission to finally rid medical practice of homeopaths and all other sectarians who strayed from science once and for all.

The story goes like this: Simon Flexner's older brother, Abraham, was an educator with a solid reputation. In 1910, Abraham Flexner was hired by the Carnegie Foundation for the Advancement of Teaching to survey North American medical schools. Visiting every medical college in operation, he found conditions to be generally deplorable. Professors were financed by dividing up the money obtained through tuition, so standards were made as low as possible to encourage a large number of paying students. Two-year programs with 16-week terms were the norm, as opposed to the intensive four-year degrees that were standard in Europe. It was easier to graduate from medical school than from a liberal arts college, and students who had failed liberal arts programs often turned to medicine as an option. Clinical research was barely existent, and was discouraged as a waste of time and money. Equipment was shabby and old. Most of the country's medical schools remained in the dark ages in terms of teaching and facilities.

The Flexner Report resulted in the closure of 100 of North America's 155 medical schools, including all of the remaining institutions devoted to homeopathy. While modern critics hold that this was devastating to under-funded but valuable rural, minority, and women's hospitals, most saw the assessment as having a tremendously positive impact overall. Frederick Gates used the Flexner Report as an impetus for launching a renaissance in American medical education. Tapping the great resources of Rockefeller's philanthropy, Gates recruited Abraham Flexner to direct that money toward the upgrading of medical schools and hospitals around the country. Flexner used Johns Hopkins, Vanderbilt, and the University of Chicago as the benchmarks of innovation, and replicated those best practices everywhere, establishing four-year medical programs with full-time teaching and strict graduation requirements. In total, a billion dollars in today's money was devoted to the transformation. In the process, Rockefeller, Gates, and Flexner gave birth to modern American medicine and the physicians, specialists, and surgeons we know today.

The Golden Age?

If you read the historical accounts of doctors making house calls and applying the latest science with a tender hand while delving deeply into their patients' lives, you might think that medical care had better balance once upon a time. However, there were enough complaints and criticisms even a century ago to cause us to question that nostalgia.

A report in the September 1926 issue of *California and Western Medicine,* for example, admonished physicians for relying too much on science at the expense of human connection. "A generation or so ago the physician treated the patient," the report declared. "Today the tendency is strongly for the physician to treat the disease . . . and to either forget the patient or to treat him as a sort of secondary accompaniment or case." The article went on to advise doctors to see their patients as promptly as possible, and to administer personal attention and reduce anxiety by explaining the illness and the tests that would go on at the laboratory and the treatments that would be required. Throughout, the writer complained that doctors once did such things as a matter of course but today barely acknowledged their patients as human beings, declaring that few remembered their patients' names or any distinctive personality characteristics. "I doubt the average busy physician or surgeon realizes how little personal consideration he gives his patient as a human sufferer who is hungry for sympathy and companionship."

The reasons the article gave for this development will be familiar to people today. First, the drive for money skewed the relationship with the patient ("the $ is too frequently the veil through which the patient is seen"), forcing the doctor to examine the patient as quickly and efficiently as possible. This was justified, however, because "the economic conditions of modern life appear to render a measure of commercialism almost necessary for the medical man." Second, the medical education system had created an emphasis on science over social skills, particularly as doctors became more specialized and the hospital replaced the home as the center for care. While specialization was unavoidable, the writer noted, the specialist could not comprehend the whole individual. "Present-day medical teaching is ultrascientific, specific, and exclusive. . . . It is impossible to know people intimately or sympathetically."

It would seem that in creating an "ultrascientific, specific, and exclusive" medical education system, Flexner had sounded the death knell for the golden age of care. Of course, this wasn't Flexner's fault. Medical practice was so complicated that it demanded intense study over many years. Four-year programs had become standard, but it was nearly impossible to squeeze in all of the necessary scientific and clinical training during that time, so starting in 1910, medical schools and state licensing boards began requiring an additional year of internship at a hospital. By the 1920s and into the 1930s, two more years of study were added to the basic medical education. After World War II, eight years was the norm for any physician who decided to specialize.

The unintended consequence was that teaching hospitals and medical schools became more laboratory than care center, and doctor contact with patients emphasized clinical practice over bedside manner. At the same time, while their brains were being stretched by the vast increase in technical knowledge, doctors were still taught to be self-reliant and utterly independent of support staff. My friends who were trained in the 1950s and 1960s tell me that they were instructed to never rely on the validity of even the simplest blood tests in making their diagnoses. The reason: because they had not conducted such tests themselves.

The public was starting to complain about doctors by the late 1950s, voicing criticisms that might sound familiar today about unnecessary procedures and fees and the lack of personal care. By the early 1970s, on the back of a social movement that brought more questioning of author-ity figures, we entered the era of the second opinion. Suddenly, patients were demanding more understanding of their own condition and a greater say in how they should be treated. Most important, they felt empowered to shop around for another doctor if they weren't satisfied with the answers.

Today, the doctor–patient relationship seems to have been turned on its head. In many ways, the pressure is now on the doctors. Small-practice physicians, emulating the mythical Dr. Welby, may have gone into the business because of their interest in helping patients but find that they are overwhelmed by the burden of meeting administrative and through-put demands. Consider that the average primary care physician has 2,500 to 4,000 patients, works five to seven days a week, takes emergency calls 24 hours a day, and often sees patients in the hospital from nine to five o'clock on weekends. Taking even a few minutes extra with each patient in the clinic can put a doctor out of business. Meanwhile, patients, better informed or bombarded by drug advertisements, have more questions and demands for treatment than ever.

To get ever-shrinking reimbursement dollars from private insurers and Medicare, physicians are overwhelmed with paperwork. What's more, both public and private payers have taken away doctors' autonomy to treat patients as they see fit. It's also increasingly difficult to be both a scientist and a care provider now, because administrative demands steal away whatever free time the physician might have to spend in the lab or in the hospital. Extra education time has been crunched and reduced to the minimum, despite the impossibility of keeping up with new treat-ment and drug developments in even ideal circumstances. The cost of making a mistake has also never been higher. Malpractice suits are such a threat that doctors are trained to be evasive about taking responsibility for decisions or actions that might have led to bad outcomes, even though it is rare that a medical error can be linked to one individual and not the system as a whole.

It shouldn't be a surprise, therefore, that the rate of medical school applications, despite a recent rise, has been declining overall in the past 10 years. At the same time, new doctors are avoiding the general practitioner role and shifting toward nonsurgical specialties with regular hours. The number of salaried physicians is rising, because it is easier to work within an administrative institution than to set off in private practice or even join an established partnership. The most successful physicians and surgeons are drastically reducing the number of Medicare and Medicaid patients that they see; and the superstars—those providers who have great press or following—are establishing boutique practices. At the same time, however, the altruism measure of those entering medical school has never been higher, as though new students recognize the detriments of their profession but are choosing it anyway. It would seem that the urge to be Dr. Welby remains strong after all.

Putting the Doc Back on the Team

The business model for health care is broken. If we are going to upgrade the health care system and bring all the benefits of technology to the patient, then physicians, as the linchpin of care, need to be part of a team.

The model of the heroic solo practitioner, rooted in our national tradition since Benjamin Rush, is an impediment today from the standpoint of cost, quality, and innovation. The best oncologist in the world, with the most innovative surgical technique, cannot ensure the health and recovery of a patient if not supported by a strong team. The oncology surgeon does not prep the patient or handle aftercare, cannot help the patient avoid a deadly staph infection or postoperative pneumonia, and is probably not even involved in follow-up visits. Beyond the surgical event, the surgeon cannot control any outcomes.

From society's point of view, star doctors operating on their own benefit only a limited number of patients, because you can't scale the expertise of individual contributors if those individual contributors refuse to allow their expertise to be automated. In the end, our ability to bring an innovation to scale and expand its application throughout hospitals all over the country is the only way to lower cost while improving the quality of health care systemwide.

For the most part, in medical school and in their internships, doctors are trained primarily as individuals. Chances are they are overachievers and strong individual contributors by nature, traits that are magnified through the very hierarchical weeding-out process of medical school. Along the way, they're rewarded for being the best academically and for outcompeting their classmates and colleagues. They're taught to think for themselves, to be skeptical of the judgments and capabilities of others, and to rely on their own skills and intellect. As interns and residents, they're encouraged to outperform the other residents, work harder, go longer without sleep, and show up those around them with better diagnoses or treatment ideas. This does not lend itself to team-oriented behaviors in the operating room or on the hospital floor.

The evidence shows, however, that the star doctor cannot compete with the best system. In fact, the best doctor is the one who is installed in the best system. The reason a particular hip surgeon has the best outcomes is because that doctor has the best hip surgery team. They perform more hip replacements than any other hospital, so they know what hip technology works best and what protocol needs to be followed. They're purchasing their artificial hips at volume, which reduces costs and the variabilities that lead to errors. The well-trained prep team gets the patient ready for the surgery and the well-trained physical therapy group is ready when the surgery is finished. The end result is high-quality care at the best cost without error.

I am not saying that physicians and surgeons need to learn to play better with others. This is not about emotional intelligence or playground behavior. I'm saying that a well-coordinated system needs to be in place to ensure successful outcomes at the best cost. You can compare the way hospitals are run to the way industries conduct manufacturing, NASA sends space shuttles to the space station, or the military conducts operations. The bravest soldier or the most accurate shot doesn't make an army squad successful. Instead, all the members of the squad, through practice and rehearsal, learn their roles and understand what to do in specific situations. And after each mission, they debrief and determine what went right and what went wrong, and then install those changes into the tactical plan to get a better outcome next time.

The reason why such stellar institutions as the Mayo Clinic, Duke Medical, Vanderbilt, Cleveland Clinic, Kaiser Permanente, Group Health Cooperative (Puget Sound), Health Partners (Minnesota), and the Veterans Administration (VA) system have such great patient outcomes is because they have installed systems that rely on team-based medicine. The Mayo Clinic has been using this approach since the 1930s, employing coordinated teams of salaried doctors. At the VA Hospital in Arizona, the five vascular surgeons work as a team, each sharing responsibility for the patients in their care. Before every surgery, all five surgeons meet to discuss the case together and decide what's best for the patient. Each day, the surgeon doing the rounds will visit every patient, even ones he didn't operate on personally. This is relatively unheard-of in most hospitals today, where a surgeon is typically given ownership over a particular patient, and no other surgeon would dare to question that surgeon's judgment or to intervene. The same thing is even more rare in small clinic and home settings, where the provider is even less a part of a system than in a large medical center.

Historically, there has been great reluctance to give authority to any decision maker except the physician. Nurses, in particular, have borne the brunt of this prejudice. During the Great Depression, care centers turned to nursing students over graduates as a way of reducing costs. The American Nurses Association lobbied hard to extol the value of trained nurses, but they were forced to agree to perform menial nursing chores, at a reduced salary, during lengthy shifts while covering a patient load rather than caring for individuals. In contrast, the famed management experts Frank and Lillian Gilbreth conducted time-and-motion studies of hospitals in the 1920s and concluded that nurses were critical to smooth hospital operations. One result of the Gilbreths' work was that a surgical nurse was assigned to hand instruments to the surgeon as he called for them. Another was that nursing teams developed internal hierarchies to divide hospital duties under the supervision of the registered nurse (RN).

We can go a lot further than that. A new division of labor in health care is starting to change the established system wherein the physician must do all the heavy lifting. Is it really necessary for a doctor to sign every prescription even when the symptoms are clear or the course of treatment is on a continuous long-term basis? Is it really necessary for a patient to visit the doctor's office or a hospital just to see a care provider? As retail health care facilities in pharmacies, shopping malls, and even airports are proving, convenience and reduced cost are powerful factors in getting necessary treatment and maintaining health. Not surprisingly, we are seeing the ultimate authority of the physician being dispersed to other members of the care provider team. Physician assistants, who have graduate degrees in medicine, can assess and treat patients under a physician's remote supervision. Similarly, nurse-practitioners (registered nurses with advanced training and degrees) can prescribe medication, as well as treat acute and chronic conditions. They often specialize and typically emphasize healthy behaviors and informed decision making in their patients. Safety studies show no detriments to relying on nurse-practitioners and other non–MD trained specialists; and there are major benefits in quality of care—in particular, more consistent contact, more interest in the whole patient, better convenience, and, of course, reduced cost. It goes without saying that expanding this approach can help alleviate physician shortages; and it can also improve the coordination of care. The vascular surgery team at the VA hospital in Arizona, for example, includes a nurse-practitioner whose primary role is to ensure continuity of care. She runs the operating room schedule and communicates with patients on a daily basis, acting as the flow-through for channeling questions or information to the surgeons or the appropriate care providers, including the pharmacist, the personal physician, and whatever chronic care specialists are involved in a particular patient's case.

In order to achieve a team-based approach, however, we must make changes to dismantle the sovereignty of the doctor. Not only is the doctor heralded as the heroic practitioner by social bias, but by law and policy as well. Laws protecting the authority of doctors as decision makers have done a great deal to reinforce this sovereignty and preserve the status quo. As I mentioned earlier, the outdated regulation of preventing pharmacists from discussing effects and composition of therapeutic drugs with patients served as one such example. As we contemplate moving to an integrated team-based systems model, we have to deal with the deeply entrenched protections for the medical profession that reinforce the status quo and are based on outmoded ideas of the way medicine is practiced in the twenty-first century.

At the Veterans Administration, the effort to instill a team-based approach has had a remarkable impact on safety and quality. VA hospitals use the same safety policy as NASA wherein anyone, anywhere, at any time can raise a concern. If a nurse doing his rounds thinks that a patient is not looking good, he doesn't have to call the intern first to confirm his suspicions but instead contacts the rapid response team to intervene immediately. Time-outs occur routinely in the operating room when some member of the team is worried that an error is about to be made. This would not happen in a typical civilian hospital where the presiding physician or surgeon is the sole decision maker.

To further track and improve on safety, the VA implemented the National Safety Quality Improvement Program (NSQIP). This program has dedicated nurses to monitor surgical outcomes. Every patient receives a NSQIP history before an operation so that morbidity can be accurately incorporated into outcomes. Every fiscal quarter, the surgical team gets those results in what is called the OE report, meaning observed outcomes over expected outcomes. If the O to E ratio goes up one quarter, outcomes are worse than anticipated and changes need to be made. Using the team-based approach, the surgeons and other care providers examine why, implement the necessary innovations, and pay special attention to the next quarterly report. Typically, the OE ratio drops back to the norm within two quarters in whatever area needs attention. In such a way, quality outcomes are consistently delivered systemwide.

Wiring It Together

The Veterans Administration's ability to employ team-based medicine is hugely facilitated by its use of electronic medical records. The full medical records of any patient in the VA system are available at the touch of a button. If patients move to another VA hospital or new primary care provider, their medical records can still be accessed just as easily as before. All members of the care team can view the same records and communicate with each other accordingly. When a surgeon orders a drug for a patient, the selection comes up on the hospital pharmacist's screen, and the pharmacist can confirm the choice or draw attention to any issues like allergies, incompatibilities with other medications, or dosage problems. If a surgeon or specialist sees a health issue unrelated to the current examination but worth checking out further, he or she is able to note that in the patient's electronic medical records and flag it so the appropriate care provider must acknowledge that concern when seeing the patient later.

This kind of longitudinal care is currently rare in our health system, but it will become the norm in the future. When you consider today's patient experience and what a patient goes through, you begin to understand the value of digitizing health records in a standardized way. When patients are diagnosed with colorectal cancer, for example, it's frightening. Today, their experience is that they have to go to their family doctor, then a gastrointestinal specialist, then a colorectal surgeon. The patient has to get tests, lab work, CAT scans, chemotherapy, and radiation therapy over the course of months, often involving hospital stays and follow-up visits. All of the physicians, clinics, and testing centers have to coordinate, but they have no procedure for communicating with each other. In today's world, much of the work a patient does involves managing the communication among the players. Few patients have the confidence or the certainty that they will obtain the best care with the best possible outcomes under such circumstances.

In tomorrow's system, when health care goes fully digital, the connectivity required to support complex care will be part of the infrastructure and taken for granted, like broadband and wireless is part of the infrastructure of most communities and offices. Communication—meaning education about your condition and treatment—won't happen through handwritten charts and paper that gets faxed and filed. It will happen face-to-face with the doctor, and later at home on your computer, when you can revisit your health record, check on links, delve further into the details, and even send the doctor more questions by e-mail. If you haven't been through a serious crisis like cancer, you might not appreciate how comforting this will be. Most patients find it necessary to bring a partner along on visits, because remembering everything the doctor says is next to impossible. But with the power of technology at your fingertips, the mental burden on the whole team will be alleviated.

This connectivity extends to the hospital. Doctors, nurses, and technicians at the hospital will have access to the same information. They will be treated to frequent reminders regarding a patient's health characteristics. For example, if a patient is currently on several different medications with unique interactions, a call system will check in to ensure that the nurse or doctor is aware of this and has consulted the records.

After the hospital stay, the doctor will not have to ask you what happened. He or she will be able to see your personal records, your lab results, and the progress that you're making online; can make decisions based on shared facts; and can record those decisions for all others on the team to follow. In this high-tech age, doctors should be able to access data concerning their patients wherever and whenever they need it. This means we must be able to provide them with portals and devices for doing so. In the near future, your doctor will be able to view your 3-D MRI scan on a laptop in the kitchen or office, and will be able to check up on your pharmaceutical records via the digital display on a mobile phone. In fact, you'll be able to look at the same scan and the same records, communicated to you at the same time in ways that a nonexpert can understand.

Soon, you'll also be able to make more informed decisions about your treatment. You'll be able to access your data the way you access your e-mail—on your computer, television screen, BlackBerry, or cell phone. This information can be tied into searches organized around your specific condition, medication, or demographic. Those who are concerned about privacy need not lose any sleep at night. In a world where we can sign online and do our food shopping by submitting credit card information, there will be great lengths taken to ensure the same safety with regard to your individual health records. Encryption advances are making it easier to protect against hacking, and Congress is already on the move to ensure access to insurance for those who fear rejection based on preexisting conditions. To make such a system successful, universality cannot be sacrificed.

But many doctors and hospitals are proving to be more resistant than patients to digitizing health care. For hospitals, the up-front investment costs are the major impediment. But in the future, those hospitals and health plans that offer seamless coordinated care and successful outcomes are going to be the market leaders and benchmark organizations. Those that fail to modernize will be unable to compete. Young doctors tend to be tech savvy and eager to use efficiency-improving technology like electronic medical records. But until recently, their voices were drowned out by the older physicians who are more reluctant to adopt innovations. Recently, Kaiser Permanente has begun to digitize health care records. To establish the system quickly, physicians are now required to fill out their patient charts electronically. This allows the doctor or care provider to pull up a patient's health record instantly, even during an emergency, no matter where the patient is being seen. Some doctors don't like it, finding it difficult to interface with technology while trying to connect with a patient. But once upon a time, CEOs refused to type, let alone use a computer. Today, you can't pry the BlackBerry from their hands.

At the same time, I anticipate that providers will be much more receptive to some of the other benefits that come along with digitization and connectivity. The automation of health records and information access that will help patients and doctors alike will be coupled with great advances in administrative, claims management, and revenue cycle support. Small clinics, without having the time, expertise, or scale of operations to efficiently handle complex administrative procedures, can already outsource these tasks to companies like McKesson that will take care of everything, from payer negotiations to managing accounts and revenue processing. Along with the real-time information that comes with electronic health records, this will mean fewer repetitive tests and more high-quality patient interactions.

The Medical Home

Consider the impact of team-based medicine and electronic medical records in the area of chronic care.

Today, medical care, particularly in the outpatient setting, is based on acute care. This means that it is essentially the diseases or symptoms that are treated. In other words, the system is built around the "What seems to be the problem today?" mentality. Doctors have that mentality because of the way health care has evolved. Treatments have been developed to cure specific diseases or to lessen specific symptoms. If you have an infection, you receive antibiotics. If you are anemic, you get a dietary supplement. But the problem is that acute care management doesn't meet the needs of people with chronic disease.

Assume, for example, that you have type 2 diabetes. You go to the hospital with a high blood sugar level and get treated with insulin and told to watch your diet. But that does nothing to treat your risk of associated heart disease, and a year and a half later you're being medevacked to a hospital on the verge of a massive heart attack. People who have diabetes need to do much more than watch their blood sugar levels. They also need to be very careful about their cholesterol and blood pressure levels. Most diabetes patients aren't aware of the risk of heart disease. According to the Centers for Disease Control and Prevention, only 7 percent of diabetes patients get all the treatment they need.

Around 20 percent of the people admitted to hospitals suffer from chronic diseases. However, this 20 percent accounts for 60 to 70 percent of the total costs to hospitals. About half our population has some form of chronic care need. Chronically ill people who are uninsured wait until they are eligible for Medicare benefits before seeking treatment, thus exacerbating their conditions and making their treatments more costly.[1] In general, when untreated or poorly treated, chronic conditions fester and give rise to other even more expensive health problems. Fifty-four million Americans are at risk for diabetes, even as diabetes and its complications accounted for $132 billion in direct and indirect health care costs in the United States in 2003, and 73,000 Americans die from diabetes annually. Five million Americans are living with heart failure, even as heart failure cost $25.9 billion in direct and indirect health costs in 2004. Seventeen million Americans suffer from lung disease, and asthma rates continue to jump, even as the annual cost to treat asthma was $4,900 per person in 2003. If there was ever a textbook case of the economic value of prevention and maintenance, chronic care fits the bill.

Currently, chronic patients who visit the hospital emergency room don't leave with integrated, specific plans for their health. Instead, they typically walk out with their acute symptoms treated and their chronic conditions untouched; or, in the best case, they are sent to a specialist or a technician for more testing. Ideally, chronically ill patients do not just need acute treatment; they need a long-term approach that incorporates many different types of care providers, ensures engagement in healthy behaviors, provides monitoring, and supports maintenance.

Imagine if chronically ill patients were to walk out of the hospital emergency room with one plan that covered everything they would need to fully manage their health. The ideal plan would incorporate the hospital, the home, the physician clinic, the rehab center, and the pharmacy. Imagine if the plan was implemented immediately, setting many different parties into action to examine the patient, determine a daily course of treatment, monitor the progress, and manage compliance. Imagine that information about the patient's condition and progress was able to be stored electronically, and shared and viewed remotely by everyone who needed the access.

Today, disease management (DM) programs are in place to help make such plans real. The typical structure of a DM program involves identifying the patient, getting the patient to agree to participate, doing an initial health assessment, developing a care management plan, educating the patient accordingly, and identifying and engaging with providers who can be part of the team. In McKesson's DM program, we have qualified nurses who provide follow-up visits and phone calls, assess symptoms, and continue to communicate with providers. Heart failure patients who participated in such a program had 22 percent fewer emergency room visits and a 45 percent reduction in 30-day readmission rates. The participants in the asthma management program had fewer hospitalizations, bed days, and emergency room visits compared to patients not in the program.

By coordinating care and focusing on preventive medicine, we can keep people out of the hospital and reduce the nation's overall health care bill dramatically. Taking disease management to the next logical step, we can put the primary care physician in the center of the care team, with a highly trained case manager in charge of referrals, payment and reimbursement issues, basic monitoring and evaluation, and coordination.

Right now, physicians are not sufficiently equipped to coordinate patient care because they lack the staff and technology to do the job. But they are expected to do so despite the fact that they are not given adequate resources. Much of the prevailing thinking in the medical community operates under the assumption that, because they have obtained nearly a decade of medical training, the physician is the ideal candidate to handle care management. But this isn't actually the case. It is true that the physician is generally among the most highly trained on the care team, but physicians' vast expertise makes them an unnecessary and expensive option for this task. Today, we are beginning to see the case manager absorb every aspect of the patient's medical history and manage the care team. These individuals require less medical training than the physician but are often more capable of handling the tasks of care management as it applies to common or simple conditions. Meanwhile, physicians will become the hub of care for more complex or debilitating medical concerns, and will be allowed to use their considerable expertise in a way that does not stretch them too thinly. Together, the physician and case manager will handle the responsibilities of monitoring care, making referrals, and engaging whatever medical and community resources are necessary.

When such a medical home becomes a reality, we might not pine as much for the golden age of Marcus Welby. Longer-term relationships with a physician who knows us like a close neighbor and has the proper resources to manage our health from start to finish would go a long way to reestablishing the trust and bond between doctor and patient, while giving us a sense that we are in control of our own health care and know how to access the answers and resources we need.

The Algorithm Will See You Now

In the near future, not only will you be better connected to your doctor and your care team, but your doctor and care team will be better connected to the best medical knowledge and treatment protocols in the world.

That was Dr. Ernest Codman's dream for expanding the benefits of end results medicine. As I mentioned in the previous chapter, in the early 1900s, Codman envisioned a system in which the most effective treatments (as evidenced by the best results) are assessed by a panel of experts and then that knowledge is dispersed to all other physicians. He imagined that physicians would then rely on those proven approaches, which would constitute a new baseline standard for medical care. Codman knew that science never stands still, so his system of best practices was designed for continual improvement through fresh innovations, again assessed by experts and dispersed to all.

The reason for Codman's proposal was simple. Medical care in the early 1900s was haphazard and uncertain. A patient with a particular condition was treated differently depending on the hospital visited; indeed, there was great variation between doctors in the same hospital. Other than medical school, there was no established system to spread the cumulative advances of medical understanding. Meanwhile, treatment innovations occurred too fast for the medical curriculum, let alone for individual doctors isolated from their peers. In Codman's dream, if all doctors and hospitals could be linked to each other with a common understanding of best practices, the quality of health care would be raised across the board, while the cost would drop because a patient could receive the best treatment at more institutions.

It was a dream that took shape only in rudimentary form. Elite organizations like the American College of Surgeons and scientific periodicals like the *New England Journal of Medicine* assess, debate, and publish the latest, most effective medical knowledge at great volume. Most of us assume when we are examined and treated by a doctor or at a hospital that we are receiving the benefits of that advanced medical science. In fact, the chances that you are receiving the latest, most up-to-date and comprehensive medical care when you see a doctor are no better than 50 percent. Most physicians believe they are offering it to us, but they are simply not aware of what has happened since they were last at medical school or cracked a journal. While we're conditioned to believe that the experienced and senior doctor is the better bet, the longer physicians have been out of medical school the more likely it is that they are unaware of the latest clinically proven treatment practices. How could they possibly keep up? To stay abreast of the latest advances, a general practitioner would need to read 19 articles per day, every day of the year. And they simply don't have that time.

Today, tapping into best-practice knowledge is largely hit or miss. How many times have you read a story of a doctor making a shrewd diagnosis of a mystery illness or complication? All too often the correct diagnosis seems to arise from an absurd mix of experience, random connections, and luck. A condition reminds the doctor of something remembered from years ago; this ties in with a journal article the doctor vaguely remembers and needs to find in a stack of magazines, or a lively conversation with a colleague at a convention the previous month. Digging in, the doctor uncovers the latest thinking on the illness, runs a different set of tests, and finally identifies the problem—a drug incompatibility, a new virus, a complication due to gender or race. Presto, the patient gets the right treatment. The patient is left feeling extremely fortunate for having run into this particular doctor, and grateful to the doctor for having been diligent and curious enough to provide the right care. Unspoken go the fears: What if the patient had gone to a different doctor? What if the doctor had been too busy, tired, or cranky to go beyond the normal routine? What if the patient and doctor hadn't connected on a personal level, or the doctor had viewed the patient as an annoying complainer?

The amount of variation between doctors and hospitals is still as astounding today as it was during Codman's time. One could argue that this variation allows for a great deal of experimentation in approach— but as any researcher knows, without applying clinical experiments across a large enough sampling and without control populations for comparison, no innovation is scientifically valid. Nor are we diligent enough about spreading or adopting the proven innovations that have been discovered.

Cancer patients know what this is like. Visit four specialists and you may receive four different treatment plans combining different regimens of drugs, radiation therapy, chemotherapy, surgery, and so forth. Which path and which doctor do you choose? When your life is on the line, the decision is an agonizing one. If you haven't visited more than one doctor, you may not know that another doctor might make a different prognosis and advise a different course of treatment. In 1999, the Institute of Medicine noted that there is no national system of standards and protocols in existence, and therefore quality of care is very inconsistent. The National Quality Forum, which advocates publishing quality measurements based on patient outcomes, launched a program in March 2007 to evaluate how many hospitals are providing patients with the latest care for breast and colon cancer. The concern is that many hospitals ignore even very basic established procedures.

We see the impact of this kind of variation in a number of different ways. Our high error and hospital infection rates are due to a lack of standards. If care teams were trained to follow protocols, the variations and uncertainties that lead to errors and infections would be eliminated. We also see the impact in the fact that patients typically receive 20 to 30 percent more care than necessary. If protocols were being followed, it wouldn't be necessary to overprescribe or overtreat, because we would have clinical proof. It is very difficult to realize that too much care does not lead to high-quality care. It is very easy to prove, however, that too much care leads to higher cost. Best-quality health care does not mean that everything that can possibly be done for the patient has been done; it means that the patient has received the appropriate care at the appropriate time from the appropriate source.

We have a way to give physicians and care providers a means to employ the latest best practices, while at the same time preserving the freedom of innovation and clinical judgment. They are called algorithms. A clinical algorithm is a list of clear and scientifically delineated boundaries that determine the range of what is acceptable care. These are valuable tools, as they limit variation to proven, evidence-based approaches, but at the same time allow for innovation within those boundaries. It is a way of taking the results of clinical research and applying them to the patient. For example, if you have a heart attack and a paramedic diagnoses your condition correctly, the paramedic should be able to follow a care algorithm that leads to the same level of improvement in you as it would in thousands of other people. The paramedic does not have to be a world-famous cardiologist to stabilize you and improve your chances of full recovery.

Thirty years ago, clinical algorithms were literally written in booklets. Using branch logic formats, they enabled care providers to assess your condition and follow the advised treatment steps accordingly. Algorithms are essentially the way computers work, providing a means of dealing with variables that are too complex and multistaged to be processed by the human brain. Today, more sophisticated algorithms can be processed with computers or handheld devices to enable physicians, nurse-practitioners, and other care providers to access best-practice medical care at the patient's bedside.

McKesson has a system called Horizon Expert Order that provides connective technology to link doctors with best practices. When the patient exhibits a set of symptoms, the physician makes a number of assumptions around those symptoms and typically orders a series of tests to support or refute the assumptions. Today, those laboratory results can be viewed in real time, and the physician can compare the results to precedent tests and make a diagnostic decision. Here's how it works. Imagine you have been sent to the hospital for an emergency. The doctor looks at your vital signs and conducts a few blood tests, then inputs those results and an initial diagnosis into a tablet PC with wireless Internet access, along with some of your demographic details like age, gender, and ethnicity; your allergies; and your medical condition. Instantly, a database appears with a wide variety of recent scientific studies conducted on people like you with your condition. The studies involve large-scale, randomized controls using homogenous populations, and they are rated based on quality of research.

If the diagnosis is a certain type of pneumonia, for example, a series of care protocols will come up on the screen that basically say, based on this type of pneumonia, the following drugs should be ordered and the following tests should be conducted. The treatment data also includes information on side effects, needed dosage, frequency, and success rates. You and the physician can then discuss your options in depth, and the physician can make further decisions based on your preferences, condition, and personal circumstances.

The benefits are tangible. The physician does not have to be up on the latest journals or remember that conversation at the most recent convention; she just has to consult a handheld computer and combine that with her diagnostic and clinical experience. The rest of the care team—the nurses, pharmacists, technicians, and case managers—no longer have to remember 20 different sets of care delivery methods from 20 different doctors. With set algorithms in place, doctors and care teams can focus on those treatment methods that fall within the given boundaries and incorporate the most sound scientific research and outcomes. For you, the patient, the care protocols represent the best-practice approach to treating your condition. As a result, you know that you can make informed decisions about your course of treatment with confidence and real data.

When physicians incorporate algorithms into their practices, we call it evidence-based medicine. For some doctors, the term is loaded with negative connotations. They call it "cookbook medicine" because they believe it means following a set of explicit instructions while disregarding their many years of schooling, their lifetime of clinical experience, and their gut intuition. They believe that it alienates the physician from the patient by making the patient's condition a statistic rather than an individual case. They are suspicious that standardized approaches benefit cost cutters while suppressing the freedom of the physician to make a diagnosis and treat accordingly. Often, those same doctors are technology averse. They have their own way of doing things and don't like to be instructed by an electronic device. They also argue that innovation will be frozen if standards are implemented.

Let's debunk some of those arguments here, starting with the idea that evidence-based medicine takes the care decisions out of the doctor's hands and freezes innovation. When my mother passed away, I took a couple of her cookbooks and tried to re-create some favorite recipes from childhood. Interestingly, I found plenty of detailed notes scrawled in the margins. Where the recipe called for a half teaspoon of salt, my mother had jotted down a note for a quarter tablespoon. Where it called for bottled lemon juice, my mother substituted fresh squeezed with a zest of rind. In other words, my mother's cookbook was a living document that changed as she experimented until she created the recipes I loved so much.

Algorithms are inherently designed in a similar way. Rather than setting specific protocols, or instructions as to how care should be given based on scientific observation, algorithms establish a set of boundaries that give doctors a valid starting point while also allowing a basis with which to watch for exceptions. As many professionals suggest, these exceptions are nuggets of gold. If there is a mistake, it is an opportunity to educate. If an algorithm is wrong, there is the opportunity to improve it. If new information becomes available, there is a chance to change previous algorithms.

In the same way, best-practice protocols evolve, too. A physician who is astute with evidence-based medicine knows that it is combined with strong clinical expertise. The physician's primary role is to act as a diagnostician. Nothing can supplant the skill and knowledge required to form the initial assumptions that lead to the appropriate tests. The protocols that result do not take away control; they provide input. They are not administered without considering the particular circumstances or needs of the patient. The difference, however, is that any variations in treatment are recorded and logged, then compared with the actual outcomes later. Any innovations that produce better results can then be incorporated into the standard protocol. In this way, the system becomes more and more intelligent.

The idea that protocols and technology benefit cost cutters misinterprets the needs of payers, whether they be private insurers or Medicare. Evidence-based protocols reduce costs in several ways. First, when best-practice treatments are applied, more successful outcomes are likely. This means that you spend less time in the hospital recovering from your surgery, you are less likely to get an infection as a result of treatment, and the chances are lower that you will need to return as a result of relapse. Second, since the protocol is clear, you receive the appropriate amount of care, reducing the likelihood of overtreatment and increasing the efficiency of the treatment. This notion of efficiency includes the idea of receiving care from the appropriate provider. There's no reason to get treatment from the best vascular surgeon in the world when the nurse-practitioner provides the same quality of care in the most efficient way. There is no cost benefit to undertreating, cutting corners, or relying on a provider who is not expert enough to handle the job. In fact, such tactics would cost the payer more, not less, in terms of extra care, longer hospitalization, increased infection rates, and the like.

Indeed, the adoption of protocols is making pay for performance a viable possibility. Pay for performance is a model for payment that requires care providers to adhere to specific standards of practice. Are the patients getting their antibiotics prior to surgery? Have they been evaluated within 24 hours of the operation? Evidence-based medicine uncovers very specific standards that have been proven to have an enormous impact on the quality of outcomes. As a patient, you want care providers and hospitals that have an incentive to make sure those protocols are being followed, and that have the technological tools and well-trained teams to enable them to do so. Still, this model is incomplete and we have not arrived yet. The biggest concern around pay for performance models today is that they award based on the process rather than the outcome. In other words, it isn't so much pay for performance as it is pay for compliance. Although this is better than simple capitation reimbursement, we still will not maximize performance until we reach a system that incorporates desired outcomes and reimburses doctors by their results.

So where do we stand right now? Although we've come a long way from algorithm books, we're still in the early stages of evidence-based medicine. The content of the system—meaning the protocols, guidelines, and automation of the information—isn't in place on a large scale, and not many providers have access to it yet. Furthermore, we must be aware of its limitations if we are to use it correctly. While extremely beneficial in most circumstances, we must understand that some conditions are so complex that they are not able to be translated into protocol. In such cases, it is the expertise of the caregiver that is invaluable. But when used properly, protocols enhance the expertise of the provider, not replace it. If we can understand and play to this precarious balance, then we can greatly improve care for all constituents.

With both the benefits and the restrictions of evidence-based medicine in mind, we are rapidly migrating our health care system toward it. The amount of information available to physicians today is already overwhelming. In the future, that best-practice care data will be exponentially larger. Fortunately, even as the database is getting larger, our hospitals, physicians, and care teams are getting better technology to access and implement best practices.

Does this make medicine more or less personal? In my book, best-practice care, improved efficiency, and better technology give doctors more time for connecting personally and meaningfully with their patients. This is not a new concern. A 1925 journal of medicine worried openly about the increasing emphasis on science and standards of medical care at the expense of bedside manner. As the writer noted, "That wholesome mass service is but the lengthening shadow of a man, is particularly true in bedside medicine. It is quite as true with machine-made doctors today as it was in those days when students starved to follow and absorb the personalities of great leaders. It was more the human qualities of the immortal Osler than his scientific attainments that endeared him to his disciples and patients. Fortunately, he was super-endowed with both a knowledge of the humanities and of science."[2]

In the future, doctors will be better equipped to deal with the whole patient and to bring their own art and talent to bear on the patient's condition. And as patients we will feel cared for, understood, and informed to a level that is rare today.

Chapter 5

Accounting for Care

My fear is that this time the physicians will give in. Every 15 or 20 years we have a debate in this country about nationalizing health care. Each time the argument is generated by crisis—escalating costs, problems with access, dissatisfaction with service—and each time the argument comes at a moment when the system appears to be on the verge of breaking down, prompting those in favor of radical transformation to raise their voices. Generally, their proposals involve some form of government-run health care, either a system in which insurers and providers are forced into regulated markets or one in which the government pays for everyone's health care coverage outright. At each previous such juncture, physicians have been among the most stalwart opponents of a nationalized or highly regulated scheme, because they see the interference as having a negative impact on quality of care. This time, however, I worry that the physicians are ready to give in.

After all, if you are a doctor, you've trained in medicine for much of your adult life because you want to treat people and improve lives.

In order to do so, you've taken on tremendous debt, knowing that the sacrifice is counterbalanced by prestige, satisfaction, and above-average compensation. Now that doctor incomes are actually falling, however, this part of the bargain doesn't look so great, but that very discrepancy reinforces how committed you are to the profession, as opposed to something more lucrative like finance. But recently, many of the doctors I speak with are wondering if it's worth it. Convoluted reimbursement schemes have been encroaching on their practices for years, shaping decisions, directing care. The paperwork and bill-processing demands of an entrepreneurial practice have grown arduous and frustrating. The amount of time a doctor gets to spend with patients is being squeezed by the pressure to funnel more customers along the conveyor belt. In other words, it is becoming more difficult to resist the allure of a nationalized health insurance system in which, theoretically, the government takes care of administration and directs treatment, freeing the doctor and patient to concentrate on the medical problem at hand.

Physicians have always known, however, that the danger in fixing health care by putting it under government control is that we make it much, much worse. I think that American citizens understand this danger, too, which is why wholesale change has been rejected politically at several significant moments over the previous 100 years. American health care consumers, however, are just as tired of our current situation as physicians are. The simplest solution, many believe, is to mandate quality, cost, and access through some form of nationalized health care system. If Canada, France, Japan, Germany, and the United Kingdom can survive under government-run systems, why can't we?

It's incredibly easy to propose national health care as the solution to all our problems. It's much more difficult and nuanced to make the argument that a less regulated system serves us all better; but I hope to convince you of that in this chapter by explaining how a health care system that is too reliant on government intervention impedes innovation, reduces quality, and hides costs. In my experience, market-based solutions, in which the government's regulatory power is integrated appropriately, work far better in solving our problems. I also believe that the new ideas and technologies on the horizon will realign our current system in ways that reduce costs and inefficiencies, while emphasizing quality of care throughout the life cycle of the health care consumer. I am aware that being a proponent of a health care system that is motivated by profit is not a very popular position to hold at this time. But profit doesn't come from greedy businesspeople wringing their hands and scheming over how to con consumers out of their money. It comes from serving the consumer—the patient. Profit is a by-product of a happy customer. After all, it is the consumer who has the money, and it is the consumer who chooses to whom he or she wishes to give it. It's critical that we understand what is at stake, and how the current system can be improved through relatively noninvasive ways in order to bring us closer to our goals.

We need the government to take a central role in the oversight of health care and, for some people, the financing of our care, but remain clear of legislating the care process. The risk in shifting to some form of single-payer, nationalized payment scheme is that such systems often further exacerbate inefficiencies, freeze innovation, and fail to capitalize on the incredible medical and administrative technologies that are just becoming available. Instead of debating how our system compares to the national programs in France or Canada, I believe we should be asking a different set of questions. What is the dream? What is the vision of perfect health? My dream is a system in which consumers are able to take charge of their own health, in an intelligent and informed way, through a lifelong engagement instead of during isolated interventions and emergencies. I want care providers and payers to work in tandem and be forward-looking and preventive in focus, in making sure that each person has the best care at the appropriate time through the most appropriate source.

At present, we have a system that actually impedes personal responsibility and informed decision making. Because of a convergence of opportunities, however, it is now becoming possible to better align our health care system with our values and ideals, and produce results that will make us all proud of the system once again. How are we going to get there? By the end of this chapter, I will have shown you some options. At the outset, I want to show you how we've arrived at our current predicament.

Warring Impulses

No other industrialized country has taken the same journey as ours in developing its health insurance system. To understand why publicly administered health insurance has never caught on in this country and yet continues to be debated and desired, it helps to think of the opposing views of two of the founding fathers.

Alexander Hamilton, the nation's first secretary of the Treasury and an accomplished economist, viewed government as a vital tool for stimulating economic development and protecting the rights of the people. Thomas Jefferson, one of our most celebrated presidents, believed that "government is best which governs least." When it comes to health care as well as a variety of other social concerns, we continue to be influenced by both of those principled philosophies simultaneously, sometimes to our betterment, sometimes to our confusion. Culturally, we're wary of putting too much authority in the hands of the few, and favor the benefits of market competition. Yet we are also a nation that enthusiastically supports programs, charities, and philanthropic efforts that aid the underprivileged. Given those sometimes contradictory impulses, it has never been easy to enact significant reform at the political level. Even popular presidents at opportune times have failed to promote nationalized health insurance because balancing all of the interests and fears of the many different constituencies has been so difficult.

Our earliest hospitals, as we've seen, were founded to help the vast numbers of people who could not help themselves. At the same time, our best philanthropic leaders and most progressive thinkers worried about making people too reliant on charitable institutions—a popular nineteenth-century concern known as "pauperization." One group of individuals who were clearly incapable of paying for medical care were the sailors who frequented the nation's ports. Injuries went untreated and diseases spread rapidly aboard self-contained ships, at sea for many months. When the ship docked, the port city often found itself inundated with men who needed medical care but had no family or finances to provide it. The first health insurance initiative in U.S. history—the Marine Hospital Service (MHS)—was established in 1798 by none other than President John Adams, father of Nabby Adams. The MHS included a loose network of hospitals in American port cities that agreed to care for sick and disabled seamen. Funds were appropriated by taxing 20 cents off of each sailor's monthly pay, and the money was collected by U.S. customs officials. Not surprisingly, the system was not perfect or sufficient. To cap costs, sailors with chronic or incurable conditions were excluded from hospital treatment, and even those who were eligible were often placed on waiting lists that could last as long as four months.

By the 1850s, a number of voluntary programs had sprung up to provide a form of health insurance to citizens. For the most part, these were offered by cooperatives or fraternal beneficiary associations like the Elks or Lions clubs. Doctors were hired by such associations so that they could offer free care to their dues-paying members. Some commercial insurance firms experimented with offering coverage at this time, as did a number of communities, churches, and corporations, but few lasted long. Around the same period, in 1847, the American Medical Association (AMA) formed to give doctors collective power in ensuring adequate compensation and treatment standards. The AMA has been a strong voice in every policy debate around health care ever since.

It wasn't until the early 1900s that the idea of nationalized health insurance started to gain momentum. The reasons were simple. Hospitals were becoming the focal point of health care and costs were escalating dramatically, making it harder financially for the average person. In 1912, Teddy Roosevelt proposed national health insurance in his unsuccessful Bull Moose run for president. In 1915, the American Association for Labor Legislation (AALL), a group of economists at the University of Wisconsin, made its own push for universal health care. The AALL included nearly 3,000 professionals (physicians, lawyers, professors, and social workers, as well as business, labor, and political leaders), so its proposal had considerable sway. AALL pushed for reform incrementally at the state level, across the country, advocating a "standard" health insurance to protect low-income workers during times of injury or illness and to provide hospital benefits. A well-coordinated campaign was launched to win over the public and pass laws in a number of state legislatures. But in 1918, both California and New York rejected the AALL bill, and the reform drive was defeated.

One explanation for the defeat was that the nation's appetite for idealistic reform had been reduced by the ferocious conflict in Europe. A series of terrorist bombs and socialist-organized strikes shook society in 1919, hardening popular suspicions toward anything that smacked of socialism. All in all, the country was in no mood for national health care. Nevertheless, because of the deaths of 130,000 American soldiers in the war and the return of many injured, Congress established a hospital system for veterans in 1921.

Society changed dramatically in the 1920s, shifting almost overnight from a kind of Victorian age to a modern lifestyle we would recognize today in terms of its consumerism, advertising, work habits, mass media, and family structure. As the extended prosperity of the Roaring Twenties picked up its pace, technological advances took root in hospitals, doctors began charging more, medical costs rose, and cracks in the health care system started to show. According to Henry H. Moore, author of several influential reports for the *American Journal of Sociology* at the time, the problems included "the shortage and inaccessibility of personnel and equipment in private practice; the inability of the people to pay the cost of medical service; the extensive employment of inferior types of treatment; the unfairness to the private physician of the present system of charges; and the insufficiency of interest among private practitioners in preventive medicine"—all problems that sound similar to the challenges we face today. Moore concluded in one of his reports that "There may be a few influences now at work seeking to bring about the adoption of compulsory health insurance or other measures that might be considered radical. It is believed, however, that an intelligent and progressive attitude will prevail and that the investigations inaugurated and continued in 1927 will result in steady progress toward a more efficient and economic organization of medicine in the United States." In other words, Moore predicted that although we would be tempted by a nationalized system, more efficient organization of our current system would serve us better.

By 1929, health care was costing Americans $3.66 billion per year, 4 percent of national income. Families were feeling the pinch. In response, a number of private initiatives were launched to help people pay for care. In 1928, for example, in Elk City, Oklahoma, a prepaid cooperative was established so that community residents could contribute regular monthly fees to an organized group of physicians in exchange for treatment. This was one of the earliest examples of managed care. In 1929, the Los Angeles Department of Water and Power negotiated a similar contract with a group of doctors. Around the same time, the industrialist Henry J. Kaiser negotiated with doctors to provide health care for workers at shipyards and steel mills. After World War II, Kaiser exported that system to the general public as the Kaiser Permanente Health Care System. There was plenty of opposition to such an approach from all sides, however. Doctors in Elk City protested vigorously, and the AMA and hospitals let it be known that prepaid plans would give business too much say over health, while freezing innovation. The AMA, in particular, held that doctor-run systems were practically unethical, since they mixed business and health care too closely. Many opponents also feared that private insurance schemes would serve as a stepping-stone to a nationalized system.

After the stock market crash in 1929 and the beginning of the Great Depression, the health care market shrank, and consumers, with less money in their pockets, became more discerning about when they sought treatment and how much they were willing to pay for it. To deal with reduced demand, the AMA made efforts to reduce the number of new doctors, but some hospitals reacted to the financial crunch in a different way. For example, Baylor Hospital in Texas, in an effort to cushion itself against bad debt from patients who could not afford care, developed the idea of offering full hospital services for up to 21 days for a nominal monthly fee. By 1932, the Baylor Hospital idea had become the nonprofit health insurance system known as Blue Cross. In a few short years, it expanded rapidly to include many other organizations and tens of thousands of members. Blue Shield, a similar program, started in 1939, and the two groups later merged to become Blue Cross and Blue Shield Association.

During the Depression years, social security was a bigger political issue than health care. Then the start of World War II jolted the economy. Suddenly, employers needed workers but they were not able to offer higher salaries, so they began to offer health insurance plans instead. In 1943, the Internal Revenue Service (IRS) made such benefits tax exempt for the employer, encouraging widespread adoption. Our employer-based private health insurance system springs from those events.

Still, the idea of radical reform surfaced again after World War II, when President Harry S. Truman pushed for a nationalized system that would include coverage for services from doctors, hospitals, nurses, labs, and dentists. His "Fair Deal" program drew on ideas that had been percolating during Franklin D. Roosevelt's presidency, but once again, the nation's taste for government intervention was at a low point just as its fear of socialism was resurfacing. This sentiment only intensified throughout the 1950s, as the Soviet Union tightened its grip on the nations of Eastern Europe, and the Korean conflict brought American soldiers to battle once again, this time against communists.

A Step Back from the Marketplace

The most significant shock to our health care insurance system occurred in 1965 when President Lyndon Johnson signed into law Medicare and Medicaid, which provide coverage for the elderly and poor, respectively. These two groups had fallen through the cracks with the rise of employer-based health insurance. The retired, the unemployed, and those with low-paying or intermittent jobs were shut out from a private system that resisted dealing with individual customers. Johnson's two massive social programs were designed to close that gap.

Despite admirable intentions, the large-scale intervention into a market-based system had unintended fiscal and social consequences. In a snap, insurance companies were no longer under pressure to provide coverage for those outside their desired customer pool. Because of Medicare and Medicaid, the old and the poor (who were far more likely to have high medical costs) were covered by tax dollars instead. Doctors and hospitals had always charged patients according to what the market would bear, but to participate in the new Medicare and Medicaid systems, they were now permitted to charge their usual and customary fees, as long as those fees were "reasonable." In practice, this effectively meant that prices were detached from any market reality, enabling doctors and hospitals to decide their own fees without competition. What's more, since Medicare and Medicaid patients had no concerns about the total cost of care, doctors and hospitals were encouraged to administer the most expensive treatments they saw fit. As a result, Medicare and Medicaid expenses exceeded projections almost immediately, and health care costs became greatly inflated over the ensuing decades. The resulting hybrid of public and private insurance coverage has interfered with the market, reduced competition, disguised variations in quality, raised costs, and exacerbated many of the problems we now face.

As health care expenses began to accelerate once again, political leaders struggled to find a new solution. The Nixon administration introduced an innovation called health maintenance organizations (HMOs) in 1973. HMOs were forms of managed care, harking back to the concept of prepaid cooperative plans, in which patients subscribed to a system as a means of containing costs *and* producing better care outcomes. In an indication of their popularity, the HMO idea was quickly adopted by California and New York, the two states that had rejected the AALL proposals 50 years earlier.

Soon, many employer-based health insurance plans were offered in the form of either HMO or preferred provider organization (PPO) plans. Today, around 60 percent of us receive our health care coverage through such a managed care system. Many large insurance companies offer HMO plans because they provide some advantages over traditional indemnity insurance. Employers like them because they offer a less expensive form of insurance that is reasonably comprehensive. Insurance companies like them because they provide a very effective means for containing costs. In theory, doctors and patients should like them because the HMO places the personal physician at the hub of care, determining the treatment the patient needs. Well visits are encouraged to detect illnesses early and thus prevent more expensive treatments later. Members with chronic illnesses are often assigned a case manager to ensure they receive cost-effective treatment and do not get any sicker and thus become more costly to the system. The containment of costs and the emphasis on keeping patients healthy should make us all happy.

In practice, managed care plans haven't proven to be our dream solution. The complaints range from the trivial to the frustrating to the life-threatening. Patients are required to choose a primary care physician (PCP) from a list that may or may not include their preferred doctor. The PCPs either work directly for the HMO or are part of its network of providers, and receive a flat fee based on how many members they service every month. Thus, PCPs have an incentive to see as many patients as possible—reducing the amount of time spent with each one. In addition, HMOs are often criticized for rationing care by restricting referrals and expensive treatments deemed unnecessary, regardless of how important they may seem to the doctor or the patient. Moreover, these decisions do not seem to be made based on established protocols but on the whims of office workers without medical knowledge. Finally, HMOs have proven to be more costly than expected, mostly because of the administrative bureaucracy involved in running them.

In the 1980s and early 1990s, high costs and lack of coverage continued to be major political issues. In 1983, to contain hospital costs, Medicare introduced the idea of Diagnostic Related Groups (DRGs) in which hospitals would be paid a fixed fee for patients with a particular condition. In theory, DRGs helped simplify the cost structure and cap it. And yet problems quickly arose. The simplified fee structure did not account for differences in patients. For instance, the hospital was forced to charge the same amount for someone with mild diabetes as for someone with a more complicated and costly condition. As a result, treatment decisions were influenced by cost more than quality. In addition, hospitals were still able to bundle services into a kind of cost-plus format that inflated prices further—like having the contractor building your house hire all the subcontractors at whatever cost he wants.

In 1984, and later in 1992, the federal government tried to freeze Medicare-based physician fees around the same time that private insurers tried to hold doctor fees steady, too. But fixing costs this way had an unintended inflationary impact as well. The problem with fixed fees is that they encourage the doctor to prescribe additional or more expensive procedures, tests, and treatments in order to generate more income, no matter how unnecessary. In a competitive market, the patient serves as a brake on runaway costs since it's the patient's money that is being forked over. But when fixed fees are covered by insurance or Medicare, the patient has no skin in the game and thus no financial reason to object. As we've learned, higher-cost care doesn't necessarily mean better care; in fact, it often leads to worse outcomes.

An even better lesson about the difficulties of reforming health care through radical policy came in 1993 when President Clinton proposed a bill that weighed in at 1,342 pages. Designed to contain costs, improve quality, and cover the millions of uninsured, Clinton's proposal rearranged our existing system into a complicated mix of private health insurance cooperatives and health care service providers. At the time, it was met with fierce resistance from a number of different sides, including big business, those who feared government control over the private sector, and those who did not like the idea of mandating health care coverage.

After the wreckage of the Clinton health plan, no one was interested in pursuing comprehensive reform for the next 15 years. Instead, incremental measures were introduced. To counter the power of HMOs, the idea of a "Patients' Bill of Rights" got bandied about. Different versions were passed by Congress but never reconciled. In 1997, as part of the Balanced Budget Act, Congress passed the State Children's Health Insurance Program (S-CHIP), the biggest expansion of public health insurance since Medicaid. S-CHIP was designed to provide coverage to families below a certain household income who can't afford private health insurance yet earn too much to qualify for Medicaid. Also, as part of the Balanced Budget Act, Medicare recipients were allowed to obtain coverage through private insurers for the first time.

In his second term, President George W. Bush introduced two new health care coverage initiatives. The first, Medicare Part D, focused on prescription drugs coverage and relied on private insurers to provide prescription drug plans for Medicare consumers to choose from. This program was criticized by those on the right as being a huge expansion of government, and by those on the left as not going far enough in covering drug costs. Regardless, the result has been steep inflation in overall drug prices.

President Bush's other initiative, passed along with Medicare Part D, was health savings accounts (HSAs), which are a tax-advantaged means of banking money that will go toward future medical expenses. Like an individual retirement account (IRA) or a 401(k), they can be contributed to by employer and employee, and the funds can be invested and grown over time. HSA funds are tax-deductible up to a certain amount as long as they are not used for anything other than approved health-related expenses, including expenses not currently covered under health insurance like co-payments, deductibles, dental work, eye care, and equipment such as eyeglasses and hearing aids. Right now, HSAs can seem like an esoteric financial tool that has no direct impact on our daily lives. However, 401(k)s were once equally obscure. Financial institutions are making progress in turning HSAs into a standard financial product that consumers will be able to use in everyday fashion, accessing their HSA accounts with a debit card the way we tap into our checking accounts at the ATM machine or online today.

HSAs are fundamental to those who want to use tax incentives to implement large-scale privatization of our health care system while encouraging a more consumer-directed approach. On the other side of the fence, as has been the case throughout our history, there are those who are adamant about expanding government to make sure everyone has insurance coverage. Significant progress in this arena has taken place at the state level in Massachusetts, where health insurance coverage will be required for everyone. Companies with more than 11 workers will either provide insurance or pay into a state fund. For those citizens who don't get employer-based health insurance or cannot afford health insurance, the state will provide heavily subsidized coverage. The third important piece of the puzzle is that insurers are forbidden from electing not to cover someone based on preconditions.

Today, health insurance is at the heart of much political fervor. We sit amidst a sea of choices that cover the entire spectrum from privatized to nationalized solutions, advocated by strong leaders willing to fight for each approach. Given our history, the chances are slim that a nationalized health insurance system of the single-payer variety will be implemented. But clearly, the desire for reform is widespread and strong emotional arguments can be made by all sides. What is for sure is that the debate is only beginning. In the rest of this chapter, I want to explain what's at stake and what opportunities are on the horizon to radically improve the road forward.

Fixing the Breakdowns

We need health care insurance. A century ago, health care costs were manageable, but today, because of many complicating factors we should be happy to be burdened by—such as a thriving society, advanced medical technology, and breakthrough treatments—health care is too expensive to pay out of pocket. Although fee-based health care is making a comeback and HSAs have great promise, catastrophic care will always require insurance. One of the fundamental problems our society faces right now is how to improve the system so that everyone can access quality care.

Some people say that we need "Medicare for all," or that we should extend the VA health care system to the general population, or that we should all be able to access the same quality health plan that our elected representatives in Washington are offered. Despite these easy platitudes, we also need to recognize that health care is not free, and any nationalized or government-subsidized system disguises the price we all pay. As it is, we can barely afford the Medicare we now have. With increased enrollment by the baby boomer population, higher fees for medical care, and the growing costs of chronic illnesses, Medicare is under serious strain and is estimated to run out of funds by the year 2018. Those who advocate privatized insurance are worried about this kind of crippling financial drain and the care rationing that will inevitably result. President Bush recently took a stance to veto an expansion of the S-CHIP program to include the children of families with incomes of up to 400 percent of the poverty line. His stance elicited a great deal of controversy. But regardless of his intentions, the situation itself highlighted one of our deepest and most genuine fears that the creeping growth of a nationalized system is one that we cannot afford. If we were to expand S-CHIP or Medicaid to include people who already have private insurance coverage or who could afford such coverage, we would see a migration of people from the private realm to the government-funded realm, putting us one step closer to nationalized medicine.

What's wrong with nationalized medicine? In Canada, the United Kingdom, France, Germany, and Japan, care is available to all, emergency room lines are shorter, and per capita health care costs are lower. What's not to love about that? Doctors, from an administrative standpoint, benefit from an easier system of interacting with only one payer as opposed to many. Each day is simpler; when they show up for work, the waiting room is full and the job of seeing patients begins.

Unfortunately, nationalized systems have many serious problems, including long waits and endless bureaucracy. Many doctors in nationalized environments, despite having an easier time administratively, often leave for private systems where the potential for income is greater. The lack of economic incentive typically offered in a private system also reduces the drive for innovation, and thus many countries with nation-alized care utilize medical technology that comes from the United States. All in all, it is difficult to compare the two systems, but what is clear is the fact that neither works as well as our standards of quality and access demand. I see no sense in trading one system for another that will not offer any real benefit above what we already have. Instead, we should utilize the gift that we have—innovation—to leverage our system's strengths and fix its many flaws.

So, what policy choices should we make in order to safeguard what is good about our system while correcting its faults? Let me tell you about some worthy initiatives you may not have heard about in the din of the current political outcry. In 1974, a group of corporate CEOs, called the Washington Business Group on Health, met to take common positions on the health care crisis then facing the United States. At the time, one of their most prominent positions was against any form of national health insurance. Much has changed in 30 years, however. In 2007, I joined a group of business leaders at the Coalition to Advance Healthcare Reform (CAHR). The organization, led by Steve Burd, the chairman and CEO of Safeway, was created to promote market-based health care reform, with universal health insurance coverage as one of its cornerstone proposals.

Why have business leaders shifted their stance so resolutely? Primarily because the cost of providing employee premiums has become such a bur-den for large U.S. corporations that it is making it difficult for them to compete in a global marketplace. Many business leaders also see the oppor-tunities that are available for our society if business-minded, market-based reforms are implemented in a system that currently operates on such anti-business principles. But it goes even further beyond that. We recognize first that if we do nothing, the rising number of uninsured, and the rising cost of our overall system, will be a crippling social and economic prob-lem. By bringing together leaders from all industries, representing all sides of the political spectrum, CAHR has shown that it is possible to achieve an agenda based on agreeable principles that are immune to partisan bias.

The primary goal of CAHR is to promote a health care system that produces better outcomes at lower costs. As the first step in doing so, CAHR recommends universal coverage. The Massachusetts proposal has shown that our system as a whole is better off if everyone is required to carry health insurance, regardless of employment status. Society requires every car owner to have car insurance for the same reason. With more healthy people contributing to the risk pool, the burden of catastrophic care will be greatly diminished. Low-income individuals who can't afford mandatory care should receive financial assistance to pay for it. In other words, we're not advocating that people receive health care as a free service of the government, but that they obtain it themselves through private insurers with the necessary financial assistance. Along the same lines, CAHR holds that health care costs should be tax deductible, not just for employers, but for everyone.

With universal access, however, CAHR believes there should be individual responsibility. Fifty to 70 percent of an individual's total health care costs are behavior driven. There are some aspects of behavior that are a function of environment and economics—aspects that are not easily changed and not easy to hold others accountable for. However, a good percentage of unhealthy behaviors are those that are preventable. Overeating, smoking, a lack of exercise, not following a prescribed drug or treatment regimen—are all glaring and expensive contributions to poor health. For that reason, health care consumers should have a financial incentive to lead healthier lives and take care of their health in proactive ways. Financial incentives alone will not solve all the preventable health problems, but even the smallest effort on an aggregate scale has the potential to save costs across the board. Prevention and wellness should become cornerstone features of doctor visits and checkups. And for people with chronic conditions, the team-based approach I described in the previous chapter should be adopted. All of this can be facilitated with the implementation of information technology systems such as portable electronic medical records and e-prescriptions, as well as by the removal of regulations and the introduction of more market mechanisms. Given more skin in the game, patients will take a more serious approach to their wellness, and it becomes in the best interest of all players to do everything possible to keep the patient healthy for the long term.

The Market Mind-Set

Where should the line between government and market be drawn? I am not against government oversight of our health care system, but I am against government intervention into the market. The role of government is to set certain minimum standards and provide oversight so the insurance companies and providers are forced to play fair and people have the care they are paying for and need. Many articulate and well-meaning people blame business and the profit motive for trampling on the better interests of sick people. In my view, the unintended consequences of well-meaning but interfering health care regulations have caused great harm also. I believe that the government should have a role in mandating that certain standards be met, that access to health care be universal, and that bad guys be held accountable for illegal or unethical misdeeds. But I think the government does a terrible job and does significant damage whenever it gets into the business of regulating the actual marketplace.

The vital task of overhauling our health care infrastructure is impeded by government intervention. Regulations have diluted competition in the industry and created an artificial kind of status quo while intensifying the problems. Monetary controls instituted by the government are like an artificial dam blocking a great and powerful river. The river itself is the market, a force that acts naturally. Some seasons there is rainfall and some seasons there is drought—the river rises and falls—but this is all part of the natural cycle. Dams can provide needed safeguards and help moderate the harshness of nature, but they can also unintentionally impact the entire ecosystem downstream for hundreds of miles. The same is true for price controls that disrupt or divert the flow of the economy when used incorrectly. For example, if a price ceiling was placed on golf clubs, companies would produce fewer because they wouldn't be getting as much money for them as before. (Perhaps those companies would produce something else in greater quantities instead, like tennis rackets.) Meanwhile, customers who wanted golf clubs would be happy for a time with the low price, but perhaps less happy about the reduced availability of golf clubs or their quality. Next, assume the price of steel or titanium rises in some unrelated event, and the profit margins for golf clubs are squeezed even further as a result. Any incentive to produce golf clubs has been reduced that much more. If the government doesn't mandate that manufacturers continue producing the item, the industry might otherwise move on to some other product entirely. Eventually, through such convoluted reactions and counterreactions, you create a market that is so compromised and unnatural, it may as well be determined in five-year plans by a state agency.

In a more complicated fashion, this has happened within the health care industry. Take the impact of Medicare. I am not so brave or foolish as to advocate that we stop offering such support, but I think it's important we understand the consequences of it and choose better means of integrating it with the marketplace. In their book *Redefining Health Care*, Michael Porter and Elizabeth Teisberg point to the introduction of Medicare in 1965 as the moment in which we, as health care consumers, stopped looking for low-cost, high-quality products and services as we would in any normal market like consumer goods, and started associating low-cost health care with the idea of low quality. To say that Medicare was the sole catalyst for a movement in consumer oversight of health care costs is too grand a statement. The real argument and mine is that the consumer needs a greater line of sight regarding price and quality or value. After all, if cost is no object, why pay less? Over the years, the government has fiddled with the marketplace, in knee-jerk and after-the-fact ways, to adjust and compensate for its own regulated remedies. Today, many doctors are becoming reluctant to care for Medicare or Medicaid patients, because the reimbursement they receive from the government is minimal.

In fact, we are paying for Medicare twice—once through our taxes, and once through the higher prices required by private coverage. Medicare is such a major health care payer that the extensive rules and regulations the government puts in place force doctors and hospitals to modify price structures for the entire market. Most physicians have around 50 percent of their patient load in a price-controlled system through Medicare or Medicaid. The other half of their practice is subsidized by private health plans. Patients with private health plans actually pay 50 or 60 percent more than what the government is willing to pay through Medicare or Medicaid. In other words, the government's efforts to cap costs mean it doesn't reimburse enough for the services it demands of doctors and hospitals—and gets a free ride as a result.

A fundamental reason for this problem is that the government chooses cost-based reimbursement as its measure rather than price-based reimbursement. In other words, in order to be fair and to prevent providers from overcharging, the government dictates a maximum cost that it is willing to reimburse for a service, rather than determining what the average price for a service is in the marketplace and allowing doctors to charge accordingly. If we change the mechanism for reimbursement so that the market is setting the price rather than the government, we will be able to equalize compensation across the board, bringing private and public coverage into line, even without taking the drastic step of doing away with Medicare and Medicaid. In other words, Medicare should not be forcing the market to adjust to its cost controls and reimbursement strategies; it should be forced to adjust its reimbursement methods based on the marketplace.

If a market-based system is allowed to function, compensation for health care will be based on demand and the quality that is delivered to customers. When there is a lot of demand, prices will go up, but so, eventually, will supply of those services. With the rising number of baby boomers entering Medicare, for example, we can expect a sharp rise in cardiac defibrillator implant operations. In a market-based system, this would mean that more doctors and hospitals would be drawn to this form of surgery as a lucrative service, and those doctors and hospitals would also compete among each other in terms of quality. The hospitals with a better track record of defibrillator implants would attract more patients. Conversely, if the best cardiac hospitals charged too much for their service, consumers might decide to go to a hospital that is nearly as good in terms of its outcomes, but charges less.

Given the way Medicare currently operates, however, we can expect that the government will not allow price to be set by the market, but instead will cap costs that it's willing to reimburse hospitals for cardiac implants. As an unintended consequence, even though the need for the service is growing, the incentive for doctors and hospitals to provide that service goes away. At the same time, because of the rationing of care, the quality distinctions do not come to the surface. Customers will be more concerned with getting the surgery than with determining which hospital is the Lexus and which is the reliable Honda Accord. In other words, in a semi-regulated system, the government steps in to make sure prices do not get too high. Supply of those services is therefore discouraged, and demand goes unmet. When market forces are dampened, services are not distinguished by price, and there is less incentive to make a competitive distinction based on quality.

Does this mean there is no place for government in the health care industry? Absolutely not. In health care, I believe that government can and should create standards for safety, but that it should not determine how those standards get met or how much should be charged. Take an example from the auto industry. Decades ago, seat belts were not mandatory. The government, as the people's advocate, was a tremendous positive force in requiring cars to have certain safety features. Then came the air bag. At first, only luxury cars were equipped with air bags because they were an expensive item that not every consumer could afford or deemed worth paying for. The government decided, however, that air bags represented an important technological innovation that could help us take another great leap in terms of safety. To enforce their use, however, the government did not decide to subsidize the cost of air bags, nor did it put a cap on the cost borne by the consumer; instead, it mandated that all companies put air bags into every single one of their cars while allowing those companies to charge consumers for the air bags' inclusion. This enabled the prices of cars to stay where the market intended, and also encouraged further innovation in terms of cost or efficiency. Companies marketing cars to low-end markets, for example, were forced to develop cheaper ways of including air bags while still meeting safety standards. It is these kinds of market pressures that create constant evolution in an industry and lead to more efficient practices.

The 65-Year Drop-Off

My one radical policy suggestion for the government is to change the terms under which we offer health insurance coverage. The current employer-based health insurance system is predicated on the idea that you, the private health insurance customer, will disappear at the age of 65. After all, when you retire, your employer-based health insurance comes to an end, and your Medicare coverage begins. However, 80 percent of a person's health care expenses come in the last few months of life. For most of us, since death comes after 65, this means that the burden falls to Medicare. Incidentally, years ago, when we picked 65 as the retirement age, our odds of living longer than that didn't look so good. Today, many people are living 15 or 20 years longer—all of those years increasingly expensive from a health care standpoint.

This is a pretty good deal for insurers. They get paid to cover health care expenses during the customer's most healthy years, and they get to pass the customer over to the government just as the customer is becoming less healthy and more expensive. In blunt terms, private insurers are motivated to see us live at minimal health care expense until age 65. It follows that private insurers have no incentive for the insurer to create programs around preventive and wellness care that could keep us healthier post-65 even though expensive chronic conditions or even acute illnesses like cancer are more likely then.

Please understand that I am not claiming private insurers are callous about their customer's lives or cut corners with care in the knowledge that Medicare is waiting. I am saying, however, that it is only natural and understandable that decisions about how to organize and provide care are made knowing the 65-year handoff is inevitable. It is a little bit like leasing a car for a set period of time. Imagine that after a two-year period you are obligated to return your car, but you are under no obligation to return it in good shape. With six months left in your lease, I bet you forgo rotating the tires or even changing the oil because the car, in your mind, is now a disposable item. As you get closer to the end of the lease, you won't get the tune-up it needs, and you may not even bother to bring it through a car wash. Why incur the expense yourself? However, for the rental firm, a car returned in such condition is going to be much less profitable to lease or sell to another customer.

Consider the ramifications if the customer remained in the private sector. In our current Medicare-based system, the private insurer knows with certainty that a 45-year-old customer has a 20-year maximum "life span" remaining as far as monthly payments go. But if the customer were to remain with the private insurer after age 65, the rules of the game would change significantly. Suddenly, the insurer has less certainty. Will the patient live to 66 or 86? Who knows? What the insurer does know is that it can continue to collect monthly premiums from that customer for a longer time. As a result, it is now motivated to keep that customer alive and in good health for as long as possible.

We all want to live a long and healthy life, and we want care providers and insurers working with us who feel the same way. Suddenly, by encouraging patients to stick with their private plans rather than switching over to Medicare, we align the health care consumer's interests (longer, healthier life) with the private insurer's interests (more monthly premiums over longer period of time). How does the insurer make a longer, healthier life possible? It begins to organize services around encouraging healthier behaviors earlier. It wants to avoid costly treatments later, so it guides customers to cheaper preventive measures. It wants the customer to make informed decisions about the quality of care offered by providers in its network, encouraging choices based on quality results—not the cheapest doctor, hospital, or treatment, but the best doctor, hospital, or treatment for the dollar. If the insurer encourages the customer to see a bad doctor or get surgery at a hospital with poor practices, then the insurer will be penalized when the customer ends up visiting the emergency room later or spending extra weeks in intensive care. When payers must focus on patients' health over a long period of time, they will reduce costs to themselves by working to maximize the health of the patients. As the aggregate health of the beneficiary increases and emergency procedures become less commonplace, the prices of premiums across the board will drop.

Again, I am not saying that private insurers are disinterested in helping their customers lead healthy, high-quality lives. I *am* saying that we have no chance of changing our health care focus from an episodic and crisis-oriented system to one in which health care is a lifelong engagement where healthier behaviors are encouraged unless we create a shift in economic motives. That's what a market-based approach can do.

The Consumer in Charge

Ultimately, market pressures will come from the consumer being informed and engaged. We need a health care system in which consumers, or their representatives, have real information about the hospitals, care providers, and insurers they choose to work with, and real incentive to make better decisions about their health.

Some of this is cost and quality related. What do you mean it's going to cost $50,000 to have cardiac surgery done at your hospital? It costs only $5,000 to get my arrhythmia corrected with electric stimulus at the other hospital, and their results and recovery times are better! Some of this is safety related. Why would I go to a neighborhood hospital with

10 times as many staph infections as the hospital three miles away that has eliminated staph infections? If we, as consumers, are aware of the issues and challenges that are most critical, and if we have a freer market in which to operate, we can make decisions that have real impact on health care quality. I envision a day in the near future when consumers question a hospital or a pharmacy because it does not use electronic prescribing or evidence-based medicine. I imagine such consumers taking their business elsewhere, like they might avoid a coffee shop that does not allow debit cards, or a grocery store that does not date its perishable items.

A consumer's market-based decisions will impact the way service providers operate. A hospital without automated medication administration will lose customers to a hospital that has a seamless radio-frequency identification (RFID)-based system for prescribing, ordering, and delivering medications. A physician group that performs 100 flawless stent implementations a month will gain business over a physician group that performs 10 such procedures at a higher cost. Market economics is the best vehicle to force change, improve quality and efficiency, and lower price. Government mandates or regulations can never keep up with demand in the marketplace.

Is this putting too much responsibility on the individual health care consumer? Some believe that we need government to make our decisions for us because consumers don't have the expertise to make choices that are in their own best interests. I think that is a profound misunderstanding of where government can add value, and how markets actually work. I want the government to ensure that the car I buy meets very specific safety and emissions standards; but I do not want the government telling me what kind of car I can buy, how much I should pay for it, how many vehicles I should own, or where I should get them serviced. This doesn't mean or require that I am a car expert. I don't necessarily need to know how engines work, what kind of systems the automotive factory has in place, or whether the guy who sold me my car is compensated by commission or salary. But I do need to educate myself about certain basic details, and I need to make a judgment based on my own needs and desires.

Of course, it is true that buying a car and getting the best care for yourself and your family are entirely different matters. Transparency is a powerful tool that will empower consumers to set their own standards for quality of care, but one that, in and of itself, will not be a sole catalyst for needed change. Nor will it appear instantaneously. As change theory suggests, such an implementation would not result in immediate and linear improvement. It will be gradual, and it will not be predictable given the variables that affect consumer rationality. However, given ample time, a transparent system will make a difference. It will place into the hands of consumers power that they have never known before—the ability to choose their own care and, in so doing, improve the quality and efficiency of health care across an entire system.

Many believe that some consumers simply will not be able to make the best choices. If that's your point of view, then you will have a hard time believing that government should step back from the decision process. I am not claiming that we will need to be medical experts to make a more transparent system work. But we can receive help from various sources. The Internet provides a remarkable infrastructure for making informed decisions. Our ability to shop—to research products and services and to find out how other people review them—has been radically transformed in recent years. We will always need experts to provide us with decision-making services. For example, not many of us have the time, the intellect, or the desire to understand the financial markets and invest our retirement savings accordingly; but we can determine which financial adviser we want to work with based on our goals and values, develop a trusting relationship with that person, and feel in control of our financial future regardless of who is hitting the buy or sell button on the trades that get made. In the same way, we can be in control of our health future, too.

Transparency is obviously the critical component. Right now, we live and work in a system that has almost none of the information available to make informed choices. I believe this will be radically transformed in the near future. At the moment, we can get far more consumer information comparing vacuum cleaners than cancer hospitals. One hundred years ago, Dr. Ernest Codman proposed a system in which hospitals and care providers would publish their care results so that patients and doctors could make informed decisions about where to go for the best, most cost-efficient care. We need to be able to know whether Dana-Farber's cancer care is significantly better or worse, and cheaper or more costly, than the care that can be obtained at Sloan-Kettering.

The reason we don't have access to that information right now is because we haven't allowed our health care system to evolve according to market principles. In a mistaken belief that we would receive poor-quality health care if economics were to rule the day, we allow the government to police our markets. In fact, we need the government to police the behaviors of the businesses that provide services in any market, but markets themselves do not work when they are controlled by nonmarket forces. Consider all the wonderful innovation that we have seen in the high-tech world in the past 20 years. If the government had been placed in a position to direct and control that marketplace, we would not have the rate of innovation we have seen in personal computers. We would not have millions of web sites offering information and services. There would be no incentive for teenagers and college dropouts to make new products, because there would be no Google billionaires.

Our health care system would experience a similarly astonishing rise of innovation and service if true market incentives were in place. As it is, the incredible advances we have already seen are evidence of the bottled-up demand that exists among health care consumers, and the passions, intellect, and vision of the men and women working in health care today.

Getting the Payer–Provider–Consumer System Aligned

Payers will play an integrated role in helping consumers navigate and providers inform. Currently, there exists a somewhat adversarial relationship among payers, providers, and patients, and a lack of transparency is intrinsic to the way money gets made. Payers offer insurance products to employers based on their understanding of how much it will cost to provide health care to the employee base plus their families. Complex formulas and calculations go into making such an offer, which is why it is incredibly difficult to obtain individual health insurance. It is simply not cost-effective for an insurer to determine how much to charge you for coverage when the risk of your coverage is not pooled within a larger population.

On the other side of the market, payers negotiate with providers to obtain care for the kinds of claims they project the employees and families will need. In this, they have great power to set prices because the customer base—those employees and their families—will not be able to go outside of that realm of providers to make better market decisions. Between providers and payers, there are many complex dynamics at play, in which providers try to be included in the benefit book at the highest possible price.

A consumer with three young children knows exactly how much she owes for a co-pay but never finds out exactly how much the pediatrician charges, or how much other pediatricians charge for similar services. If she's done her homework, she gets anecdotal information about whether the pediatrician provides quality service, but she does not get to compare measures of quality in any meaningful way. Nor does the insurance company or the care provider have any interest in the consumer knowing these things. They are not competing with the consumer for their service; they are negotiating with each other, and the consumer is kept out of the loop of that transaction to the benefit of the provider and the payer.

In a health care system that functioned on the principles of market-based transactions and transparency, a type of payer would arise that functions more like an administrative coordinator of financial and clinical transactions rather than a traditional insurer. That payer's role would be to inform the consumer of the cost and quality of the services available and make the financial transaction happen.

At present, the current system is a nightmare of paperwork and confusion. When the patient visits the provider, the provider makes a manual record of the services provided, and sends that invoice to the payer. In a perfect world, the payer reimburses the provider promptly and at full value. In the real world, payments are delayed, and the amount that is reimbursed is less than the amount invoiced. The difference needs to be covered by the patient, so the provider informs the patient of the billing discrepancy, and the patient is prompted to call the payer and try to work out the problem. None of these discussions take place electronically with commonly viewed documents. If the patient is lucky, eventually the situation works itself out or simply goes away; but it is not an experience that inspires a lot of faith in the system, and there are many examples of people who do not get the coverage they thought they had paid for.

In the near future, transactions will take place in a much improved way. When a patient visits a doctor, the doctor will get online authorization for services. The insurer will respond instantly with the amount that the insurer is able to reimburse and the amount that is owed by the patient. The doctor will collect the patient's portion on the spot. When the visit is over and the clinical record is documented, the information is sent to the payer, and the doctor will be reimbursed electronically for the agreed-upon amount. The entire transaction will take place through the "locked box" of a financial institution to ensure that the payer does not have access to the provider's accounts.

Installing this kind of system will have a ripple effect on the relationship between payer, provider, and consumer. The increased transparency and the instantaneous communication of commonly held information will lead to a more cooperative mode focused on shared goals. To explain what I mean, let me tell you a little about what is happening now.

One of the biggest concerns in health care today is the amount of administrative inefficiency and the lag time with regard to transferring patient health information. As things stand, most hospitals and almost every individual office or clinic uses a paper-based system, effectively ensuring that medical records not only will be difficult to transfer and interpret, but will be recorded in incompatible formats. The resulting complications are a tremendous impediment to upgrading and improving the efficiency of the American health care system.

This is not breaking news to anyone working in health care; but all of the solutions proposed to alleviate the problem require major up-front investments and a vast improvement in on-site technological infrastructure. Here we have a chicken-or-the-egg type of problem. There is no financial incentive for hospitals, let alone individual doctors and clinics, to make such a technological investment until everyone else is doing it, too. Until then, the average American home or office where Internet access, e-mail, and online shopping and banking take place is far more sophisticated than the average clinic where the fax machine is still the administrator's best friend. Even a simple thing like formulating a full medical record for a single patient on one template requires checking the records of every single doctor and hospital the person has ever visited, and manually transferring that data to electronic form.

So, if we can't retrieve patient records from paper files, where can we get them? One short-term solution driven by McKesson and other companies is to obtain the information through payer-based health records. Instead of relying on providers and patients to supply critical data, we go straight to the most reliable source—the insurance companies. By using data from insurers, particularly claims data, it is possible to establish a record for a patient's entire medical history. Information from insurance companies is much easier to track down because of the simple fact that patients switch insurers less frequently than they change physicians or hospitals. On the downside, claims data has a tendency to be somewhat vague and can lag events by several months, so it may not yield the most accurate and up-to-date information, but it is the most efficient way of obtaining patient records given the poor organization of data today.

The end goal is standardization. This will bring more transparency, greater administrative efficiency, and easier transference of data. When you consider what a patient goes through, you begin to understand the value of digitizing information flows. When patients are diagnosed with colorectal cancer, for example, it's frightening. Today, their experience is that they have to go to their family doctor, then a gastrointestinal specialist, then a colorectal surgeon. The patient has to get and pay for tests, lab work, CAT scans, chemotherapy, and radiation therapy over the course of months, often involving hospital stays and follow-up visits. All of the physicians and clinics and testing centers have to coordinate, but they have no procedure for communicating with each other. In today's world, the complex health care system is a mysterious landscape navigated without a map; much of the work a patient does involves managing communications among the players, in addition to the complex payments that generally follow such communications. Understandably, few patients have the confidence or the certainty that they will obtain the best care with the best possible outcomes at a fair cost. Too often, they feel as though they are lost in some absurd bureaucratic nightmare.

In tomorrow's system, when health care goes digital, the connectivity required to support complex care will be part of the infrastructure and taken for granted, like Internet broadband and wireless is part of the infrastructure of most offices and communities. Communication—meaning education about your condition and treatment won't happen through pieces of paper that get faxed and filed. Increasingly, it will happen—and in some cases it is happening—face-to-face with the doctor, and later at home on your computer, where you can revisit your health record, check on links, delve further into the details, and even send the doctor more questions by e-mail, track your co-payments, and schedule your next appointments. If you haven't been through a crisis like cancer, you might not be able to imagine how comforting this will be.

This connectivity extends to the hospital. Doctors, nurses, and technicians at the hospital will have access to the same information. They will be treated to frequent reminders regarding a patient's health characteristics. For example, if a patient is currently on several different medications with unique interactions, a call system will ensure that the nurse or doctor is aware of this and has consulted the records.

After the hospital stay, your personal doctor will not have to ask you what happened. He or she will be able to see online your personal records, your lab results, and the progress that you're making; can make decisions based on shared facts; and can record those decisions for all others on the team to follow. As a result, you will be able to stop worrying about navigating the system, and focus on managing your own health.

Virtual Health

Digitization will create paths of communication between provider and patient that will be so natural and seamless in the future as to sound like science fiction today. Currently, at every doctor's office, there are countless administrative tasks that have to be taken care of with each and every patient. In most locations, this is done with good old-fashioned paper and pencil. The biggest and most important concern is making sure every single patient visit is well documented, a process that most insurance companies require in order for you to receive reimbursement. Apart from this, appointments need to be scheduled, payment has to be collected, prescriptions have to be written, insurance information has to be shared, and medical files must be viewed. Each of these tasks is its own time- and money-consuming nuisance in a paper-based world.

One of the most glaring inefficiencies burdening the health care system today is that a good percentage of the patients that primary care physicians see exhibit symptoms that could easily be addressed and treated from home. Unfortunately, most doctors do not make house calls anymore, and most people don't have the expertise to make an assessment and prescribe a course of treatment. Because of these unnecessary visits and follow-up visits, customers are spending extra money, doctors are using up valuable time, and payers are forced to reimburse for an expense that could and probably should have been avoided.

E-visits allow patients to fill out online interview forms related to their symptoms, send them via secure link to a trusted primary care physician at any time of the day or night, and access the diagnosis from home. All of this is done for a modest fee that is much cheaper than having to pay for a check-up. In fact, more and more insurance companies are covering e-visits because, from a cost standpoint, they are simply more efficient than paying for frequent trips to the doctor's office. Best of all, e-visits are done without time constraints. Patients fill out the online form whenever they have a free moment, and doctors can respond at a time that is convenient for them. This allows caregivers to devote more of their day to patients with more serious needs that require intense personal care.

Using the same secure system, appointments can be scheduled, prescriptions renewed, health records updated, lab results viewed, and referrals requested. Here's an example. A busy advertising account manager named Sophia develops a sore throat. Dr. Lang's office staff schedules an appointment and e-mails her the confirmation. Sophia fills out her pre-exam paperwork online and heads to the doctor's office. Dr. Lang's office checks Sophia's insurance eligibility with her health plan prior to her examination. At the examination, Sophia and Dr. Lang are able to spend a few minutes catching up on each other's lives, until Dr. Lang, prompted by Sophia's digital records, asks about a condition Sophia has been treated for recently. Then, moving on to the sore throat, Dr. Lang does an exam and submits an e-prescription to the pharmacy near Sophia's office.

With the examination complete, Dr. Lang's office sends the reimbursement request to Sophia's health plan, and receives an electronic payment from Sophia's health savings account for her co-pay. On her way back to work, Sophia stops at the pharmacy to pick up her medication. The pharmacist, who already has her prescription and has checked it with Sophia's records to avoid medication errors, confirms her benefits with her health plan, bills her accordingly, and submits the remainder to her insurer for reimbursement.

We're not there yet, and we will not make the shift in one leap. But as of today we can install systems that do enough to bring us closer to digitized health care and greatly improve our current situation. A full electronic medical records system is like a top-of-the-line BMW, but most clinics and even some hospitals do not need all of that capability right away—a simple and economical Honda or Toyota will do. Small practices can easily work with a data repository, an e-mail communication piece, and the luxury of a physician-supported e-prescribing tool. Everything else is a nice-to-have but not a must-have. But obtaining that base of operations can be a springboard for technological advancement. Eventually, we will achieve a system of standardized electronic data management across every level of care.

In the future, when providers, payers, and consumers are connected, health care episodes will be streamlined and enriched. Patients will be able to manage their own health at their own convenience, at a cost that fits their budget, and in a more informed and engaged way. The insurer or health plan will be able to reduce costs by streamlining paperwork and administrative operations, and advise the patient on treatments and providers with the best, most cost-effective outcomes. The pharmacist will partner with the patient, advising on medications, checking for adverse drug interactions and allergic reactions, and supporting a healthy medication regimen. And the hospital and clinic will be able to make better care decisions, while gaining convenience, flexibility, and that feeling of high touch that health care consumers will come to see as vital components of good health care service.

With the adoption of digitized care, we will be miles closer to a system that is truly about serving the consumer and maximizing the value of the last two feet.

Chapter 6

How Technology Is Putting the Patient at the Center of Care

So where do we stand now? The history of our health care system is an incredible story of scientific and technological innovation, driven by entrepreneurs, corporations, caregivers, and government policy. Our current situation is marred by gaps and disconnections, but as I have tried to show in the previous chapters, we are on the verge of experiencing a reconnection through technologies already in existence that will integrate health care services and put the patient back into the center of care.

The Gap

In the past 10 years, 12 Nobel Prizes in Medicine have gone to American-born scientists, while three were awarded to foreign-born scientists working in America. The rest of the world benefits from our new drugs, our diagnostic technologies, our treatment advances, and our facilities. In 2003, $94.3 billion was spent on biomedical research in this country, an amount that no European country can come close to matching. The National Institutes of Health's annual research budget is roughly $28 billion, compared to $3.7 billion spent on research by the European Union governments. The reason we are replete with innovation is because of the energy of our market-based system. The reason we are plagued with disconnects, gaps, and inhibited service is too often due to the restraints put on providers, hospitals, and businesses through market interference.

Despite our technological advantages, too many health care consumers see too few of the benefits. Rather than experiencing the empowered connection of the medical home, they feel medically homeless, as Darrel Kirch, the president of the Association of American Medical Colleges, has put it. There are many hospital systems in this country leading the way in terms of innovative approaches for those who have access to them. Institutes like Boston Children's Hospital, Brigham and Women's, Cleveland Clinic, Spartanburg Regional, Presbyterian, Eisenhower, and Covenant Health are among the systems that stand out as renowned centers where you can receive state-of-the-art care, with all of the quality and efficiency benefits of the best-run businesses. However, these are exceptional institutions that are not representative of the status quo, and their achievements ought to be much more widespread. What needs to be done? Some of the most important technological solutions available to us are not yet widely adopted. Only about 10 percent of modern hospitals use electronic medical records, for example, a necessary technology to improve the efficiency, quality, and safety of care. And, as I mentioned earlier, the problem goes deeper yet. So many hospitals struggle to implement even the most basic of best-practice protocols and fail to achieve the consistency of quality that can be produced through an aligned system that utilizes the best that technology has to offer. But this is changing. As we continue to drive new innovations throughout the health care industry, we will be able to put more tools into the hands of consumers. Consider the following seven factors necessary for an integrated, consumer-centered system and how technology is reshaping our health care experience for the better.

Transparency

During my research for this book, I decided to go online and do a Google search in an attempt to see how easy it would be to find objective safety and performance ratings for providers across the country. Having found several sites that boasted doctor quality ratings, I decided to do a search for my primary care physician. After 20 minutes of research, I found a total of three web sites that actually had my physician listed. Of these, two offered little more than contact information, while the third wanted to charge me $30 for a "doctor report." While patient reviews and comments were encouraged in some cases, feedback simply didn't exist for most of the providers listed.

A search for hospital ratings had slightly better returns. Within a few minutes I was able to find two national hospital review web sites, as well as several state-operated ones. But these sites, helpful as they were, did not even come close to covering the huge variety of concerns that patients face. They didn't provide the easy-to-interpret combination of objective and subjective data that can be found on comparable web sites rating computers, cars, or sporting equipment. Each used its own unique rating system. Of the two most notable, one used statistical data while the other used a subjective scale. It is quite possible that more sites exist, but in today's fast-paced world, anything that takes more than 20 minutes to locate simply isn't accessible enough to become widespread.

We have all seen what technology can do in terms of transparency. If we go onto Amazon.com, we are greeted with professional reviews from multiple sources, sample content from popular books, numerous reader reviews, and an easy-to-operate list of the "most popular" items. Health care review sites have not even come close in terms of usability and pure quantity of information, but they will. Consumers and payers both realize the value of transparency in a market-based system, and have already started to take action. Providers, businesses, and hospitals that anticipate this demand will be the market leaders in the future, and we will soon achieve clarity such that consumers will be informed and empowered like never before.

Connectivity

Transparency will revolutionize the role of the consumer. Connectivity is the handmaiden necessary for transparency's full benefits to be realized. After all, the output of transparency is that consumers make better choices, so pathways, if not superhighways, need to be established to enable consumers to access the care that appeals to them most. Connectivity will streamline every transaction in the system, allowing consumers to make more educated decisions in real time. Patients will be able to communicate with their doctors remotely; doctors and payers will be able to use technology to settle claims and free up manual time normally spent on revenue cycle management; and providers will be able to instantly communicate with each other to exchange patient data. In the near future, the hospital will be made more efficient as pharmacists, doctors, and nurses will be talking over wireless voice transmitters and submitting medication orders through RFID trackers—monitoring the status of every drug, instrument, device, patient, and caregiver at every moment. The less time that must be spent on transactions, communications, and monitoring, the more time may be devoted to the patient.

Productivity and Efficiency

One of the major failings of our health care system is the massive amount of money being lost in the cracks. Every year, some $400 billion to $500 billion is wasted on rework and error. This waste of money relates directly to a waste of time and consumer productivity. All of the paper handoffs, systematic errors, and variability of care create a great deal of waste. But when your health care providers are connected and capable of sharing and viewing data in real time, health care will enter the modern age.

But not all productivity improvements will sound like science fiction. Some simply involve bringing established business processes into the age-old cottage industry of health care. For example, why is it that we must wait months for a doctor's appointment and an hour when we arrive at the clinic? At a clinic in Sacramento, Kaiser Permanente has been able to reduce an average 55 days' wait to one day by offering "open access" or "same-day scheduling." This requires a logistical understanding of how patients flow through a clinic, and what combination of set appointments and open appointments are optimal to maximize efficiency. Despite this remarkable improvement, the vast majority of clinics in this country do not see patients on the same day they call.

Spreading Medical Best Practices

When Kevin Everett, an NFL football player for the Buffalo Bills, suffered a catastrophic and life-threatening spinal cord injury during a game on September 9, 2007, it looked as though he would never walk again. The doctors gave him no better than a 5 percent chance of living anything close to a normal life, and said in all likelihood he would be a paraplegic. Then, one day after surgery, a minor miracle happened: Everett could move his limbs and was able to breathe on his own. How did this miracle occur? Because Everett's doctors followed the latest, most advanced protocol in treating spinal injuries. The protocol says to intravenously treat the injured patient with ice-cold saline solution in order to put the patient in a hypo-thermic state. The protocol exists because doctors at the Department of Neurological Surgery at the University of Miami School of Medicine have discovered that doing so reduces swelling in the damaged tissue and thereby significantly reduces the damage to the spinal cord. As Dr. Barth Green, head of the Miami project, said, "We've been doing a protocol on humans and having similar experiences for many months now. But this is the first time I'm aware of that the doctor was with the patient when he was injured and the hypothermia was started within minutes of the injury. We know the earlier it's started, the better."

Note that the patient did not need to be flown to Miami to access the best treatment, nor did the most knowledgeable clinical practitioner need to be flown to Buffalo to administer the protocol. A team doctor working for the Buffalo Bills who was aware of the protocol was able to save the patient from a lifetime in a wheelchair with a breathing tube.

Patients with any common condition can be treated with the best evidence-based medicine if their physicians and care providers are trained to access and follow the protocols. Technology can give them access to that data, while a team-based approach can help them system-ize the processes. We can lower the cost of high-quality care throughout our health care system by doing so. This is not about turning doctors into mechanics—it's about bringing the productivity, efficiency, and quality gains of every other industry to health care.

Innovations in Diagnostics

Several years ago a new diagnostic test was approved in Chicago for a number of esophageal and gastrointestinal (GI) disorders: a simple vitamin-sized pill containing a microscopic camera. After being swallowed, the pill travels through the esophagus and the GI tract taking 14 color digital pictures per second. Those pictures are transmitted instantly to a recording device on the patient's wrist. After 20 minutes, the doctor has enough information to make a diagnosis, and the capsule is passed naturally and painlessly two to three days later. Before the advent of this technology, the patient would have received a very uncomfortable endoscopy, involving the insertion of a long tube and requiring sedation and several hours of recovery.

In another example, David Piston, director of the W. W. Keck Foundation Free-Electron Laser Center, uses biophotonics as a demonstration of the world to come. The term refers to the application of light to illuminate and manipulate the hidden worlds of living organisms, and is the direction many research hospitals are taking. Using national funding, the Keck Foundation is looking into several different areas of minimally invasive procedures:

- *Materials science*—allows scientists to go deeply into the chemical components in our biological cells.
- *Laser surgery*—working with researchers from Vanderbilt, Duke, and Stanford on new ways to develop smaller and less expensive light scalpels.
- *Proteomics*—helps scientists better understand the functions of proteins and thus identify the proteins that will advance the mapping of the human genome—ultimately finding new ways to treat and prevent disease.
- *In vivo imaging*—allows scientists and physicians to watch the movement of a single molecule, which will provide important information about diseases such as cancer and diabetes.

Given a choice of either undergoing anesthesia and some form of an exploratory procedure or swallowing a pill, which would you choose?

Robotics

It's hard to imagine what an operation will look like in years to come. Replacement parts today are becoming standard: hips, knees, even faces. How good is your surgeon? In the future, if you have a heart operation or a kidney transplant, your surgeon's hands might not even touch you. Instead, you may be operated on by a robot.

Take heart surgery. The surgical team includes a caterpillar robot. This tiny device, a mere two centimeters long, can move around the surfaces of the heart 18 centimeters per minute. Instead of having your ribs split open and your inner chest exposed, you will have a small scar as this robot is inserted under the rib cage and maneuvered onto the heart by a remote control device through the manipulations of skilled surgeons. Tiny suckers on the caterpillar hold onto the heart gently as it moves around to the exact location where treatment is needed. The robot can do a number of procedures, including injecting stem cells and growth factor genes. It can also take samples. It has a little camera added to its tool chest and a magnetic tracker.

Dr. Cameron Riviere, who led the research and ran the initial tests at Carnegie Mellon University Robotics Institute in Pittsburgh, explains that this device avoids having to stop the heart, pry open the rib cage, or deflate the left lung, thereby reducing lots of risk linked to the bypass procedure. Although this technique has been performed only on animals, scientists say it is a mere two to three years away from being used on humans.

Nanotechnology is an even more futuristic approach that will one day be commonplace. Imagine being injected with a vaccine containing countless numbers of microscopic, molecule-sized nanomachines. These robots, because of their small size, will be able to cross over cell membranes and be absorbed into any cell, permeating the entire body. They will act as suppressors of foreign bacteria and viruses, identifying unnatural pathogens and destroying them. They will be able to deliver specific doses of drugs directly to desired cells for faster and less harmful delivery. They will be able to find and destroy cancerous cells throughout the body. They will even be able to repair damage done to the body's natural cells by fixing broken or misaligned patterns in the DNA.

Imagine being able to live to three times your normal life expectancy without showing any signs of aging, as almost all infection and cellular damage is prevented and repaired from within. Nanomedicine itself is already here. Researchers at Rice University used such technology to effectively kill cancer tumors in mice using gold-coated nanoshells. By conjugating antibodies or peptides to the gold-plated surface, these tiny particles were able to bond to cancerous cells. The area of the tumor was then irradiated with an infrared laser that alone simply passed through flesh without heating it. Because gold is such a good conductor, the nano-particles were sufficiently heated to kill the cancer cells to which they were bound.

Today, using cameras, lasers, and robotic arms, surgeons already oper-ate with incredible precision. An estimated 100,000 surgical procedures were performed through robotics in 2007, from kidney transplants to prostate removals. Robotics also allows surgery to be performed remotely. Surgeons in major cities or hospitals can operate on patients thousands of miles away. This will further reduce the cost and inconvenience for patients who would normally need to travel to receive medical care.

Convenient Retail-Like Health Experience

Why do we even need to go to a doctor's office or hospital? So often the treatment we go to the doctor to receive is unnecessary. We know what is wrong with us, the administrative nurse knows what is wrong with us, and the doctor listens for 10 seconds and knows what is wrong with us, then gives us a prescription to see the pharmacist who could have diagnosed what was wrong with us in the first place. Now consider this: What if you didn't even have to see the pharmacist?

I have already mentioned throughout this book the convenience that pharmacy retail health clinics will bring. MinuteClinic, a company that is now part of CVS, is a perfect example of convenient care close to home. This retail service has generated more than 850,000 visits since its found-ing in 2000. It now has upwards of 175 locations. It requires a finely tuned technology system to run efficiently and effectively. Because examinations take only 10 to 15 minutes, it manages to greatly distin-guish itself from the hospital emergency room—no wait, no paperwork. Of course, to work seamlessly with the existing health system, medical record keeping and the ability to have interactive interface with hospitals' ambulance services and the like are critical success factors.

AmeriClinic and AeroClinic are two other great examples of retail experiences that are entering the scene. Through these new venues, patients will be able to receive affordable, high-quality, and professional care in locations as convenient as an airport or a shopping mall. When you can disembark from a flight and get a full checkup, or receive testing for an ear infection with your grocery list in hand—and pay with your credit card—you are truly getting the full retail experience.

But why should you even have to leave your home in the first place? Telehealth is the delivery of care using telecommunications technology. According to the American Telemedicine Association (ATA) guidelines, this unique practice can take the form of audio and visual remote communication between a patient and provider, self-testing for things such as blood glucose levels, remote transmission of clinical data, or even laboratory tests conducted from across the world using advanced equipment. Telehealth also makes chronic care management and the medical home a reality because it allows the patient to receive therapy or treatment whenever needed. Using e-mail, it will be possible for a nurse or some other trained professional to send you frequent reminders regarding medication adherence, wellness tips, and other important information. Soon enough, we will have our own health channel on TV where we can view our personal records and see reminders, messages, and videos posted by our care team.

Fast-Forward

So far, I've been talking about the significant changes in health care we'll all be experiencing within the next five years. Many of those changes involve a transformation in how care is delivered. Although that system upgrade will feel radically new—in terms of the quality of care you receive, the overall reduction of errors and cost, and your ability to be informed and in control of your health decisions—those changes actually represent an evolutionary rather than a revolutionary shift. They are being driven by the health care industry adopting the technology and business processes that are already in existence in other industries today, receiving similar quality and efficiency improvements as a result.

Now I'm going to tell you about some longer-term changes that are even more exciting, more bewildering to imagine, and more disruptive to our current health care system. I'm talking about the advent of genetic diagnosis and treatment in what is known as personalized medicine. As we've learned, evidence-based medicine involves bringing the latest, most scientifically advanced medical standards to the care you receive from your physician or hospital. But those standards are based on applying your diagnosis to the clinical data associated with your particular demographic, meaning your age, gender, and condition. Personalized medicine will be based on treatments that are particular to your individual genetic makeup. This will allow for unbelievable precision when treating your condition, prescribing your medication, or even managing your predisposition to a condition not yet presented.

To understand the ramifications for our health care system, consider the way a child is cared for now. If you are a parent, you know that continuous health monitoring becomes part of your child's life even before birth through prenatal care. Following birth, your child's life becomes marked by a regular series of appointments with your pediatrician that include checkups, status comparisons, and vaccinations, in addition to all of the minor aches and illnesses associated with early childhood. Until your child is six or eight years old, the health care system is engaged in active intervention and monitoring, all toward the objective of maintaining health, preventing serious illnesses, and catching conditions at the earliest possible stage.

Then, after the age of eight or so, the health care system stops monitoring you. For approximately the next 40 years, it is as if you have passed beyond the light of the sun to the dark side of the moon. During that blank period, however, a combination of lifestyle, environmental influence, and genetics may evolve into some kind of chronic condition that is likely to adversely affect your health. Occasionally this condition is fatal, and sometimes it merely requires a change in lifestyle, but most often it's somewhere in between those extremes. Regardless, the cost of dealing with such a condition escalates because it has not been prevented, monitored, or maintained. We all pay a price as a result.

All of that is going to change within the next 10 years. By the time my young daughters have their first children, this 40-year gap will be eliminated. The most advanced medical thinkers I know are leading their institutions to prepare for a genetic revolution. When that revolution arrives, every newborn will receive an inexpensive genomic profile that will provide a blueprint of that child's health propensities. Such blueprints will shape and guide the care individuals receive throughout their lives. The kind of postnatal and early childhood monitoring we receive now will stretch from birth to death.

Some people, with visions of science fiction dystopias, think it's scary to imagine a society in which every person has a genomic profile and knows what diseases and even life span they are predisposed to. I hope to satisfy those worries by the end of this chapter by giving you an understanding of how personalized medicine will impact your health and quality of life. For me, the only scary part is that many of our health care providers, our medical schools, and our public and private systems of reimbursement are not preparing for the change to come.

Technology that enables us to more clearly understand what is going on within the body has always seemed radical upon its introduction, only to become utterly ordinary and commonplace soon after. Before we could see inside the body, there was no science to medicine. At best, we could inspect a person's condition on the surface and derive some suspicions about an illness from feeling the pulse and checking the pallor of the skin. When Benjamin Rush practiced medicine, there was no stethoscope to listen to the heartbeat or the lungs, no thermometer to check for temperature, no microscope to examine infection, no X-ray machine to view a broken bone or a chest cavity, no anesthetic to enable exploratory surgery.

Surprisingly, when these inventions did eventually come about, they were not regarded with the same reverence that they are today. New technologies comprising the clinical tool kit have rarely been eagerly adopted by physicians, nor have new support systems of analysis and treatment arisen at hospitals overnight. Even the stethoscope, that device so symbolic of medical practice, took a great deal of time and persuasion for physicians to come to appreciate and use it with expertise.

The word *stethoscope* comes from the Greek words for "I see" and "the chest." It was invented in 1816 by a French physician who, out of embarrassment, wanted some way to examine a female patient's chest without actually pressing his ear to her skin. Rolling up a stack of paper, Dr. Rene Laennec created a cone, placed it near her chest, and was amazed to hear the sound of her heartbeat loud and clear.

Following up on his discovery, Laennec bored a small hole in a piece of wood, narrowed at one end for the ear and funnel-shaped at the other end. Three years later, Laennec wrote his classic treatise on mediate auscultation and began selling stethoscopes for two francs, a price that included the treatise. The stethoscope enabled doctors to study illnesses such as tuberculosis.

Despite the actual advantages of using Laennec's stethoscope, the device was not widely adopted by physicians for some time because it was feared that the lack of physical contact with the patient would negatively affect the doctor-patient relationship. Older physicians complained that they did not have the touch and failed to see the true usefulness of the device. Younger physicians were more eager to obtain and try out the stethoscope until their practices began to bear clinical fruit.

The famous Dr. Oliver Wendell Holmes wrote a mock ballad warning doctors against relying too much on the stethoscope lest they be fooled by odd sounds like flies buzzing. "Now use your ears, all you that can, / But don't forget to mind your eyes. . . ." This satiric warning against placing too much faith in technology was not meant to discredit the stethoscope, however, as Holmes would later become one of the leading proponents of the new technology of chest examination. Still, it wasn't until the 1960s that the stethoscope we know today came into existence.

Over the twentieth century, we have greatly improved our ability to understand the inner workings of the human body and treat illnesses and injuries accordingly. When the X-ray was discovered in 1895, it took three decades for X-ray machines to be widely used in American hospitals. The X-ray's modern progeny, computed tomography, otherwise known as the CAT scan, was first used at the Mayo Clinic in the 1970s. Although we are in an age of rapid technological advancements, it is interesting how long it takes for scientific discoveries to be applied to technology, and then to be incorporated into the practice of medicine. It's not enough for individual physicians to seize upon a device or a treatment innovation; an entire system must develop around it.

A half century ago, in 1953, James Watson and Francis Crick unlocked the structure of DNA. Their work was based on a half century of explorations by scientists before them. Watson and Crick determined the elegant double helix structure, that interconnecting strand of A, T, C, and G that provides the instructional language for the cells in our bodies. It was the starting point of the genetic revolution, which is about to explode into new technologies and new treatments today.

The Human Genome Project was proposed in 1986 at Cold Spring Harbor Laboratory on Long Island, where James Watson was director. Dr. Eric Lander, a geneticist at MIT, described the decoding of the human genome as the starting point for our ability to understand the basis of disease. Medicine without genomic understanding, Lander said, was like a mechanic trying to fix a car without understanding the parts. "We bring our bodies in to doctors all the time and they don't know the parts list and they are not even as advanced as the auto mechanic. The genome project is an attempt to change that, to give medicine that parts list. It's not going to cure all diseases but it's a foundation for more rational approaches to medicine. I think it's going to transform biology and medicine."

In order to get that parts list, the Human Genome Project was launched in 1990 with the goal of identifying and mapping all the genes in the human genome. The technology for doing so evolved along the way, and progress was slow though steady for many years. In 1998, a private venture named Celera Genomics, headed by Dr. Craig Venter, aimed to accomplish the same task more quickly and at reduced cost, while patenting the genetic information that was uncovered as a result. This spurred increased urgency within both organizations. In 1998, when President Clinton decided that the human genome could not be patented, the biotech industry lost $50 billion in market capitalization overnight.

On Charles Darwin's birthday, February 12, 2001, both groups published their significant results to date, knowing that filling in the gaps was only a matter of time. The Celera group had decoded the genome of Craig Venter. It was revealed in 2007 that the Human Genome Project had decoded the DNA of James Watson.

Personalized Medicine

Until recently, the idea of using an individual's genome to aid in their medical treatment was still science fiction. Sequencing genes was far too expensive and time consuming, and the technology for linking specific genes to specific diseases was in its infancy. Scientists realized, however, that human beings are nearly genetically identical except for a small fraction of their genetic material, and it only requires sequencing that difference, or haplotype, in order to provide an individual genome. The International HapMap Project, aimed at identifying the genes involved in common diseases, began publishing data in 2005, and has brought the future to us much more quickly than expected.

Today, genetic tests are available for thousands of diseases, and genetic screening has become cheaper and faster. People who learn that they are susceptible to certain diseases like colon cancer and diabetes are able to get regular tests in order to catch the onset of such conditions early and change their behavior and diet to prevent or minimize the negative impact.

Personalized medicine, however, goes beyond the idea of genetic testing to an entirely new level of care, and in turn a higher quality of life. When my oldest daughter has her first child, I believe that baby will get a genomic profile for roughly $800. The data obtained through that profile will be stored in a central information system, called an Integrated Delivery Network (IDN), to which primary care physicians and specialists will have access throughout the course of my grandchild's life. Within that IDN database there will be a kind of artificial intelligence search engine—based on the principles of semantic knowledge and driven by complex algorithms—that can support physicians in their decision making and recommendations.

My grandchildren's doctors will know from the moment of birth the likelihood that they will develop some form of chronic condition, cancer, or other significant illness. This knowledge will shape and form their health care for the rest of their lives. Compared to today's 40-year gap in treatment, my grandchildren will receive constant monitoring and prevention. Tapping the database's artificial intelligence, their doctors will know which clinical interventions will be most effective, which cardiology or cancer drugs they will respond best to, and when care should be delivered.

Personalized medicine will allow doctors to treat us with a level of precision never before possible. As Health and Human Services secretary Mike Leavitt has said, "Personalized health care will combine the basic scientific breakthroughs of the human genome with computer-age ability to exchange and manage data. . . . Increasingly, it will give us the ability to deliver the right treatment to the right patient—every time." One of the most difficult aspects of patient care is dealing with variability. Some patients respond differently to drugs and treatments than others do. Sometimes this variability can be considered broadly on a demographic scale, but health care is largely experimental and the margin of error rates are extremely high. In the future, having precise genomic information about a patient will enable a doctor to more accurately know what medicine or treatment will have an impact. This kind of targeted treatment ability is already being felt in the area of certain cancer drugs, for example. A few years ago we treated most lung cancer patients with the same series of protocols, but now we understand that there is a genetic basis for why some drugs are effective in some people and not in others. The cost and time savings in this regard are as enormous as the assistance provided to doctors in making better treatment decisions.

As many doctors will tell you, genomics is only the beginning in a vast technological revolution. An even more complex solution is already in the works and is set to deliver equally promising results. The technique is called *proteomics,* coined to make an analogy with the term *genomics.* Rather than focusing on an organism's set of genes, proteomics focuses on proteomes, a term referring to the entire set of proteins produced by an organism during its life. Whereas the body's genome remains constant, proteomes represent much more of a challenge, as the body's protein production tends to vary depending on environmental and biochemical interactions. Not only that, but while the human body contains about 25,000 gene variations, those genes account for the production of over 500,000 different proteins. The effects of this scientific knowledge will be similar to that of genomics, but will allow for understanding at a much more specific level. Although proteomics has many potential uses, some are already being used today. Currently, it provides an incredibly accurate method of diagnosing pervasive diseases. For example, a process called immunohistochemical staining is used to identify buildup in beta-amyloidal protein, which causes plaque buildup in the patient's brain, resulting in the onset of Alzheimer's. Other diseases that have already been identified by their protein biomarkers are heart disease and renal cancer.

With the advent of these tremendous scientific discoveries, we will have an ability to understand disease in a different context than ever before. No longer will we see an individual disease, but we will see how it interacts with each unique person. We will be able to predict it before any symptoms begin to occur and develop treatments that are more effective with less residual impact on the body's natural processes.

Today, very few medical schools are preparing for the advent of personalized medicine. It is my belief that great changes will be made in the training curriculum for doctors, resulting in new skills. In terms of historic impact, this shift will be comparable to the post–Flexner Report era, in which the medical education practices of Johns Hopkins and other top schools were replicated around the country in a few short years. Vanderbilt Medical School is one of those institutions already planning to include personalized medicine and genetic counseling as part of their core curriculum by 2010. Today, personalized medicine is barely taught at all.

Technology is not going to be the true challenge as we transition to a personalized medicine age. As we have seen with the issues of connectivity and evidence-based medicine, the challenge will be people and systems. Building a genetic software infrastructure to support a physician to make appropriate medical decisions is relatively simple. More complex are the changes we will need to make in the way health care is delivered in order to create a system in which a patient receives the appropriate genetic counseling and therapy from a physician.

A genome profile today is typically 8 to 15 pages in length. Few primary care physicians can understand much of what it says, let alone answer the kinds of questions that a patient might have as a result. Nor is it even possible for a human mind to cognitively process all of the knowledge generated by such data. Only computers, with their complex algorithms, can do that. But if we consider the primary care physician as the center of the so-called medical home, then in the future the role of a general practitioner will mean being a kind of genetic counselor and technological expert, the control central for referring the patient to the appropriate specialists and physician extenders as needed. This will create renewed interest in the position of primary care physician, as practitioners and patients come to see the general practitioner as the essential linchpin of care.

Today, health plans are not organized around the idea of personalized medicine. We treat and pay for acute care, based on incidents and stand-alone events, and undervalue the long-term advantages of preventive medicine. While we are currently having our debate about how to pay for health care in this country, it would be helpful if we could keep the future of personalized medicine in mind. As I've suggested, eliminating the 65-year cutoff would go a long way to making private insurers think in terms of their customers' entire life spans. Evolving primary care practice into the medical home model will also establish the kind of system we need to put patients at the center of care. And a connected system of electronic medical records will enable physicians, nurses, technicians, and the entire medical care delivery team to work as a team while putting patients in the center of the health care hub.

And finally, there are the reasonable concerns of people who worry about privacy and genetic discrimination. Like issues of ethical and proper business conduct, this is an area where the government has a strong role to play. Unfortunately, politicians in general and the U.S. Congress in particular rarely debate issues in time spans that accommodate the needs of the medium-range future. Fortunately, in this particular instance, the government seems to be ahead of even the private sector and health care providers. The Department of Health and Human Services, headed by Mike Leavitt, has formed a personalized medicine team that is working on the legal, clinical, and reimbursement issues involved. As a result, I believe laws will soon be in place that protect individuals from genetic discrimination, and that the technology to encrypt data will be more than adequate to protect privacy.

Immanuel Kant said the field of philosophy could be reduced to four questions: What can I know? What ought I know? What can I hope? What is man? These are questions that echo in the mind when we consider the level of knowledge that will be obtained through our rapidly developing capability to decode the human genome. Yet, it seems that we've reached a cultural tipping point when it comes to the acceptance of genetic knowledge. Currently, patients who are admitted into Vanderbilt Medical Center sign a consent form to agree to provide their genetic composition to a DNA data bank. Interestingly, fewer than 10 percent of people have chosen to opt out of such a program.

Many physicians are eager to take advantage of the power of personalized medicine. I asked a core project leader at Vanderbilt what motivated him to advance this work. As an oncologist, he had a ready answer. "I was tired of treating cancer patients and knowing that every one of them was an experiment. I could never tell them with any certainty what their outcomes were going to be, what their chance of recurrence was going to be." The more he thought about the possibilities of genomic therapy, he realized that's what his life's work should be. A lot of geneticists I've met say the same thing. They do not want to give their patients partial answers anymore. They want to be able to tell the 35-year-old woman with breast cancer the percentage chance of recurrence based on her genetic makeup, and to know that one specific protocol will benefit her much more than another. The cardiologists, the nurse-practitioners, the surgeons—they're all hungry for certainty. They want the best tools available to give you the appropriate treatment in the appropriate way.

Chapter 7

The Blueprint
for Change

We've seen where our health care system has come from and why it is saddled with its peculiar and intractable problems, and we've seen the technological innovations that are available to transform it. So where do we go from here? When tradition collides with the future, the challenges that result create opportunities for vision and progress that can culminate in something exceptional. What's needed is leadership. We live in a country where we possess something special in our advanced medical capabilities and the quality and talent of the men and women who provide us with care, innovation, and support. The uniqueness we have created, however, cannot make us afraid of doing what must be done, to massively upgrade the system we rely on without tearing it down, to fix what's not working while preserving what is, to bring quality to every aspect of care, and to make it affordable and accessible to all.

The great medical maxim of Hippocrates is well known: First, do no harm. That is the predominant argument of those who believe that we should not try to fix health care for fear of making it worse. In fact, there are plenty of examples where health care has done lots of harm already, and compelling reasons to make significant changes before it's too late. The preface to Hippocrates' famous maxim is less known: "Declare the past, diagnose the present, foretell the future. . . ." Going forward, that's the kind of clear-minded assessment and call to action we will need.

Resistance to Change

The most tantalizing option, of course, is to do nothing. First, do no harm. Don't break what is working well for a very large number of people. Leaving aside the matter of 47 million uninsured, as well as the fact that we will no longer be able to live up to our Medicare commitments within the next decade, doing nothing is not a strategy that will even maintain the health care quality we currently have.

There are those whose self-interest rationally and reasonably lies with the status quo. From that camp I frequently hear arguments that health care is too complicated to tamper with, or that health care is unlike any other industry and not responsive to the quality or efficiency improvements of a normal business. Supporting the do-nothing debate, there is a view that we already have outstanding health care. Our top surgeons are the most advanced in the world; our best transplant, cancer care, and trauma centers are unsurpassed anywhere. Why mess with whatever has produced such stellar results? While I also believe that we need to honor our achievements in health care, those who say nothing should be done to improve matters remind me of the famous boiling frog experiment. Placed in a pot of lukewarm water, a frog, it's said, will not find a temperature change uncomfortable as long as it is gradual, and will remain in the pot even until it reaches the boiling point.

In hospitals, we hear such arguments all the time. If we change X—which is escalating costs to untenable levels—then someone will die. While it is true that health care is a huge responsibility and cost is no issue when our loved ones' lives are on the line, efficiency improvements save lives, improve health, and increase the intimacy of care. Understanding that premise is necessary, I believe, for us to shake off old thinking about health care and to upgrade the system.

The real worry is regression. In statistical theory, regression is the concept asserting the relationship between dependent and independent variables. Take an example from game theory to illustrate. Suppose you are betting on a person winning at cards, and continue to increase your bets along the way; you will ultimately lose if the person uses the same betting method over time. The reason for this is because the dependent variable—the strategy of play—is stagnant, and the independent variable—the cards and how they turn out—is changing. In health care, we are increasing our bets by levying more monies on a system that is not significantly changing operational strategy, even though our use of that system is becoming increasingly overwhelming. Regression theory suggests that if we keep doing what we are currently doing without improving the core processes, we will gravitate toward the average. Furthermore, if we remain stagnant and stay at this point while all other variables evolve, we will begin to fall below par. This means we will see fewer of the tremendous breakthroughs and accomplishments we're so proud of, and more of the bureaucracy, long lines, mediocre care, and errors that we dread.

As we have seen throughout this book, our health care industry has a long history of silos and separated interests. Achieving consensus in moving health care forward is, of course, a heroic task. So many well-organized bodies have representatives in Washington: hospitals, insurers, physician associations, nursing unions, and niche organizations representing particular patient interests. Quite often, these groups are in fierce opposition to one another because their competing agendas threaten to swing the economics of health care.

There are some who will criticize in knee-jerk fashion the claims that economics is at the core of those arguments. But health care, despite that word *care,* is a business. Patients are not widgets—but they are customers. Physicians and other care providers may have a more altruistic calling than do bankers and stock brokers, but they still make decisions about patients and care as part of an economic system—including their own incomes and what can be reimbursed. Most hospitals are non-profit, but they still succeed or suffer based on budgets and revenue. Technology suppliers that make dialysis machines or colonoscopy probes may be regulated by the government as to what they can charge in the market, but they do take those regulations into account as a business condition and leverage all of their options to show returns on their investments. Forget about arguments that health care is unlike any other industry; health care is the largest and most important industry in the U.S. economy.

Of course, the one component being left out of this overview is the patient. If you exchanged the word *patient* for *customer* you would see that, in one aspect at least, health care *is* unlike any other industry in the country. After all, in what other industry would the customer put up with no options for service? In what other industry would customers not care how much they are charged or how well the quality of that provider's service compares to that of other providers? If we are going to change health care for the better, we need to turn all of our assumptions around and put the customer-patient first. Right now, customer-patients are treated like children or invalids who are incapable of thinking for themselves; who are given few choices, if any; and who are kept deliberately in the dark regarding the data needed to make rational economic decisions.

Putting the patient in the center is where health care reform needs to start. Technology will give patients the capability to take control of their own health.

Designing the Scorecard

Let's put aside any question of who is going to lead a change in our health care system, and even the nature of whatever agenda any such leader would hold. The most important thing I can do in this book, I believe, is offer a blueprint for transformation. If we change health care, how will we know whether our efforts have met with success? How can we evaluate whether we did no harm and made things better instead? I believe that in order to truly improve American health care we need to run health care organizations with clear scorecards so we know what we are doing well and not doing well. From scorecards we can create focus and align our energies and resources at specific targets.

In order to make any journey, it's critical to have an end goal. I believe that for the first time in our history we actually have clarity in this country around what our health care end goal should be. Regardless of political spectrum, regardless of whether you are a teacher in an elementary school or the CEO of a Fortune 50 company, it is my view that Americans want: *accessible health care for all that is cost-effective, safe, reliable, and patient-centered, while always improving in quality and delivery, and provided in a way that encourages the quest for new medicines and improved standards of best practice.*

If every American can receive such care regardless of one's geographic location or economic situation, and if our health care system continues to improve over the years so that our children receive even better care than we do, then I think we will deem our change efforts a success.

Having defined our end goal, it's necessary to break the objective into manageable categories that can be measured and improved to drive our efforts. I've come up with four categories for measurement in an overall scorecard (AQEI):

1. *Accessibility (A)*—care that is available to all regardless of income, age, or employment status.
2. *Quality (Q)*—care that is safe, error-free, and at the highest standards of current medical understanding, with both short-term and long-term effectiveness.
3. *Efficiency (E)*—care that is provided at the lowest possible cost, in the timeliest and most appropriate manner.
4. *Innovation (I)*—care that is constantly improving in delivery and process while also generating advancements in diagnostics, medicine, treatments, delivery, and back-office operations.

First, for argument's sake, let's consider the U.S. health care system as a whole and grade it according to the AQEI scorecard. This assessment measure, utilizing natural categories to which most can agree, was constructed with careful attention given to previous evaluations that still hold great credibility. It is not meant to displace previous work or to take the place of valuable data created in earlier reports. Rather, this scorecard is meant to build upon them and provide a simple approach from which we can build an agenda for change to move forward. For instance, the Commonwealth Fund Commission on a High Performance Health System created a national scorecard that rated U.S. health care delivery overall as 66 percent out of 100 percent, a grade of D. The researchers did this by "comparing actual national performance to achievable benchmarks." Their report acknowledges that this flies in the face of the overall long-standing perception by those living in the United States that this country is the best in the world at health care delivery. The reality in the report, a conclusion that I have also found to be true, is that this perception is valid only when considering the *best* health care delivery in the country. The score on overall delivery is a mere 66 percent! According to the Commonwealth Fund Commission, the United States is experiencing 100,000 to 150,000 preventable deaths on an annual basis and spending more than $100 billion per year needlessly.

Our research team took a different cut at rating the U.S. health care system independently from the findings of other studies like the Commonwealth Fund Commission. Although we selected similar categories, the significant noted difference is that we placed innovation equally alongside of quality, efficiency, and accessibility. This has been done to recognize the importance of innovation and the power of technology to improve our delivery system through new medicines, cures, and methods of general practice. Overall, we rate American health care delivery higher than the Commonwealth Fund Commission did as a result of the inclusion of innovation. We agree with the Commission on a number of conclusions, including the point that quality and efficiency can be best improved together. I feel strongly that if we work hard to improve the efficient delivery of care and clean up the areas that get in the way of providing care, then our quality scores will improve.

Notwithstanding, I present the scorecard because I am a firm believer in a market-based approach and a major proponent of using technology to the fullest. My conclusions stand beside the Commonwealth Fund Commission's report in its statement about the importance of harnessing technology by creating "investment in data systems . . . [Using] electronic medical records and modern health information technology we will cut expenses." A scorecard is all about creating transparency whereby the power of decision making is put in the hands of consumers—patients and families. Only when we view health care as a supply chain, or a complete system, do opportunities that improve the system holistically present themselves. In this example, transparency is driven by the scorecard, which puts more control into the hands of customers.

Because my confidence in America's technological innovation is reflected in its own category on the scorecard, the overall health care delivery score is higher—albeit still unacceptable. The world looks to the United States as the system that provides innovations with far greater impact than those produced by any other nation on earth. Technology will be a fulcrum forcing the United States to a call to action, because it will enable the patient to be at the center of care decisions. Patients with information and access will accept nothing less than total quality.

Accessibility

I give accessibility a C– for several reasons. First, 47 million people in this country do not have health insurance. This puts a tremendous burden on our system in terms of costs, long waits in emergency rooms, and inappropriate use of providers. Hospitals cannot turn down the uninsured, but at the same time cannot receive reimbursement from them. What business can operate like that? Imagine going to the airport, finding your seat on the plane, and informing the flight attendant that you do not have a ticket—and yet the airline is required to fly you to your destination anyway. Every other passenger around you bears the burden in terms of overcrowding, higher ticket costs, and less incentive from the airline to provide quality service. Second, the fact that every person in this country, regardless of financial need, is eligible for Medicare at age 65 has some negative economic implications. Private insurers, realizing they will lose their customers at age 65, do not do as much as they should in terms of encouraging preventive medicine and healthy behaviors that reduce long-term costs. In addition, private citizens, knowing that their health care will be taken care of post-65, forgo treatment until that age, exacerbating expensive chronic conditions.

Quality

I give the U.S. health care system a B– in terms of quality. At its best, the U.S. health care system holds first place in the world. If the best U.S. health care were standard in every hospital and among all care providers, we would deserve an A+. Unfortunately, such excellence is not practiced equally across the country. Because health care is not run like a normal business, we do not see innovations scaled, reduced in cost, and spread throughout the industry or even within hospitals and clinics. When I asked doctors and hospital administrators, "Would you go to your own hospital for treatment?" The answer most often stated was: "It depends." Some hospitals demonstrate high-quality results in some areas but not in others. Some doctors within hospitals practice higher standards of care than others in the same hospital. This incredible variation within the system is part of the reason why our error rate is so high. Finally, the emphasis on acute care over long-term or continuous care is emblematic of low quality even as it leads to high costs.

Efficiency

Based on my personal and professional experience, I would give the U.S. health care industry a C in terms of efficiency. As I've described in this book, and as most people are now well aware, our health care system is extremely wasteful in terms of cost. Providers are inefficient because they have not embraced technology. In a paperless society where even the most sensitive and valuable information can be transmitted instantly and securely, we remain a paper-based industry. Furthermore, defensive medicine, the focus on acute over chronic care, and the lack of a team-based approach mean that our health care delivery model is top-heavy and short-term focused. We use very expensive physicians where nurse-practitioners would provide more timely and efficient care. We use emergency rooms when pharmacies or telecenters offer what we need. We perform expensive MRIs out of the fear of a lawsuit when all that is warranted is an aspirin. We treat acute conditions and fail to follow up on treatment or medication or provide guidelines for behavior change that will reduce economic burdens. It's interesting to note the conclusion in the Commonwealth Fund Commission's report that the American system is wastefully inefficient because of the failure to build payer processes for preventive care. This results in the minority of people accounting for the majority of cost.

Innovation

With technological innovation we score our first A. By any standard, we lead the world in terms of medical advances and our rate of innovation will be accelerating in the coming years. Every year, the leaps are astounding. Our technological advances in diagnosing and treating illnesses, generating new drugs, and developing technologies for improving the delivery of care are also astounding. Innovation is the crown jewel in our health care system, and the entire world benefits as a result. We must find ways to leverage and share innovation through technological advances so that the American deficiencies in access, quality, and efficiency improve. This will happen best when the patient becomes the consumer and has choices.

Getting to A+

While based on experience and research, my assessment of the four categories is naturally subjective; but I think that few would argue with the criteria or the overall grades. Having scoring systems provides us with a baseline for where we are now, and where we need to be. I believe that there is no reason why a country with the ingenuity, economy, and energy of the United States can't achieve A+ in every category. So that is my end goal.

My own prescriptions for achieving an A+ may differ from other views, but I offer them here for clarity's sake with the hope that we can collectively create a call to action.

A+ Accessibility

Catastrophic accidents are an unfortunate fact of life, and the financial burden of such an event is mitigated by those who pay into the pool of money but don't draw from it excessively. Note that the insurance pool is adequately handled by private insurers. The amount of catastrophic insurance you need is debated and then regulated by the government, but the amount you pay is dictated by the market. Private insurers compete for your insurance dollar by providing you with some combination of quality, price, and service. You decide what balance is important to you.

Private health insurance, in a similar sense, should invoke a precarious balance between the market and the government. Both must play an essential role. One of the biggest problems facing consumers in the insurance market today is the fact that insurance companies stretched with escalating costs are forced to find ways to reduce reimbursement risks and to attract healthier members. I believe that the government has a necessary and critical role to enforce the moral imperative here. A baseline level of coverage must be defined so that no patient is left without coverage when it is most needed. At the same time, though, the price, delivery methods, efficiency, responsiveness, and quality of service should be left to the dynamics of the market where private insurers compete with each other for your insurance dollar. Individual insurance buyers should receive the same tax benefits as employers using pretax dollars, which will level the economics with employer-purchased insurance. For those whose incomes do not reach a certain level, the government should provide vouchers so that such people can purchase their own coverage from a private insurance firm. In this way, the validity of the market is maintained. If we agree on paying for the health care of all Americans over the age of 65, the government-run Medicare system should be modified by providing seniors with the funds to buy insurance in the private market. In this way, insurers will no longer see an automatic drop-off at age 65, but will be encouraged to help manage their customers' health for the long term while distinguishing their offerings from each other through price, quality, and service innovations. In addition, the pool of insurers should be expanded beyond the state in which we live. If insurers from all over the country can compete for our business, we will see innovators in service arise, just as the airline system, once dominated by the big airlines, have had their business models overturned by the likes of Southwest Airlines and JetBlue. This will also allow health care consumers to keep their health plans, no matter where they live or who employs them, and give insurers the right to modify their prices and offerings as needed to compete in local markets.

Finally, our system of accessibility needs to include a system of accountability. It's not fair that everyone pays the same price. Those with unhealthy behaviors that lead to poor health cost the system more, and these costs should be reflected in the price of their insurance.

A+ Quality

The quality of care in this country will be influenced by a number of important shifts in the industry: the organization and integration of care, the use of evidence-based medicine, holding the system accountable for outcomes, monitoring impact on health status of populations, and so on. Among these, though, one of the most immediate steps we must take is to provide patients with the means of making care decisions based on quality, price, and convenience. Patients must make their own decisions regarding the best value in health care, the way they might assess the best value in other purchase decisions they make every day. Right now, it is difficult to know which hospital provides the best care in general, let alone for particular procedures. We don't know what a hospital's error rates are. We don't know what protocols it has in place, whether its medical staff is organized into functioning teams, or how many kidney transplants it performs in a week. And if you think it's a challenge to understand what hospitals are doing, realize that access to such data concerning individual doctors is impossible to get. Best-doctor lists are meaningless except as social status indicators, because they do not provide measures of quality based on actual results. Try to do your own research online someday. I bet you can get more information about a relatively meaningless consumer good than you can about the hospital where you will be undergoing heart surgery or about the physician who will be wielding the scalpel.

Some private insurers are pushing for transparency and choice because they understand that it is the best customer-directed way to drive down costs. Patients who receive high-quality and appropriate medical treatment cost insurers less in the long run than those who receive poor-quality care, receive too much care, or are refused needed treatment. And yet, because of physician and hospital lobbying groups, some state governments act as the last defense against those pushing for transparency. People who argue for more government control of health care take note: The government does not always have a patient's best interests in mind.

Providing transparency to patients will eventually result in a system in which consumers actively seek the best-quality care, balanced with cost and convenience. This will encourage hospitals and care providers to compete based on quality, cost, and service. I believe this will ultimately bring health care into practices that emulate the way business works in other industries.

In business, when a company develops a profitable innovation—whether in terms of product, process, or anything that improves competitiveness—it seeks to bring that innovation to scale. This means the company strives to replicate the innovation with reduced effort and cost and spread it as widely as possible throughout the business. For example, when Apple came out with a new touch screen for its iPhone, this was widely heralded as a benchmark in elegance and ergonomics. Apple did not restrict that unique interface to its iPhone, however; it soon brought it to its line of iPods. At a hospital today, if a surgeon develops a new approach that improves the quality of outcomes, reduces errors, or makes a procedure more efficient, it is rare for that approach to be spread to other surgeons even in the same hospital. Instead, solo practitioners draw fame and fortune to themselves, the hospital gains indirect credit as the institution where the technique is practiced, and the rest of the health care industry is unlikely to see much benefit.

If hospitals were competing transparently in terms of quality, cost, and convenience, they would seek to capture that innovation and replicate it so that other surgeons could adopt the same best-practice approach. This would improve the baseline of quality across the board for that kind of surgery. And because more surgeons would be practiced in the innovation, it would also reduce the cost and increase the convenience for consumers. Some argue that this would imply a reduction in health care quality because lesser surgeons or physicians would be seen by patients. This is a fundamental misunderstanding of the way advances are absorbed into a system. Today, every physician is skilled with a stethoscope. When the invention was developed, few physicians had any mastery over the new device. In the airline industry, at one time only former combat pilots were hired to fly commercial planes. Today, we recognize that automated systems and training can expand the pool of potential pilots, thus reducing reliance on the superstars and lowering the cost. In health care, the net result is better, cheaper, more convenient care for consumers.

Next, within industries, and to some extent between different industries, businesses copy each other. Apple's development of the iPod transformed the music industry because it combined the newest technology in portable listening devices with previously unheard-of ease of use, storage capacity, Internet connectivity, and style. Other MP3 producers followed suit as best as they could, accelerating the adoption of such features and intensifying competition, further prompting Apple and other makers to keep their pedal to the metal. As a result, MP3 players have become the industry standard. Just as horse-drawn buggies were replaced by automobiles, compact discs are becoming obsolete as music companies seek competitive advantage by adopting the latest best practices. Similarly, the practices of a hospital with outstanding outcomes, low costs, and high convenience will be emulated by other hospitals. Successful innovations that are scaled spawn competition, which in turn reduces costs and increases convenience.

At this time, other than moral imperative, there is little incentive for health care providers and hospitals to adopt best practices and bring them to scale, because there is no real marketplace in health care. Ernest Codman dreamed of a review board that would assess best-practice innovations and spread them to other hospitals so that the baseline of care would be raised across the board. He understood that the best method of doing so was to make costs transparent and publish hospital and physician end results so that patients could make informed decisions about where they wanted to receive care. Recent attempts to enforce pay-for-performance standards through Medicare amount to a stick, punishing physicians and hospitals for not following the protocols of established best practices. The carrot preferable to that stick would be to allow best-practice care providers to thrive in the marketplace at the expense of their less able competitors.

A+ Efficiency

One of the major complaints about the inefficiency of the U.S. health care system is that it is fragmented. When patients see different physicians, or switch health plans, or get tests in different facilities, there is little or no coordination in their care. Doctors don't share records. Health plans don't communicate with other health plans. Testing services don't work for doctors. This lack of integration and the inefficiency that results lends credence to the arguments of those who would put health care under centralized government control. After all, it is argued that the integrated institutions with salaried physicians like Kaiser-Permanente, the Mayo Clinic, and the Veterans Administration (VA) are the nation's top performers in many areas.

In fact, government-controlled systems can have the same communication problems with bureaucracies that are run like isolated fiefdoms, plus the added inefficiencies around costs and restricted services that go with socialized economics. Top-performing health care organizations actually have a commitment to electronic medical records in common.

Going to a paperless system is the first and most important step in upgrading our health care operating system. Enabling care providers, health plans, and patients to communicate instantly and coordinate seamlessly will result in monumental cost and time savings while also decreasing errors, reducing wait times, and improving health and satisfaction. I am fully confident that, given a market-based system, consumers will choose to gravitate toward clinics, hospitals, and medical centers that use electronic medical records and similar products. When empowered with the information to make their own decisions, people will be receptive to the drastic improvement in waiting times, efficiency, and outcomes that standardized electronic documentation provides.

Going paperless will also enable care providers to adopt other new technologies more readily. Bar-code systems tracking prescription drugs and monitoring medications, and handheld devices for consulting evidence-based best practices and viewing test results are two of the technologies that can radically and cheaply improve the efficiency of our health care system.

The seamless and coordinated care that is possible in a paperless system lends itself to better long-term care. The idea of a medical home base, where a primary care physician coordinates our health care with a team of specialists and other care providers, is really possible only in a paperless system. Shifting from an acute, event-based approach to health care intervention to one that is long-term and preventive in outlook is made possible when care providers can easily track health history and schedule coordinated treatments into the future. In addition, the existence of medical records and electronic communication makes it easier to rely on physician extenders in providing care. The best health care comes from the appropriate source. If a nurse-practitioner, pharmacist, or social worker is the best source, a seamlessly coordinated team ensures that quality and physician oversight are maintained.

In general, our health care industry will be more efficient when it focuses on healthy behaviors, wellness, and outputs with the same emphasis it currently puts on treating emergencies and illnesses. This approach will be a priority for health insurers when health care coverage is made accessible to all and portable with the individual while the 65-year drop-off into Medicare is eliminated.

A+ Innovation

How can we do better than an A in innovation? Make entrepreneurial efforts more rewarding. To me, it's amazing that we continue to achieve advancements at such a rate given the degree of difficulty posed by government regulations. The market should be the place where those decisions are made, not Washington, D.C. How can we expect innovation to continue to thrive if we cap what companies can earn? If prices are allowed to float with demand, then more companies will jump into a hot market, bringing new innovations in product, operations, manufacturing efficiencies, or service, lowering prices naturally rather than artificially. Imagine where we would be in the computer industry today if the government had determined how much Apple could charge for its original desktop computer. Would Digital Equipment Corporation, Dell, Gateway, Compaq, Hewlett-Packard, or any of the countless other companies have jumped into the market knowing that demand was strong but profits were capped? Instead, they've cut computer costs down to the bone, while computer power has increased exponentially beyond expectations, changing the way we live, work, and consume as a result.

The government's interference in the pricing of medical practice creates similar distortions and retards the spreading of best practices. If a surgeon discovers a new surgical technique, the government, through its control of Medicare and Medicaid reimbursements, distorts the market for those services and hampers the development of a new medical offering. Let the market decide the value. Physicians and hospitals do not have a monopoly over care unless we artificially create a situation in which there is no difference in cost, quality, and service among providers.

The government's role should be to regulate ethical conduct, safety, and monopoly power by any health care players. Where the government is in the reimbursement business, it should do so based on market prices, not artificial cost containment or caps.

Applying the Scorecard

You may or may not agree with my recommendations for achieving A+ in accessibility, quality, efficiency, and innovation. Nevertheless, the very existence of the scorecard will, I believe, encourage improvements in those areas. The old adage that what gets measured gets improved is true in business, in life, and in health care. Consider the Apgar score. More than any other method or approach, the simple Apgar score improved infant mortality rates around the world. Using the Apgar system, doctors, midwives, and nurses were able to examine a newborn infant, assign it a rating based on its condition, and work to improve that condition to achieve an acceptable level if necessary. This gave all delivery rooms the same base standard of excellence, and gave care providers the focus and competitive incentive to raise scores to an achievable objective.

In a similar way, people in the health care business—whether they be politicians, business leaders, care providers, insurers, suppliers, or hospital CEOs—can consider the impact of their work using the AQEI scorecard, and judge whether it does bring their corner of the world closer to an A+ in those four areas. For instance, a hospital CEO, the administrator of a physician clinic, or the manager of a health insurance division, each weighing a new technology investment, can evaluate that decision through the AQEI scorecard and know whether the investment will further the cause of A+ health care.

Let's take a real-world example to illustrate. In the early 1990s, the VA health system had sunk to an all-time low in terms of quality and service. In 1994, Ken Kizer, the VA's new undersecretary for health, led an effort to transform the organization. Examining the overall system, Kizer discovered some problems similar to the general ones we face today. There was a lack of standardization across the VA system in terms of how doctors treated even common chronic illnesses. There were serious problems with a bloated centralized bureaucracy and poor-quality outcomes in terms of patient care.

Over the next five years, Kizer instigated a number of sweeping changes. He broke the centralized bureaucracy down into 12 regional offices with their own budgets and performance objectives. He overturned the supremacy of the top-heavy and expensive hospital-centered approach by shifting to an outpatient model with hundreds of community clinics. In line with that, Kizer had each patient in the system assigned a primary care provider whose job was to oversee the patient's long-term care. Next, Kizer uncovered enough cost savings in the organization's drug purchasing program to fund a major upgrade in communication technology. The VA had long had an electronic system in place for scheduling appointments and tracking lab results. Kizer overhauled that technology, known as Vista, to handle electronic health records for every patient in the system. Finally, to reduce medication errors, Kizer installed robotic systems in hospital pharmacies to fill prescriptions, and he invested in bar-code scanners so that prescriptions could be tracked from the doctor's order to the pharmacy to the nurse administering the right dosage to the patient with the correct wristband.

The impact of Kizer's leadership was astounding. In terms of efficiency, the VA went from a bloated government bureaucracy to a more nimble paperless organization where patient records could be accessed by the right people at any time. The primary care provider and community clinic approach made sure that treatment was provided through the appropriate source, rather than via the expensive hospital or specialist. Quality of outcomes improved because the patient was tracked electronically through the system, with physicians, physician extenders, and social workers sharing information and communicating around the treatment plan. Moreover, safety was improved as errors were eliminated in the prescribing and administering of drugs. These improvements were driven by the technological, administrative, and systems innovations Kizer implemented.

On a national level, consider the changes implemented in the Netherlands. Twenty years ago, the Dutch system was a typical European-style socialized program, heavily regulated by the central government. At that time, most citizens were covered by tax-funded state-run health insurance. Hospital and doctor fees were capped, but there was little incentive to innovate or improve efficiencies. Care that cost more than the regulators would bear was rationed, and there were long waiting lists for special surgeries and treatments.

Recognizing that the situation could only get worse, the Dutch government made drastic changes to the system. The main thrust of those changes was a system in which health insurance was privatized, but made mandatory for all citizens to purchase. This put patients in the driver's seat in terms of purchasing the health plans that made the most sense to them and becoming concretely aware of the cost of treatment. Those unable to afford their own insurance have their coverage subsidized by the government. Insurers are not permitted to turn down any customers with preexisting conditions; instead they are compensated for taking on patients with more risk. Insurers, in order to maximize profits, encourage patients through financial incentives to adopt healthier behaviors. They also permit customers to seek medical care through doctors not in their system, or even outside the country, if the cost, quality, and convenience are better. Insurers are not yet able to negotiate prices fully with hospitals and physicians, but the percentage of their reimbursement that is negotiable is increasing every year. In this way, the Netherlands is migrating toward a more competitive marketplace for health care.

The Dutch health care system is still in transition, but it is moving toward better scores on the AQEI index. It has ensured accessibility for all, and it is improving quality levels by putting patients in the center of their health care decisions and making them aware of cost and quality issues. Compare patients' situation to Canada, a country whose health care has long been idealized in the United States as a socialized system that works, when it is in fact regressing because of a lack of leadership and action in its government-controlled but privately run system.

Forty years ago, the Canada Health Act established the system of socialized medicine in place today. Because costs are controlled, care is rationed and patients wait long periods for necessary treatments. Most Canadians supplement their socialized health care with private insurance, further disguising the inefficiencies. The costs of not treating illnesses or conditions in a timely and appropriate manner are ignored as acute problems become chronic. Meanwhile, as the baby boomer bolus of demand reaches retirement age, the funding for socialized medicine will fall just as the use of the system will rise. Every year, the equivalent of two medical schools of physicians leaves the country because their skills are underutilized and their salaries are capped. From having ranked second in the world in terms of doctors per patient in 1970, Canada now ranks 26th. In terms of access to new technology, the country ranks near the bottom of industrialized nations.

During an era in which medical advancements are taking place at ever-increasing rates, and globalization is making consumer choice a greater possibility for those wealthy enough to seek the best care in the world, Canada's situation is growing increasingly dire. The biggest political priority is to resist the temptation of an American-style system, but maintenance of the status quo is causing the overall accessibility, quality, efficiency, and innovation of the system to degrade rapidly. A country that prides itself on accepting refugees from all over the world may soon see its own medical refugees leaving its borders.

The Leadership Answer

As Ken Kizer's example shows, leaders in individual organizations can make a difference. Following the AQEI scorecard can provide a metric for making such improvements. As we've seen in the Netherlands, such an approach can make for improvements on the national and state levels, too. Every country and every organization has its own culture and way of doing things. In the past, we've had philanthropists like John D. Rockefeller and Frederick Gates, critics like Abraham Flexner, teachers like William Henry Welch and William Osler, and scientists like Eric Lander driving us toward change. Now we need a new generation of leaders to pick up the torch and run with it.

Unfortunately, though, the complexity of our problem is such that we will require leaders from all over the health care playing field to collaborate, which is certainly easier said than done. Just like the old analogy of asking a blind man to describe an elephant, one's take on the health care system is entirely dependent on preconceived notions and subjective perceptions. It starts with a vision statement we can all agree to—a series of goals. For this vision we can go back to accessibility, quality, efficiency, and innovation, and a grade of A+ for each of these four components.

With a standardized vision statement, we can be free to enlist all of our resources to pursue the best means of success. One of the first issues that I believe needs to be addressed is the level of involvement that we need from our government. In this time of crisis, many of us have turned to this central body to help us come out on top. After all, it seems like the easiest way to achieve rapid change. Unfortunately, this is a misguided notion. We look to the government to help contain costs and improve the quality of care, even as it battles with rising Medicare expenses and a health care budget that is next to empty. In this situation the government will naturally do the primary thing within its power: contain costs through increased regulation. This is not the answer. I believe that the lawmakers on Capitol Hill should remain deeply involved in our care, but not in a way that handcuffs the industry. Instead of using monetary regulations to contain costs, I believe we need to focus on the rules of engagement. By lessening the monetary role that government plays in the industry, we will be able to transfer some of the cost burden over to the market—and the market is more than capable of handling it. I have already identified what our country needs to do to bring our system in the right direction, but the following five points show the specific tasks that the government must own in order for us to be successful.

1. *Include everyone.* Mandating insurance is the first and most important action that the government must take in order for us to reach our goal. The reasons are many. Access only to emergency care is not enough to stay healthy. Each uninsured individual is one less person who is contributing to the aggregate risk pool, and today weighs down an already overburdened system through high emergency room costs. Hospital emergency rooms have become the de facto center for free care in the United States. For this, we need our central body to step in. Of course, it is not such a simple matter as flipping on a light switch and willing everyone to be covered. Payers must be required to accept anyone regardless of risk, and a safety net must be provided to support those in need via government-issued vouchers. The payers will adjust their prices to reflect their total risk but also be forced to compete. I have already discussed how this must be done. I have shown throughout the book that progress is already being made; now is the time to make it happen.

2. *Transition to market-based Medicare and Medicaid.* This is a step that will pose a significant challenge. How do we shift the cost burden of Medicare over to the market without diminishing the support given to the elderly and disadvantaged? Our country has begun to offer Medicare Advantage plans, private options that offer comparable coverage to that of Medicare, but it is only a start and the transition process will be slow. We must keep in mind that this isn't a factor of increasing profitability for insurers or being stingy with government dollars; it is about improving health and lowering costs for all. The goal is not to withhold support, but rather to ensure that those who need aid can receive it while also infusing the quality and cost advantages inherent in a market-based system. Our senior and disadvantaged citizens must have the ability to choose the coverage that works for them, while our society utilizes natural market prices and encourages long-term customer commitment by eliminating the 65-year dump.

3. *Equalize tax treatments.* In order for universal access to gain traction, insurance needs to be more affordable. Today, because of the high costs, it is almost impossible to get coverage without going through an employer. The first step to relieving consumers of this problem is to equalize tax treatments across the board. Why is it that a large corporation can get tax breaks on insurance options but consumers can't? Of course, this alone is not going to allow everyone the power to purchase their own plans, but it is certainly a step in the right direction. The government has already caught on to this somewhat, and has started health savings accounts (HSAs) that operate on pre-tax dollars. Now we need to take it one step further.

4. *Reform malpractice and liability law.* Each year, roughly 15 malpractice claims are filed per 100 physicians. Around 30 percent of those claims result in an insurance payment. And in most cases, reimbursement from malpractice suits is not limited. Doctors turn to liability insurance because their financial risk is too huge. Naturally, because malpractice costs are so high, so is the cost of the insurance. Providers have to practice defensive medicine, testing for everything because the cost of leaving a single rock unturned could be devastating to their practice. This means that both the consumer and the provider have to deal with the repetition of one useless test after another. Several states have already

begun placing caps on the amount of compensation that can be rewarded from a malpractice suit, so those state governments have not turned a blind eye to this problem. It is time for the rest of the states to hop on board and make this trend nationwide. At the same time, public and private plans must continue to drive down errors and promote quality through pay-for-performance approaches built around best-practice protocols, and transparency must become standard practice, encouraging providers to drive down errors by adopting the best practices of their competitors. The competitive marketplace and the transparency it will drive will put bad doctors out of business.

5. *Empower consumers with the information to make their own decisions.* As I mentioned earlier, we are seeing the nascent development of resources that allow the consumer access to invaluable cost and quality data. Many of these are privately offered, which means that they typically charge money for access and rarely use comparable rating systems. Meanwhile, the government has extensive resources that can help streamline the availability of information—resources that should not go underutilized. Several years ago the federal government unveiled the Hospital Compare web site at www.hospitalcompare .hhs.gov, dedicated to providing in-depth statistical information on hospitals in an easy-to-access manner. If you want to see what percentage of hospitals give aspirin to heart attack patients at arrival (a technique universally regarded as best practice), you can find out. But so far, the only information that is available pertains to heart attacks, heart failure, pneumonia, surgical care improvement, and infection prevention. There is nothing on cancer care, diabetes treatment, organ transplants, and many other important procedures and outcomes. And here are some other concerns: How many people know about this? And, even more important, how many actually use it on a regular basis? Because this is so important, we can't stop here and get complacent. The government must continue to use its resources not only to provide the consumer with the most accurate, in-depth, and up-to-date information available, but to make sure we know it's there.

I believe that this five-point guide can be instrumental in optimizing the extent to which the government involves itself in our care, and will set us on the right track toward a market-based system that will truly put the patient at the helm. There is a bridge that is being built right in front of us that will take us to new realms of accessibility, quality, efficiency, and innovation. Although it is far from complete, we can clearly see where it is headed, and our progress increases every day. At the same time, though, we must realize that just because our path is being built doesn't mean that we as a society will choose to take it. Underneath this incomplete bridge is a tunnel, one that has long since been completed. If we take that route, we will be following in the footsteps of so many of our neighbors—pursuing a nationalized system. Although it is the easier route at this point, it will inevitably be the wrong choice. The tunnel is dark, in that the illuminating light of information is denied us, and it is characterized by long waits, lack of innovation, and poor quality of care. To reach the potential before us, we must make the right decisions now.

For the call to action to sound loudly enough, there must be change at the inner and outer rings of the system. By the inner ring I refer to the patients, whose knowledge of health care is made up of their own personal experiences. Not coincidentally, this is the real source of power in most aspects of our economy, among which health care should certainly be included. I have described in depth the communications and networking technology that exists at our fingertips. Now is the time to use that technology for change. Start a blog, write an editorial letter to a newspaper, create dialogue, send e-mails—do whatever it takes to make sure that meaningful reform of our health care industry is unavoidable.

The information to make our own health care decision has been denied us for one reason or another throughout history. If we as consumers are going to become informed, we must demand that right. It is the rational majority that is the true strength of a market-based system and will have great effect in driving much-needed change. Consider global warming, an issue that has been highly contested for years. Not too long ago, no more than half of the population believed in its existence. But now it is almost universally accepted as a critical challenge in our society. The change in mentality would have been impossible if not for the people who debated the issues and spread the message through web sites and news and media coverage. With public support behind the new environmental movement, we are now seeing wildly successful business ventures in water cleansing, alternative fuel sources, and education and public awareness programs. The same thing is happening in health care today. The white spaces in the industry are steadily being filled by the Amazon.coms and Apples of medicine. With increasing support from the consumers, we will be seeing more and more incentive for innovation and development.

At the same time, at the outer ring, we have the leaders who represent the most organized power structures in our health care system today. Throughout the history of our medical culture, we have seen a balance of widely known lobbying groups such as the American Medical Association (AMA), American Hospital Association (AHA), Centers for Medicare and Medicaid Services (CMS), and many others. These leaders represent the second tier of change. It is time to organize a formal series of dialogues among representatives of these respected groups, as well as other leaders and policy makers in our society. The key to productivity lies in the market. When consumers are passionate and informed enough to make their case, industry leaders will have an incentive to serve the majority in order to preserve their own success. Market forces lead to compromise that benefits society—each player must give more to get more. Consumers will set the standard for success. It is possible to achieve shared vision among the players in health care, driven by economic and market motives to win consumers. I am committed to seeing other leaders in the medical industry meet under this common banner and create dialogue for change.

The Last Two Feet

In this book I hope to bring about the passion to encourage change in our health care system. Think of health care as a thousand-mile journey. Every drug concept must go through years and years of development to get from the manufacturing plant to the little orange bottle; every provider must endure eight to 10 years of intense collegiate and graduate education before they can enter their practice; each coverage plan that exists today has evolved from hundreds of years of medical reform; each MRI machine, defibrillator, or any other form of medical capital undergoes years of development and production. In this thousand-mile journey that brings together so many scattered players, it all funnels down to the last two feet—that distance between you and your care provider. Of the entire journey, only the last two feet are truly about the patient, the customer. I believe that the rest of those thousand miles should be, too.

During the research for this book we had the pleasure of speaking to a palliative care expert at the University of Michigan Health System. Palliative care can be described as the treatment of advanced, pervasive diseases in a way that focuses on collaboration between the patient and the provider to come to a mutual decision. This may not sound terribly unique, but it is. It has often been stated that Western medicine is too centered around acute care, the short-term treatment of a symptom or disease to deliver immediate results. Palliative care focuses not only on the disease itself, but on the person as well. It treats the disease in the context of the patient who carries it. What are patients' lifestyles like? What are their eating habits? What are their goals for the future? Most important, how can patients and doctors work together to come up with plans that focus on the patients' goals and conform to their unique styles of living?

In the course of our discussion, I was surprised to hear that research shows that doctors now are so pressed for time they are spending only a few minutes with each patient. This physician informed me that too many of his patients visit his office with the "What do I need to do, Doc?" mentality because they know that doctors have only enough time to offer a diagnosis and provide a prescription or treatment instruction. But people shouldn't be asking the doctor what to do. Instead, doctors and caregivers should be asking patients what it is that *they* want to do. Doctors should be able to take the time to share their knowledge with patients, present options, and work with patients to find a course of action that fits their needs.

The time between a caregiver and a patient is precious, never more so than near the end of life. Those circumstances make patients and families more aware of how to take charge of their dire decisions. My friend talked about how doctors, nurses, social workers, and technicians work in teams to ensure that the patient understands and can ask questions about uncertainties such as pain, medications, and alternative treatments. He spoke about how important it is that patient-centered care is delivered with compassion. I left knowing that the provider-patient relationship is strongest and most satisfying for both parties when caregivers are guides and patients are in control of the most important decisions in their lives. Going forward, our entire system needs to be focused on that premise.

In the future, significant changes will occur because we have applied sophisticated tools, the necessary information systems, qualified care delivery teams, and management necessary for the challenges ahead. We will place the consumer in the center of those discussions. We will seek the perspectives of consumers and educate them about why old delivery models are obsolete, and how they can be provided with safer, more responsive care at a better price. We will make our health a priority not just for ourselves and our caregivers, but for our insurers as well—a health care system where the consumer isn't just a short-term investment for insurers, but one that lasts well beyond the drop-off point at age 65. We will ensure that each person's care will be in the hands of an entire team of dedicated forces, and the consumer will be in command.

In the future, we will have finally embraced the notion that nothing is more personal, precious, or important than our health. We cannot delegate our health to someone else, nor can we delegate the reinvention of our health care system to the government. It must be reinvented over and over again, in constant iterations—never satisfied, never complete, like everything else in the United States. Innovation happens when consumers create demand. You have skin in this game: yours, your family's, and your friends'.

Appendix

Resources, Web Sites, Tips, and Guidelines for Educating Yourself

I t's no secret that the health care industry can be overwhelming and difficult to navigate. Our health is the most important thing we have, yet we know so little about how to obtain the best care. How do you find the best hospitals, the best doctors, and the best treatments? What can you do to feel that you are safe and protected by a team of capable caregivers? What do you need to do to better understand the payer system so you can focus on living a healthy and happy life, rather than staying up nights wondering how you will pay your medical bills?

Education is your strongest defense against the health care industry maze. Understanding the system and the resources available to you can save you a great deal of money, time, and hassle. We provide here a series of resources, web sites, tips, and guidelines that will help you.

Selecting Your Care

In this section we describe health care options.

Learning about Hospitals

The common types of hospitals are:

- *Specialized hospitals or centers of excellence.* A specialized hospital or center of excellence program is a regional referral or consultation center that performs a specialized procedure with enough frequency to be designated as the leading expert in that particular medical specialty. The purpose of these hospitals is to provide an unexcelled level of quality patient care, usually at a competitive price, to reduce morbidity and mortality. Brigham and Women's, a Boston hospital, includes centers of excellence for cardiac care, cancer treatment, neurosciences, orthopedics and arthritis, and women's health. Phoenix Indian Medical Center in Phoenix, Arizona, has an HIV center of excellence (HIVCOE) and is a clinically based center for HIV care, treatment, research, and intervention. Centers of excellence often provide extra care. For example, Wright Medical Center in Iowa offers each inpatient a complimentary massage, facial, or hair appointment, in-room menus for food on demand, wireless Internet capabilities in patient rooms, complimentary phone cards, and free meal passes for family members. Centers of excellence are usually best for complicated or tertiary procedures.
- *University-affiliated hospitals.* A university hospital is an institution affiliated with a medical school or university and combines the services of a hospital with the education of medical students and with medical research. There is often a focus on expertise and excellence, and these hospitals handle both advanced and routine cases.
- *Community/general hospitals.* These hospitals are the most common medical facilities used by Americans. In 2004, 85 percent of patients in hospitals were admitted to a community hospital. These are usually nonprofit hospitals that are funded by tax dollars and operated by a public board. They are often the most convenient and are adept at performing routine operations such as hip and knee surgeries, gallbladder surgery, and appendix removal.

- *Clinics.* A clinic (or outpatient clinic) is a small private or public health facility that provides health care for ambulatory patients or clients in a community, in contrast to inpatients treated in a hospital. Clinics are often free or low-cost and provide care for acute, non-emergency conditions.

How can you tell a good hospital from a bad one?

In addition to reading general reports and articles about the hospital, obtain the following specifics:

- Death/mortality rates.
- Complication rates.
- Success rates.
- Quality and turnover of nursing staff.
- Specialized training programs.
- Use of key new technologies.
- Average length of hospital stay.
- Frequency of effort for improvements.

Where do I get this information?

You can obtain these numbers from the following sources:

- Hospital administrator.
- Medicare hospital mortality rate published by the Center for Medicare and Medicaid Services (CMS) can be viewed at www. hospitalcompare.hhs.gov.
- Your health insurance company.
- Peer review organizations that oversee hospitals for Medicare programs.
- Web resources provided in this Appendix.

Choosing a Doctor

How can you tell a good doctor from a bad one?

- Credentials
- Referrals
- Level of experience
- Specialty
- Peer boards

Medical errors can be reported against your physician through the state medical society or state licensing board. A full list of state resources can be found on the American Medical Association's web site at www.ama-assn.org. Errors can also be reported to the Joint Commission via its web site at www.jointcommission.org.

Seeing a Nurse-Practitioner

A nurse-practitioner (NP) is a registered nurse (RN) who has completed advanced education (a minimum of a master's degree) and training in the diagnosis and management of common medical conditions, including chronic illnesses. The nurse-practitioner has the following roles:

- Collaborating with physicians and other health professionals as needed, including providing referrals.
- Counseling and educating patients on health behaviors, self-care skills, and treatment options.
- Diagnosing and treating acute illnesses, infections, and injuries.
- Diagnosing, treating, and monitoring chronic diseases (e.g., diabetes, high blood pressure, etc.).
- Obtaining medical histories and conducting physical examinations.
- Ordering, performing, and interpreting diagnostic studies (e.g., lab tests, X-rays, EKGs).
- Prescribing medications.
- Prescribing physical therapy and other rehabilitation treatments.
- Providing prenatal care and family planning services.
- Providing well-child care, including screening and immunizations.
- Providing health maintenance care for adults, including annual physicals.

Hiring a Patient Advocate

A patient advocate is an individual with extensive knowledge of the health care system. The position is often held by nurses, social workers, and other health care providers. The advocate speaks on behalf of patients in order to protect their rights and help them obtain needed information and services.

Health Advocate
(866) 695-8622
www.healthadvocate.com
Cost: $125 an hour

Castle Connolly Healthcare Navigation
(203) 333-2244
www.healthnavigation.com
Cost: The Professional Advocacy Service offers an annual membership program. Fees are $3,400 per individual, $4,200 per couple, and $4,900 for a family of three or more per year. Hourly rates can run between $80 and $200.

Pinnacle Care
(866) 752-1712
www.pinnaclecare.com
Cost: Pinnacle Care offers a variety of different programs that can run between $5,000 and $25,000 a year.

Patient Advocate Foundation
(800) 532-5274
www.patientadvocate.org
Cost: None. This is a volunteer-based service.

Choosing a Pharmacist

Your pharmacist:

- Is your medication expert.
- Monitors your drug therapy and checks your prescription to make sure the drug, dose, and instructions are best for you.
- Provides guidance on ways to relieve your symptoms without using drugs.
- Helps you select nonprescription medication or health care products.
- Offers advice and information on a wide variety of health issues.
- Works closely with your doctor on your care program.
- Keeps a computer record of all your prescription medications.

- Talks to you about your medication so you better understand:
  - What it is for.
  - How to take it.
  - Where to store it.
  - What to do if you have side effects.
  - How to tell if it is working.
  - What foods, alcohol, or other drugs you should avoid while taking it.
  - When you should refill it.

Questions for your pharmacist when obtaining a new prescription:

- Are there special side effects that I should look for?
- What should I do if I notice any of these side effects?
- How long will it take to work, and how will I know if it is working?
- Does this medication require special storage conditions?
- How many times a day should it be taken?
- Should it be taken with or without food?
- Should I avoid certain foods when taking this medication?
- What should I do if I skip a dose?
- Do I need to finish the entire prescription?
- Will this medicine conflict with my other medications?
- Is this the generic or name brand?
- Can I get a refill?
- Will my insurance cover this?
- How much does it cost without insurance?

Understanding the Payer Systems

In this section we describe the health care payer systems.

Medicare and Medicaid

Medicare is a federal health insurance program for people age 65 and older, certain people under 65 with disabilities, and certain people with kidney disease. Eligibility for Medicare depends on age or disability only.

Medicare covers inpatient care in hospitals, skilled nursing facilities, and other institutions under Part A, and outpatient services, physician services, medical supplies, and equipment under Part B. Home health care is covered to differing extents under both Part A and Part B. While Medicare thus covers many health care services required by its beneficiaries, it does not cover certain types of care that are important to older people and people with disabilities. The two most glaring gaps in Medicare coverage are prescription drugs and nonskilled or custodial long-term care.

Medicaid. Which is administered by the states, is a program of health coverage for certain people with low incomes or very high medical bills. Eligibility for Medicaid depends on age, disability, or family status and on an individual's (or family's) income and resources. Each state designs its own Medicaid program, which consists of both mandatory and optional eligibility groups and mandatory and optional services. Each state Medicaid program must cover inpatient and outpatient hospital services, laboratory and X-ray services, physician services, nursing facility services (which is broader than Medicare's skilled nursing facility coverage), home health services, and services of a nurse-midwife and a certified pediatric nurse-practitioner for certain groups of people. In addition to the required services, states can include many optional services in their programs. Every state program includes some prescription drug coverage.

Generally, Medicaid covers a broader scope of services than Medicare; however, Medicaid is means-tested and Medicare is not.

Eligibility
Medicare. Individuals age 65 and older with sufficient work history in the Social Security system, individuals under age 65 who have received Social Security disability benefits for two years, and certain individuals with end-stage kidney disease are entitled to inpatient coverage, Part A, premium-free; others who are 65 or older can purchase Part A. Beginning July 1, 2001, individuals under 65 receiving benefits because of amyotrophic lateral sclerosis (ALS) qualify for premium-free Part A without waiting two years. Virtually all beneficiaries pay a monthly premium for coverage under Part B.

Assets. Medicare eligibility is never based on how much money a beneficiary has, the value of other assets owned, or whether the beneficiary has given money away at any time. Medicaid is means-tested and does consider an applicant's assets and, in some instances, whether assets were given away to qualify for Medicaid.

Medicaid. To be eligible for Medicaid, an individual must fit into a category of persons eligible for Medicaid and must have income and resources under a threshold set in part by the federal government and in part by the states. Categories of people who can receive Medicaid include people age 65 and older, people under 65 with disabilities, children, parents of children in certain instances, and pregnant women.

Special rules apply to people seeking to have Medicaid pay for long-term care, whether in a nursing home or in the community. These rules address (1) penalties for transferring assets for less than fair value, (2) income and resource protections for the spouse, and (3) estate recovery.

Transfer of assets. The Medicaid agency will ask if the applicant has given any money away in the past three or, in some cases, five years. If an individual gave something away without getting fair value for it, she or he will be penalized by being denied Medicaid eligibility for a period of time. Gifts to certain people, especially spouses and disabled children, do not generally subject the individual to penalty. The rules apply to both nursing home and certain community-based long-term care services.

Spousal protections. These rules protect income and resources for the spouse still in the community when an individual goes into a nursing home (and, in some states, even when the individual remains at home to receive services). The amounts of income and resources set aside for the at-home spouse are greater than those generally allowed to be kept by other categories of people eligible for Medicaid. Though the rules are intended to *prevent* impoverishment of the community spouse, they are often referred to as the spousal impoverishment rules.

For More Information

For more information on Medicare services and plans, access the Medicare web site at www.medicare.gov. Additional information can be found in their various publications such as "2008 Choosing a Medigap Policy: A Guide to Health Insurance for People with Medicare," which can be accessed online through their Web site or ordered by phone at 1-800-MEDICARE.

General info on the Medicaid program can be found on the Medicaid web site at www.cms.hhs.gov/home/medicaid.asp. Because Medicaid is a state-operated program, additional information can be found through your state health department. A list of state health departments is provided by the Center for Medicare and Medicaid Services and is accessible via their Web site.

Summary

What follows is a summary of Medicare and Medicaid.

Medicare
- Health insurance for seniors.
- Individual needs to have contributed to Medicare system to be eligible.
- Pays for primary hospital care and related medically necessary services.
- Generally, individual must be over 65 to be eligible.
- May have a co-pay provision, depending on the services received.
- Federally controlled, uniform application across the country.

Medicaid
- Needs-based health program.
- Pays for long-term care.
- Individual must meet income and asset test to be eligible.
- Individual must be over 65, disabled, or blind.
- Requires mandatory contribution of *all* recipient's income.
- Individual state-by-state differences create a different program in each state. (Programs are generally similar, but may be different in specific applications.)

HMOs and PPOs

A **health maintenance organization (HMO)** is a collection of health professionals, doctors, hospitals, mental health care workers, and other specialists, who work for a set fee. There are independent HMOs where all the staff members work directly for that private HMO. A broader spectrum of doctors and other health care workers can agree to a set fee for service with many different HMO plan companies and are not actually employees of the HMOs themselves. HMOs are designed to save people money while getting the entire health care they need. Co-pays for visits and prescriptions are usually very low, and there is no deductible to be met. However, HMOs do have their downside. HMOs are in business to make money, so if you have many health care issues, you may not be accepted or may have to pay more. If you have a chronic medical condition that requires many visits, tests, and treatment, you will cost the HMO lots of money. The HMO balances this out by keeping a tight hold on your health care. All visits must be approved ahead of time.

HMOs are often restrictive and have lots of rules that must be followed if you want the HMO to pay. You can see only the doctors on your HMO list, and you must see your primary care doctor first, no matter what is wrong with you. If you have to go to the hospital, you must have your primary doctor's permission prior to going. Many people find that way too restricting and choose not to go with HMOs for that very reason. When and if you need to see a specialist, you must have seen your doctor first to make sure the HMO can't treat you instead of going to a more expensive doctor. The HMO makes sure it is its doctor who has control over all your medical needs, not you. Most doctors are excellent and will hand out referrals, and most doctors these days are enrolled in HMO plans, so this isn't a problem for many people. If you are not one of the lucky ones, getting the care you need could be difficult or impossible. HMOs can also be a bit fussy about you wanting to change your primary doctor. So be sure that you like your doctor and you have spoken to other people who are patients of his or hers.

Most HMOs also have a patient quota that the doctor has to comply with. He or she must see a set number of patients per day to avoid being penalized or removed from the group. This is why there is never enough time to talk with your doctor past your examination point. The doctors need to keep it short so they can see more patients. There is also the concept of capitation, which gives contracted doctors a set amount of money for each patient each month, regardless of whether the patient is sick or well. Last, you must make sure any laboratory tests you need are specifically covered with your plan or the HMO won't pay for them. But for most people who have HMOs this is not a problem.

A **preferred provider organization (PPO)** is a collection of private-practice doctors, labs, care facilities, and hospitals that contract with insurance companies and receive an agreed set rate for their services. These plans have much less restriction but cost the patients more. Patients have more control over their own medical needs and don't need a referral as long as the doctor they are seeing is a member of the PPO. The co-payment is higher because the plan usually covers only 80 percent of the fees. So that makes you, the insured, responsible for 20 percent of all your fees from all medical treatments, including hospital stays. You may also have a deductible to meet before your coverage starts each year. PPOs hire nurses and medical professionals to handle patient cases and make decisions about hospital visits and diagnostic tests. You have more freedom, but you end up filling out claim forms.

PPOs are ideal for people who have the money and want to have more freedom in their health care choices. If you are a person with many health issues that require several different opinions, extensive tests, or complex treatment, and you need specialists, this plan gives you a better choice and fewer restrictions on what you can do. You won't have to wait months to see the specialist; you will be able to just go. It will cost you more money, but you will have your needs met faster.

Keeping in Good Health

Tests for the following are recommended:

- **Breast cancer.** According to the American Cancer Society, women in their 20s and 30s should have clinical breast exams about every three years, and every year for women 40 and over. As far as mammograms go, women over age 40 should have them every year. However, if you have a history of breast cancer in your family, you'll want to consult with your doctor about starting mammograms earlier.
- **Cervical cancer.** The American Cancer Society suggests that all women should begin cervical cancer screening about three years after they begin having intercourse, but no later than when they are 21 years old.

Screening should be done every year with the regular Pap test
or every two years using the newer liquid-based Pap test. At age 30,
women who have had three normal Pap test results in a row may get
screened every two to three years with either the conventional or
liquid-based Pap test. Women with certain risk factors (like HIV
infection, a weakened immune system due to organ transplant, or
undergoing chemotherapy) should continue to be screened
annually.

- **Colorectal cancer.** Colorectal cancer is the second leading cause
  of cancer death in the United States, so screening is very important
  for both men and women. The American College of Gastroenterol-
  ogy says that all people over 50, with no family history of the disease, should get a colonoscopy every 10 years *or* a sigmoidoscopy
  along with tests to look for blood in the stool every five years. People with a family history of colon cancer or other risk factors should
  begin screening with a colonoscopy by age 40.

- **Skin cancer.** Skin cancer is the most common cancer in the United
  States, and it is so preventable. One of the best ways to reduce your
  risk is to wear a sunscreen with an SPF of 15 or greater all year
  round. As far as screening goes, you should have your doctor examine your skin from head to toe every few years if you're under 40,
  and every year over 40. If you have a lot of freckles or moles or are
  fair-skinned, you may need to be screened more often. And if you
  have any suspicious moles you're concerned about, have them
  checked out right away.

- **Prostate cancer.** The American Cancer Society recommends that
  all men over 50 have a digital rectal exam and a prostate-specific
  antigen (PSA) blood test every single year. Men at higher risk for
  prostate cancer, such as African-American men and men with a family history of prostate cancer, should begin screening sooner. Prostate
  cancer screening has been somewhat controversial over the past few
  years, because there has been some debate over the accuracy and
  effectiveness of screening. So the most important thing is to have a
  frank discussion with your doctor about the pros and cons of early
  detection and come up with a plan that works for both of you.

- **Osteoporosis.** Women can do a number of things to reduce their
  risk for osteoporosis, including increasing their intake of calcium

and Vitamin D and doing weight-bearing exercises. The National Osteoporosis Foundation suggests that all women over 65 get a baseline bone mineral density test, and women with a family history of osteoporosis should get one sooner.

- **Cholesterol.** All people over age 20 should get a cholesterol panel at least every five years. People with a family history of high cholesterol should get tested more often.
- **Type 2 Diabetes.** Type 2 diabetes is more common in people who are overweight, people with a family history of diabetes, and women with a history of gestational diabetes. But anyone can get it. It is suggested that people get a fasting blood sugar test by age 45 and every three years or so after that. Certainly, get one sooner if you have any symptoms that might indicate diabetes.

The AMA has published these 10 health-promoting resolutions:

1. *Don't smoke.* Avoid smoking, the leading preventable cause of death, as well as exposure to secondhand smoke.
2. *Eat your fruits and vegetables.* Eat about two cups of fruit and two to three cups of vegetables daily to reduce your risk of developing heart disease, cancer, stroke, and high blood pressure.
3. *Cut back on salt.* Limit salt intake to one teaspoon per day. If you are older than 50 years of age, limit salt to half a teaspoon per day. This will help lower blood pressure and decrease your chances of getting heart disease or having a stroke.
4. *Limit fat in your diet.* Eat a diet low in fat, saturated fat, and trans fats to reduce cholesterol levels and the risk of developing heart disease.
5. *Check your cholesterol.* Have your blood cholesterol checked regularly by your doctor. Keep your cholesterol level under 200 mg/dl to reduce your risk of developing heart disease.
6. *Reduce the amount of soda you drink.* Limit your consumption of regular soda pop and other sugar-sweetened drinks to help you avoid weight gain and obesity and to also decrease tooth decay.
7. *Check your blood pressure.* Have your blood pressure checked regularly by your doctor to help reduce your chances of heart attack or stroke. If you have high blood pressure, make sure that you keep your blood pressure under 140/90.

8. *Get a colonoscopy.* People over 50 years of age should check with their doctor about getting a colonoscopy to screen for colon cancer and improve their chances of early detection.

9. *Get a mammogram.* Women over 40 years of age should get a mammogram every one to two years to help detect breast cancer early, and, if diagnosed, improve their chances for survival.

10. *Protect your skin from the sun.* Use sunblock with an SPF of at least 30, protective clothing when you're in sunlight for a prolonged period, or limit sun exposure during the peak times of the day (10:00 AM to 2:00 PM). Those who get frequent sunburns should have their doctor check their skin regularly for early signs of skin cancer.

Source: American Medical Association, "AMA Releases Resolutions for a Healthy New Year," December 26, 2006, www.ama-assn.org/ama/pub/category/17165.html.

Terminology

AARP, formerly the American Association of Retired Persons, is a U.S.-based nongovernmental organization that offers a high-deductible insurance policy that could be used with a health savings account by individuals between the ages of 50 and 64. An estimated seven million people have AARP-branded health insurance.

American Medical Association (AMA) is the largest association of medical doctors and medical students in the United States. Their mission is to "promote the art and science of medicine and the betterment of public health."

Coalition to Advance Healthcare Reform (CAHR) is an active coalition of business leaders and employers, dedicated to engaging in health care policy debates at the state and national level and finding new and innovative solutions through private sector leadership.

Co-payment is a payment made by an individual who has health insurance, usually at the time a service is received, to offset some of the cost of care.

Health Maintenance Organization (HMO) is a specific type of health care that, unlike traditional health insurance, establishes guidelines under which providers must operate. On average, an HMO costs less than traditional health insurance, but often carries limitations on the range of treatments available.

Health Savings Account (HSA) is a tax-advantaged medical savings account available to taxpayers in the United States, in which pre-tax dollars may be deposited and used to pay for qualified medical expenses at any time without federal tax liability.

Indemnity Insurance is an insurance plan that reimburses the beneficiary for medical expenses, regardless of who provides the service. This form of coverage is offered by most insurers and can vary greatly from one plan to another.

Internal Medicine is the branch and specialty of medicine concerning the diagnosis and nonsurgical treatment of diseases in adults, especially of internal organs.

Nurse-Practitioner (NP) is a registered nurse (RN) who has obtained at least a master's degree, as well as training in the diagnosis and management of common medical conditions, including chronic illnesses. Nurse practitioners provide a broad range of health care services, can serve as a patient's regular care provider, and can often perform much of the same care as physicians.

Payer is an entity other than the patient that finances or reimburses the cost of health care services. Most often refers to insurers, other third-party payers, or health plan sponsors like employers or unions.

Preferred Provider Organization (PPO) is a health care organization composed of physicians, hospitals, or other providers, which provides health care services at a reduced fee by going through a network of "preferred" providers. Services outside of the network can also be utilized, albeit at an increased rate to the beneficiary.

Primary Care Doctor provides the patient with a broad spectrum of care, both preventive and curative, over a period of time and coordinates all of the care the patient receives.

Socialized Health Care is a derogatory term for a nationalized, single-payer health care system that is publicly financed, government administered, or both. The term "socialized" is often used pejoratively by association with socialism.

Useful Web Sites

Health Care and Medical Research

These web sites provide opportunities to educate yourself about current trends in health care and to become an active health care consumer. Read about current trends in the health care industry, new medical research and reports, information about specific populations, and indicators of high quality and patient safety. Information is offered in a variety of different ways, including full reports, fact sheets, and audio commentaries.

> **Agency for Health Care Policy and Research (www.ahcpr. gov).** The Agency for Health Care Policy and Research (AHCPR) is part of the U.S. Department of Health and Human Services and provides information about research designed to improve the quality of health care by examining methods of cost reduction, issues of patient safety, and occurrence of medical errors, and to improve the overall effectiveness of the health care industry.
>
> **Commonwealth Fund (www.cmwf.org).** The Commonwealth Fund is a private foundation that aims to promote a high-performing health care system that achieves better access, improved quality, and greater efficiency, particularly for society's most vulnerable, including low-income people, the uninsured, minority Americans, young children, and elderly adults.
>
> **Doctor's Lounge (www.doctorslounge.com).** Doctor's Lounge is a large online network of doctors, nurses, and allied health professionals. Members have written over 10,000 articles and answered more than 30,000 medical questions. It includes medical forums and descriptions of medical tests.
>
> **Participate in a Clinical Trial (http://clinicaltrials.gov).** Want to participate in a clinical trial research project? The National Institutes of Health has created a searchable Web database that provides information about private and federally supported clinical research. Information on what participation entails and how clinical trials are run is also provided, as well as symptoms, drugs, medical procedures, and an "Ask a Doctor" option.

Health Care Assistance

Use these web sites to learn what resources are available to assist you with any medical or health care problems. These organizations can assist you with understanding your medical bills, selecting insurance policies, and obtaining top health care.

Health Care Coach (www.healthcarecoach.com). This site provides health information for consumers as they make decisions about insurance coverage, choosing physicians, accessing medical care, and researching medical conditions and medical treatment options.

Healthinsuranceinfo.net (www.healthinsuranceinfo.net). This site, written and maintained by the Georgetown University Health Policy Institute, has detailed, comprehensive, and easily understood consumer guides on getting and keeping insurance in each state. It also has a newsletter available by subscription, and offers consumer alerts regarding specific health insurance plans.

Lab Tests Online (www.labtestsonline.org). This site provides information on how to understand your medical tests. It includes test descriptions, testing conditions, screening guides, and in-depth articles.

Getting Medical Care

Use these web sites to get information on what kind of medical care you may need and how and when to get it. These are available resources for comparing doctors, hospitals, and other caregivers, how to go about obtaining care, and who can provide it.

UCompare Healthcare (www.UcompareHealthcare.com). The site gathers information from more than 150 sources, including Medicare reviews, state governments, and hospital discharge data on over 5,500 hospitals, 535,000 physicians, and 16,000 nursing homes. Click on the names of up to six doctors or institutions at one time; the site will e-mail you a free report that includes demographic information, hospital success rates, disciplinary actions, services, and quality.

Hospital Compare (www.hospitalcompare.hhs.gov/Hospital). Provided by the U.S. Department of Health and Human Services, this site allows users to see how often specific hospitals provide specific treatments known to be effective for specific conditions.

EyeCareAmerica (www.eyecareamerica.org). Get a free eye exam! EyeCare America has helped more than 760,000 people in the past 20 years. If you are 65 or older, have not seen an ophthalmologist in the past three years, and do not belong to an HMO, you may eligible to receive a comprehensive eye exam and care for up to one year. The program is also open to people under 65 who are at increased risk for eye disease.

HealthFinder (www.healthfinder.gov). Online checkups and assessments are the focus of HealthFinder.gov, an online health resource provided by the U.S. Department of Health and Human Services. By clicking on the link for Online Checkups, you can find over 50 self-tests that can help you assess your symptoms.

Centers for Disease Control and Prevention Immunization Schedule (www.cdc.gov/vaccines/recs/schedules/default.htm). This lists schedules of the immunization vaccinations that children, adolescents, and adults require.

RelayHealth (www.relayhealth.com). RelayHealth is a Web-based service through which doctors and patients can communicate securely about nonurgent health care matters. Through RelayHealth, you can consult your doctor about specific health symptoms (referred to as a WebVisit consultation), request a prescription refill, request appointments, receive lab or test results, access health education information, and more.

In Case of Emergency (ICE) Sticker (www.icesticker.com). The ICE sticker campaign encourages people to enter an emergency contact number in their cell phone's memory under the heading "ICE" (i.e., In Case of Emergency). This contact information will allow paramedics and police officers the ability to contact the designated relative/next of kin in the event of emergency. Stickers can be purchased for $2.00.

Public Citizen Health Research Group (www.citizen.org/hrg). This nonprofit organization is dedicated to identifying poor providers, hospitals, and drugs. Reports, action plans, medical disciplinary board list, and other resources are available to help you identify what medical resources you should avoid.

Medication

These sites can provide you with a way to check for potential drug interactions, to determine what drugs are the most cost-effective, to obtain cost-efficient drugs, and to make sure you are taking medicine that is safe for you.

> ***Consumer Reports*' Best Buy Drugs (www.crbestbuydrugs. org).** *Consumer Reports'* free web site will help you compare drug options to find what is most effective and economical.
> **Drugs.com Drug Interactions Checker (www.drugs.com/ drug_interactions.html).** The Drug Interactions Checker explains the mechanism of each drug interaction, the level of significance of the interaction (major, moderate, or minor), and, in certain cases, the recommended course of action to manage the interaction. The Drug Interactions Checker will also display any interaction between your chosen drug(s) and food.

Medical Billing

Medical billing and the payer system is often the most confusing piece of the health care industry. These web sites can assist you in understanding medical claims, medical bills, and what Medicare and Medicaid resources are available to you.

> **Claims Assistance Professionals (www.claims.org).** Claims assistance professionals (CAPs) have in-depth knowledge of the complexities of the American health care industry and act as advocates for their clients. CAPs can act as liaisons among the patient, the insurance company, and the provider, stepping in as needed to resolve problems and facilitate adjudication. They work to ensure that clients receive all the health insurance benefits to which they are entitled and provide education regarding benefits and options, make sense of the confusing paperwork, and translate all the jargon.

Medical Information Bureau (www.mib.com). Similar to a credit bureau, MIB keeps tabs on things such as test results and serious ailments you suffer. Though not everyone has an MIB record, if you have applied for individual life, health, or disability coverage within the past seven years, chances are you do. You'll see what insurance companies are told, and that will give you a good idea of how easy or difficult it may be for you to get insurance on your own. And you can correct any errors that may be costing you coverage.

Medicare Rights (www.medicarerights.org). This site offers information on Medicare prescription-assistance programs, discount-drug cards, and discount pharmacies.

Health Savings Accounts Insider (www.hsainsider.com). HSA Insider is the leading online destination for information on health savings accounts. Leveraging the Internet to provide better choice and transparency, HSA Insider informs and enables better decisions about the purchase and consumption of health care.

Insurance Information Institute (www.iii.org). Each year, the III works on more than 3,700 news stories, handles more than 6,000 requests for information, and answers nearly 50,000 questions from consumers on a wide variety of insurance topics, including health insurance.

Staying Organized

Once you obtain the medical information you need, how do you keep track of it all? These web sites provide resources for organizing and documenting your medical history, appointments, genetic history, and more.

My Private HealthCare Record (www.myphr.com). This site lets you keep track of your own test results and allows you to share your medical history with a new doctor. You can check that you are keeping up to date on current vaccinations and medical tests, and the site allows you to manage your personal data from your primary care physician, medical specialists, hospitals, and so on.

Family History (www.familyhistory.hhs.gov). Knowing your family history can be extremely helpful for a doctor. Knowing what

Know Where You Are Going

All travelers should familiarize themselves with conditions at their destination that could affect their health (high altitude or pollution, types of medical facilities, required immunizations, availability of required pharmaceuticals, etc.). While some of this information may be found in the documents listed earlier, the key resource for health information is the Travelers' Health page of the Centers for Disease Control (CDC) web site at www.cdc.gov/travel. The CDC web site also provides general guidance on health precautions, such as safe food and water precautions and insect-bite protection. The CDC also maintains an international travelers' hotline at 1-877-FYI-TRIP (1-877-394-8747) or, by fax, at 1-888-CDC-FAXX (1-888-232-3299).

Traveling with a Preexisting Medical Condition

A traveler going abroad with a preexisting medical problem should carry a letter from the attending physician, describing the medical condition and any prescription medications, including the generic names of prescribed drugs. Any medications being carried overseas should be left in their original containers and be clearly labeled. Travelers should check with the foreign embassy of the country they will be visiting to make sure any required medications are not considered to be illegal narcotics. (A listing of foreign embassies and consulates in the United States is available on the Department of State's web site at www.state.gov/s/cpr/rls/dpl/32122.htm. Foreign embassy and consulate contact information can also be found on the Consular Information Sheet for each country.) If you have any medical problems and/or are taking medications and visiting a foreign country, write down your treatment plan in the native language of every country you visit. This way if anything happens to you, you can be treated.

Notes

Chapter 1 Unmanaged Care

1. "Six Killers," *New York Times,* April 8, 2007.
2. G. Anderson, J. Hovarth, J. Knickman, D. Colby, S. Schear, and M. Jung, "Chronic Conditions: Making the Case for Ongoing Care," *Partnership for Solutions,* December, 2002.

Chapter 3 Why We Go to the Hospital Today and Why We Will Go There Less Often in the Future

1. Ira M. Rutkow, *Bleeding Blue and Gray* (New York: Random House, 2005), p. 152.
2. Ibid., p. 156.
3. Charles E. Rosenberg, *The Care of Strangers:The Rise of America's Hospital System* (New York: Basic Books, 1987), p. 5.
4. Paul Starr, *The Social Transformation of American Medicine* (New York: Basic Books, 1982), p. 73.
5. Charles E. Rosenberg, *The Care of Strangers:The Rise of America's Hospital System* (New York: Basic Books, 1987), p. 316.
6. Ibid., p. 310.
7. Paul Starr, *The Social Transformation of American Medicine* (New York: Basic Books, 1982), p. 160.

8. "Staph Infections Rampant," *Chicago Tribune,* June 25, 2007.

9. Ibid.

10. Avedis Donabedian, "The End Results of Health Care: Ernest Codman's Contribution to Quality Assessment and Beyond," *The Milbank Quartely,* vol. 67, no. 2, 1989, p. 246.

11. Ibid., p. 248.

12. Ibid., p. 250.

13. Atul Gawande, "The Score: How Childbirth Went Industrial," *New Yorker,* October 9, 2006.

14. "In Bid for Better Care, Surgery with a Warranty," *New York Times,* May 17, 2007.

Chapter 4   The Doctor Will See You Now

1. Gina Kolata, "Some Chronically Ill Adults Wait for Medicare," *New York Times,* July 12, 2007.

2. William Everett Musgrave, "How to Make a Doctor," *California and Western Medicine,* vol. XXIII, November, 1925, p. 1411.

References

Books

Adams, Samuel Hopkins. 1907. *The great American fraud.* N.p.: P.F. Collier & Son.

Asay, Lyal D., and Joseph A. Maciariello. 1991. *Executive leadership in health care.* San Francisco: Jossey-Bass.

Chernow, Ron, Sr. 2004. *Titan: The life of John D. Rockefeller.* New York: Vintage Books.

Cohn, Jonathan. 2007. *Sick: The untold story of America's health care crisis—and the people who pay the price.* New York: HarperCollins.

Goldman, Dana P., and Elizabeth A. McGlynn. N.d. U.S. health care: Facts about cost, access, and quality. *RAND Health.*

Herzlinger, Regina. 1997. *Market driven health care: Who wins, who loses in the transformation of America's largest service industry.* New York: Perseus Books.

Kissler, Gary D. 1996. *Leading the health care revolution: A reengineering mandate.* N.p.: American College of Healthcare Executives.

Lathrop, J. Philip. 1993. *Restructuring health care: The patient focused paradigm.* San Francisco: Jossey-Bass.

Lawrence, David. 2002. *From chaos to care: The promise of team-based medicine.* Cambridge, MA: Da Capo Press.

Lombardi, Donald N. 1996. *Thriving in an age of change: Practical strategies for health care leaders.* N.p.: American College of Healthcare Executives.

Olson, James S. 2005. *Bathsheba's breast: Women, cancer & history.* Baltimore: Johns Hopkins University Press.

Porter, Michael E., and Elizabeth Olmstead Teisberg. 2006. *Redefining health care: Creating value-based competition.* Boston: Harvard Business School Press.

The Road to Market. 1958. N.p.: McKesson & Robbins Incorporated.

Rosenberg, Charles E. 1987. *The care of strangers: The rise of America's hospital system.* New York: Basic Books.

Rutkow, Ira M. 2005. *Bleeding blue and gray.* New York: Random House.

Shortell, Stephen M., et al. 1996. *Remaking health care in America: Building organized delivery systems.* San Francisco: Jossey-Bass.

Smith, George Winston. 1962. *Medicines for the Union Army.* N.p.: American Institute of the History of Pharmacy.

Starr, Paul. 1982. *The social transformation of American medicine.* New York: Basic Books.

Walzer, Judith, and Ronald L. Numbers, eds. 1985. *Sickness & health in America: Readings in the history of medicine and public health.* Madison: University of Wisconsin Press.

Web Sites

AARP (www.aarp.org)

American Institute of the History of Pharmacy (www.pharmacy.wisc.edu/aihp/)

American Medical Association (www.ama-assn.org)

ATA—American Telemedicine Association (www.atmeda.org)

Bristol-Myers Squibb (www.bms.com)

CBS News (www.cbsnews.com)

Centers for Medicare and Medicaid Services (www.cms.hhs.gov)

Coalition to Advance Healthcare Reform (www.coalition4healthcare.org)

CVS (www.cvs.com)

EWeek.com (www.eweek.com)

Forbes (www.forbes.com)

Health Guidance (www.healthguidance.org)

Health Management Technology (www.healthmgttech.com)

HealthFinder (www.healthfinder.gov)

InfoPlease (www.infoplease.com)

Massachusetts General Hospital (www.massgeneral.com)

Mayo Clinic (www.mayoclinic.edu)

McKesson (www.mckesson.com)

Medicare (www.medicare.gov)

MedicineNet (www.medicinenet.com)

News Medical (www.news-medical.net)

PandemicFlu (www.pandemicflu.gov)

PBS (www.pbs.org)

Pew Internet & Life Project (www.pewinternet.com)

Polymap Wireless (www.polymapwireless.com)

Sam Houston State University (www.shsu.edu)

Soderlind Pharmacy Museum (www.drugstoremuseum.com)

Stateline.org (www.stateline.org)

TheStreet.net (www.thestreet.net)

University of Pennsylvania Archives (www.archives.upenn.edu)

U.S. Department of Health and Human Services (www.hhs.gov)

Vanderbilt University (www.vanderbuilt.edu)

West Chester University of Pennsylvania (www.wcupa.edu)

Wyeth Pharmaceuticals (www.wyeth.com)

Articles

Bahensky, J. A., J. Roe, and R. Bolton. 2005. Lean sigma—will it work for health-care? *Journal of Healthcare Information Management* 19 (1):39–44.

Benko, L. 2004. Gone shopping: More employers show interest in health savings accounts, helping to accelerate the consumer-driven health care movement. *Modern Health Care* 34 (36):28–30.

Brennan, C. 1998. Integrating the healthcare supply chain. *Financial Management: Journal of the Healthcare Financial Management Association* 52.

Breslow, L. 2005. The organization of personal health services. *Milbank Quarterly* 83 (4):769–777.

Carrigan, M. D., and D. Kujawa. 2006. The health care manager. 25 (2):133–141.

CNBC News. 2004. In depth: Health care—medical tourism: Need surgery, will travel. June 18.

Daley, A. T. 2006. Pro: Lean six sigma revolutionizing health care of tomorrow. *Clinical Leadership & Management Review: The Journal of CLMA* 20 (5):E2.

Diehl, C. Lewis. 1871. Indigenous drugs. *American Journal of Pharmacy* 43.

Donabedian, Avedis. 1989. The end results of health care: Ernest Codman's contribution to quality assessment and beyond. *Milbank Quarterly* 67 (2):238.

Elberfeld, A., S. Bennis, J. Ritzius, and D. Yhlen. 2007. Six sigma in health care management and strategy. *Home Healthcare Nurse* 25 (1): 25–33.

Hansard, S. 2007. Consumer driven care falls flat: Satisfaction rates, enrollment still low in the health plan. *Investment News.*

Health Information Technology Leadership Panel. 2005. Prepared by The Lewin Group. March.

Hospital inpatient statistics, 1996: Healthcare cost and utilization project research note. AHCPR Publication 99–0034. Agency for Health Care Policy and Research, Rockville, MD.

Johnston, P., J. Hendrickson, A. Dernbach, and A. R. Secord.

Kieke, R. 2006. Health care survey takes a closer look at consumer driven health plans. *Managed Care Outlook* 19 (24):1(4).

Liao, Rebecca. 2003. Medical apps down despite national trend. *Stanford Daily,* November 13.

Lockwood, R. 1978. Birth, illness and death in the 18th century New England. *Journal of Social History* 12:1.

Morrow, D. S. 2004. John Hammergren oral history. *ComputerWorld.*

Moynihan, J. 1997. Improving the healthcare supply chain using electronic data interchange (EDI). *Journal of the Healthcare Financial Management Association* 51 (3):78.

Parker, B. M., J. M. Henderson, S. Vitagliano, B. G. Nair, J. Petre, W. G. Maurer, M. F. Roizen, M. Weber, L. DeWitt, J. Beedlow, B. Fahey, A. Calvert, K. Ribar, and S. Gordon. 2007. Six sigma methodology can be used to improve adherence for antibiotic prophylaxis in patients undergoing noncardiac surgery. *Anesthesia and Analgesia* 104 (1):140–146.

Pear, R. 2007. Without health benefits, a good life turns fragile. *New York Times* (accessed on *NYT.com,* March 5).

Procter, William, Jr. 1871. Editorial. *American Journal of Pharmacy* 43.

Radhich, A. E. A brief history of the healthcare industry in America. Ohio University.

Roark, D. Managing the healthcare supply chain: Selecting, purchasing, shipping, storing and stocking—all links of the requisition process; can you handle it? *Nursing Management.*

Roberts, V. 2001. Managing strategic outsourcing in the health care industry. *Journal of Health Care Management.*

Scalise, D. 2003. Six sigma in action. *Hospitals and Health Networks* 77:57.

Schurenberg, E. 2006. Shedding light on health care costs. *Money* (November): 24.

Source: Most common diagnoses and procedures in U.S. community hospitals, 1999: Healthcare cost and utilization project research note. AHCPR Publication 99–0046. Agency for Health Care Policy and Research, Rockville, MD.

Speer, Tibbett. 1997. From docks to docs. *Hospital & Health Networks.*

Stockwell, D. C., and A. D. Slonim. 2007. Pediatric critical care medicine. *Journal of the Society of Critical Care Medicine and the World Federation of Pediatric Intensive and Critical Care Societies* 8 (2):190–192.

Yarborough, Peggy. 2003. Case study: A patient with type 2 diabetes working with an advanced practice pharmacist to address interacting comorbidities. *Diabetes Spectrum* 16:41–48.

Zaroukian, M. H., and A. Sierra. 2006. Benefiting from ambulatory EHR implementation: Solidarity, six sigma, and willingness to strive. *Journal of Healthcare Information Management* 20:53–60.

Index

AARP, 200
Abroad, arranging emergency medical treatment, 197–199
Access to care:
  history of, 58
  improving, 169–170
  problems with, 15–16
  rating of, 167
  scorecard for, 165
Access to information:
  choosing doctor and, 18–19
  Codman and, 65–66
  customer experience and, 15
  frustrations about, 9–10, 11
  hospitals and, 79
  market principles and, 135–136
  quality of care and, 98–101
Accountability, 170
ACS (American College of Surgeons), 63, 78
Adams, John, 51, 52, 53, 116
Adams, John Quincy, 53
Adams, Nabby, 51–52
Adams, Samuel Hopkins, 36
Administrative demands on doctors, 93
Administrative inefficiency, 138

Adverse effects of medication, 25, 26
Advertising industry, 35–36
AeroClinic, 151
Age and cost of care, 11–12
Agency for Health Care Policy and
    Research, 202
Airline industry, comparison to, 9–10
Algorithms, clinical, 107–111
American Association for Labor Legislation, 117
American College of Surgeons (ACS), 63, 78
American Home Products, 34
American Medical Association (AMA), 88, 117,
    119, 190, 200
AmeriClinic, 151
AmerisourceBergen, 40
Apgar, Virginia, 68
Apgar score, 68–69, 176
Apollo Hospital, 79
Applying AQEI scorecard, 176–179
AQEI scorecard:
  accessibility rating, 167
  A+ accessibility, 169–170
  A+ efficiency, 173–175
  A+ innovation, 175–176
  A+ quality, 171–173

AQEI scorecard *(Continued)*
  applying, 176–179
  designing, 164–167
  efficiency rating, 168
  innovation rating, 169
  quality rating, 167–168
Automating:
  health care processes, 13–14
  health care records, 98–101
  pharmacy processes, 25–26, 43–44

Ball, Thomas, 50
Bar-code system:
  distribution center and, 23–24
  hospital pharmacy and, 25–26
Baylor Hospital, 119
Best practices:
  algorithms, 107–111
  Codman and, 64–65, 67, 104–105
  consumer-centered system and, 147–148
  evolution and, 109
  implementation of, 11
  innovation and, 172–173
  knowledge of, tapping into, 105–106
  in obstetrics, 67–69
  physician education and, 91
  physicians, hospitals, and, 75
Biomedical research, 144
Blue Cross and Blue Shield Association,
  119
Boston Children's Hospital, 144
Botanicals, 27–28
Breast cancer, 200
Brigham and Women's Hospital, 144
Bristol-Myers, 34
Brooks Eckerd, 44
Burd, Steve, 126
Bush, George W., 123, 125
Business, health care as, 163–164

CAHR (Coalition to Advance Healthcare
  Reform), 126–127
Canada, health system in, 178–179
Cancer:
  management of, 99
  tests recommended for different types
    of, 198–199
Cardinal Health, 40
Carl's Drug Store, 37, 41
Carnegie Mellon University Robotics
  Institute, 149
Carrel, Alexis, 90

Case managers for disease management programs,
  103–104
Castle Connolly Healthcare Navigation, 191
Caterpillar robot, 149
CAT scan, 154
Celera Genomics, 155
Centers for Disease Control:
  contact information, 209
  immunization schedule, 204
Centers of excellence, 188
Certified diabetes educators (CDEs), 44
Cervical cancer, 200
Change, resistance to, 162–164
Choices, making, 133–136, 171, 182
Cholesterol, 199
Christian Scientists, 87
Chronic conditions:
  cost of, 12, 76, 102
  health care providers and, 84
  team-based care, electronic medical
    records, and, 101–104, 127
  treatment of, 76–77
  See also specific conditions
Civil War:
  hospitals and, 54–56
  medicine and, 32–34
  physicians and, 88–89
Claims Assistance Professionals web site,
  205
Claims data, 139
Cleveland Clinic, 79, 96, 144
Clinical algorithms, 107–111
Clinical trial, participating in, 202
Clinics, 189
Clinton health care plan, 122–123
Coalition to Advance Healthcare Reform
  (CAHR), 126–127, 200
Codman, Ernest A., 63–67, 104–105
Colorectal cancer, 198
Commonwealth Fund:
  Commission on a High Performance
    Health System, 165–166
  web site, 202
Communication:
  about condition and treatment, 139–140
  by e-mail, 14
  between health care providers, 99
  with pharmacists, 43–44
  See also Doctor-patient relationship
Community hospitals, 188
Computed tomography, 154
Connections in history of health care, 1–2

Connectivity and consumer-centered system, 146
Consumer-centered system:
  best practices and, 147–148
  change and, 164
  connectivity and, 146
  innovations in diagnostics and, 148
  productivity, efficiency, and, 146–147
  retail health care clinics and, 150–151
  robotics and, 149–150
  transparency and, 145
Consumer Reports' Best Buy Drugs web site, 205
Consumers, *see* Customers; Patients
Co-pay/co-payment, 19, 200
Cost:
  age and, 11–12
  of chronic conditions, 12, 76, 102
  of doctor visit, 8–9
  of employer-based health care, 126
  end results and, 65
  evidence-based medicine and, 110
  of health care system, 4
  hospitals and, 61–62
  of Medicaid and Medicare, 120–121, 125
  of private insurance, 129
  quality of care and, 20–21
  of retail health care clinics, 44–45
  transparency of, 19–20
Coster, F. Donald, 39, 40
Covenant Health, 74, 144
Crick, Francis, 154
Crile, George, 63
Crisis in health care, 7–8
Customers:
  alignment of payers, providers, and, 136–140
  empowering, 133–136, 182, 183
  experience of, 15–16
  frustration of, 9–10
  in market-based system, 133–136
  patients as, 3, 5
  satisfaction of, and profit, 115
  See also Doctor-patient relationship; Patients
CVS, 44, 150

Dana-Farber Cancer Institute, 73, 79
Dart, Justin, 38
Data, electronic systems of, 75–77, 98–101
Decision-making, informed, 133–136, 171, 182
Defensive medicine, practice of, 61
Department of State web site, 199
Diabetes, management of, 44, 102, 199
Diagnostic Related Groups (DRGs), 122

Diagnostics, innovation in, 148
Digitizing health care records:
  doctors and, 98–101
  efficiency and, 174
  hospitals and, 75–77
  medical home model and, 139–140
Disease management programs, 103
Dispensing medicine:
  in hospitals, 24–26
  technology and, 41–45
Distribution center and bar-code system, 23–24
DNA, 154
Doctor-patient relationship:
  evidence-based medicine and, 108–109
  history of, 91–94
  as last two feet, 184–186
  stethoscope and, 154
Doctors, *see* Physicians
Doctor's Lounge web site, 202
Doctor visit:
  e-visits, 141–142
  process of, 8, 83–84, 137–138
DRGs (Diagnostic Related Groups), 122
Drug distribution business:
  after Civil War, 34–35
  Civil War and, 33–34
  technology and, 41–45
  wholesale, 29–32, 39–41
  See also McKesson Corporation; McKesson & Robbins
Drug prices and Medicare Part D, 123
Drug salesmen, traveling, 35
Drugs.com Drug Interactions Checker web site, 205
Drugstores:
  history of, 29, 37–38, 39
  technology and, 42–43
  See also specific drugstores
Duke University Medical Center, 49, 96

Eclectics, 87
Economies of scale, 39, 40–41
Eddy, Mary Baker, 87
Education of doctors, 86–87, 88, 89–91, 92–93
Efficiency:
  consumer-centered system and, 146–147
  improving, 173–175
  rating of, 168
  scorecard for, 165
  of treatment, 110

Eisenhower Hospital, 144
Electronic medical records, 75–77,
    98–101
E-mail communication, 14
Emergency medical treatment, arranging when
    abroad, 197–199
Emergency rooms, overcrowding in, 61, 85
Employer-based health care:
    access to care and, 15
    age 65 and, 131
    cost and, 19, 126
    history of, 119, 120–121
    problems of, 17–18
Empowering consumers, 133–136, 182, 183
End results system, 63–67, 72–73, 104–105
Errors, medical:
    deaths from, 9–10, 62
    hospital pharmacies and, 25
    methods to reduce, 70–72
    reporting, 190
Everett, Kevin, 147
Evidence-based medicine, 108–111
E-visits, 141–142
EyeCareAmerica web site, 204

Family History web site, 206–207
Fax machines, 41
Fixed fees, 122
Flexner, Abraham, 90, 91, 92
Flexner, Simon, 90
Flexner Report, 91
Follow-up treatment, 76
Food and Drug Administration, 36
Forceps, 68
Franklin, Benjamin, 50
Frustration:
    of consumers, 9–10
    of health care providers, 12, 84–85

Gates, Frederick T., 90, 91
Geisinger Health System, 69–70, 79
Gelatin-coated pills, 34
General Electric, 70
General hospitals, 188
Genetic diagnosis and treatment, 152–155
Genome profiles, 158
Gilbreth, Frank and Lillian, 96
Girard & Co., 39
Goals of market-based system, 179–183
Government:
    intervention of into market, 127–128, 175
    reimbursement by, 129–130

role of in health care industry, 130–131,
    170, 175–176
Government insurance pool, 16–17
Great Depression, 39–40
Group Health Cooperative, 96

Hahnemann, Samuel, 87–88
Halsted, William, 89
Hamilton, Alexander, 116
Hammond, William Alexander, 54–56, 62,
    88–89
Harding, Warren G., 88
Harvard Medical School, 63
Health Advocate, 191
Health behavior, individual responsibility for,
    127, 170
Health care clinics, retail, 44–45, 97, 150–151
Health Care Coach web site, 203
Health care delivery, history of, 27–32
Health Care Financing Administration, 189, 194
Health care providers:
    alignment of payers, consumers, and,
        136–140
    frustration of, 12, 84–85
    shortage of, 12, 61, 85, 94
    See also specific providers
Health care system:
    as fragmented, 7–8, 26, 173–174
    goals of, 3–4
    lessons of successful, 74–75
    transformation in, 4–5, 151
    universal, 15–16, 126–127, 180
    See also Nationalized health care
HealthFinder web site, 204
Healthinsuranceinfo.net web site, 203
Health maintenance organizations (HMOs), 60,
    121–122, 195–196, 200–201
Health Partners, 96
Health records:
    digitizing, 75–77, 98–101, 174
    payer-based, 139
    web sites about, 208
Health savings accounts (HSAs), 19, 123–124, 201
Health Savings Accounts Insider web site, 206
Heart bypass surgery:
    elective, 69–70
    robotics and, 149
Heart disease, 11
Herbal remedies, 87–88
Heroic medicine, 86
Hippocrates, maxim of, 162
HIV center of excellence, 188

Holmes, Oliver Wendell, 154
Home, health care in, 49, 50, 51–53. *See also*
     Medical home model
Homeopathy, 87–88, 89, 90, 91
Horizon Expert Order, 107–108
Hospital Compare web site, 182, 204
Hospital pharmacy processes, 24–26
Hospitals:
     best-performing, characteristics of, 77–78
     as central to health care system, 48–49, 57
     changing culture of, 73–77
     civilian, 56–57
     Civil War and, 54–56
     cost burdens of, 61–62
     death in due to infection and error, 62
     electronic systems in, 75–77
     emotion in, 47–48
     end results system and, 63–67
     finances and budgets of, 59–60
     history of development of, 49–57
     in marketplace, 77–81
     obstetrics and, 67–69
     obtaining data on, 189
     problems with, 58
     six sigma and, 70–72
     teaching, 92–93
     types of, 188–189
     variation between, 106
     See also specific hospitals
HSAs (health savings accounts), 19, 123–124
Human Genome Project, 155
Hydropaths, 87

Immunization schedule, 205
In Case of Emergency (ICE) sticker web site, 204
Incentives:
     for best practice implementation, 173
     to do it right first time, 69
     for healthy lifestyle, 127
     for hospital CEOs, 61–62
     in managed care, 121
     pay for performance, 110
     for private insurance industry, 17–18, 132
     for technological investment, 138
Individual contributor model of physician care,
     94–95
Individual responsibility for health behavior, 127,
     170
Infection, in hospitals, 62, 71–72
Information access:
     choosing doctor and, 18–19
     Codman and, 65–66

customer experience and, 15
frustrations about, 9–10, 11
hospitals and, 79
market principles and, 135–136
quality of care and, 98–101
Information technology:
     clinical algorithms and, 107–111
     health care and, 13–14
     See also Digitizing health care records
Informed decision-making, 133–136, 171, 182
Inner ring, 183–184
Innovation:
     best practices and, 172–173
     in diagnostics, 148
     evidence-based medicine and, 108–109
     improving, 175–176
     market-based system and, 144
     nationalized health care and, 125–126
     rating of, 169
     scorecard for, 165
Insurance:
     need for, 124–125
     supplemental, 198
     uninsured population, 16
     See also Insurance industry
Insurance claim for doctor visit, 8–9
Insurance industry:
     alignment with providers and consumers,
          136–140
     history of development of, 116–120
     incentives for, 17–18
     market, government, and, 170
     Medicare, Medicaid, and, 129
     political fervor and, 124
     risk and, 16, 60–61
     65-year handoff and, 131–133
     terms under which coverage is offered, 131
Insurance Information Institute web site, 206
Integrated Delivery Network, 156
Internal medicine, 201
International Association for Medical
     Assistance to Travelers, 208
International HapMap Project, 156
International SOS web site, 208
Internship, 92, 95

Jackson, James, 53
Jefferson, Thomas, 116
Johns Hopkins Hospital, 56–57
The Johns Hopkins University School of
     Medicine, 56, 89, 91
Johnson, Lyndon, 120

Johnston, Charles, 85–86
Joint Committee, 78, 190

Kaiser, Henry J., 119
Kaiser Permanente, 96, 101, 119, 146–147
Kant, Immanuel, 159
Keck Foundation Free-Electron Laser
      Center, 148
Kelly, Howard, 89
Kirch, Darrel, 144
Kizer, Ken, 176–177

Labor shortage, 12, 61, 85, 94
Lab Tests Online web site, 203
Laennec, Rene, 153–154
Lander, Eric, 155
Last two feet, 184–186
Leadership, need for, 161, 177, 179
Leavitt, Mike, 156, 159
Lewis, Meriwether, 51
Liability law, 94, 181–182
Licensing of physicians, 87, 88, 89
Liggett, Louis, 38
Lilly, Eli, 34
Lister, Joseph, 55
Litigation, 61, 181–182
Lobbying groups, 184
Longitudinal care, 99

Malcolm Baldrige National Quality Award, 78
Malpractice suits, 94, 181
Managed care, 121–122
   history of, 118–119
   PPOs, 121, 196–197
   See also HMOs (health maintenance
      organizations)
Marine Hospital Service, 116–117
Market, government intervention into, 127–128
Market-based pricing, 16–17
Market-based system:
   benefits of, 114–115
   compensation in, 130
   consumers in, 133–136
   hospitals in, 77–81
   payer-provider-consumer alignment in,
      136–140
   rational majority and, 183–184
   vision statement for, 179–183
   See also AQEI scorecard
Massachusetts, 124, 126
Massachusetts General Hospital, 53, 55, 56–57, 63
Mayo, Charles, 63

Mayo Clinic, 74, 79, 96, 154
McKesson, John, 29
McKesson Corporation:
   author and, 2
   disease management programs, 103
   distribution center, 23–24
   drug wholesale business, 40
   Horizon Expert Order, 107–108
   six sigma and, 70
   See also McKesson & Robbins
McKesson Revenue Cycle Solution, 15
McKesson & Robbins, 31–32, 34, 35, 39–40
M.D. Anderson, 79
MEDEX web site, 208
Medicaid:
   cost of, 120–121
   description of, 193, 195
   eligibility for, 194
   resources for, 194
   transition to market-based, 181
Medical billing, web sites about, 205–206
Medical colleges, 86–87, 88, 90–91, 92–93
Medical errors:
   deaths from, 9–10, 62
   hospital pharmacies and, 25
   methods for reducing, 70–72
   reporting, 190
Medical home model, 139–140, 141–142,
      159, 174
Medical Information Bureau web site, 206
Medical residency programs, 89, 95
Medical tourism, 79–80
Medicare:
   cost of, 120–121, 125
   description of, 192–193, 195
   eligibility for, 193
   fixing costs and, 122
   hospital mortality rate data, 189
   impact of on health care industry, 129
   market-based pricing and, 16–17, 181
   Part D, 123
   private insurers and, 123
   resources for, 195
Medicare Rights web site, 206
Medication:
   adverse effects of, 25, 26
   dispensing, 24–26, 41–45
   gelatin-coated pills, 34
   price of, and Medicare Part D, 123
   web sites about, 205
   See also Drug distribution business; Drugstores;
      Pharmacies

Medicine:
    Civil War and, 32–34
    defensive, practice of, 61
    evidence-based, 108–111
    heroic, 86
    nontraditional, 87–88
    personalized, 152, 155–160
    team-based, 94–98
Merck, 17
Methicillin-resistant staphylococcus aureus
    (MRSA), 71–72
Military hospitals, 54–55
MinuteClinic, 150
Moore, Henry H., 118
Motorola, 70
MRSA (methicillin-resistant staphylococcus
    aureus), 71–72
My Private HealthCare Record
    web site, 206

Nanotechnology, 149–150
National Institutes of Health, 144
Nationalized health care:
    debates about, 113
    definition of, 15
    disadvantages of, 20, 125–126
    as disguising cost, 125
    history of, 117–118, 119–120
    risk of, 115
National Quality Forum, 106
National Safety Quality Improvement
    Program, 98
National Wholesale Druggists' Association, 35
Netherlands, health system in, 177–178
New York City, 29–31
New York Hospital, 53
Nightingale, Florence, 62
Nontraditional medicine, 87–88
Nurse-practitioners, 97, 190, 201
Nurses, 96

Obstetrics, best practices in, 67–69
Olcott, Charles, 29
Olcott, McKesson & Co., 31
Order entry systems, computerized
    physician, 42
Osco, 44
Osler, William, 89
Osteopathy, 87
Osteoporosis, 198–199
Outcomes:
    evidence-based medicine and, 110

    as measures of quality, 69
    National Safety Quality Improvement
        Program, 98
    sharing, 72–73
    team-based care and, 95–96
    See also Best practices, implementation of
Outer ring, 184
Outpatient clinics, 189
Overseas, arranging emergency medical
    treatment, 207–209

Palliative care, 185
Paperless system, 174
Paperwork, 93, 114, 138, 140
Patent medicines, 35–36
Patient Advocate Foundation, 191
Patient advocates, 190–191
Patients:
    as consumers, 5
    as customers, 3
    See also Customers; Doctor-patient
        relationship
Patients' Bill of Rights, 123
Payer systems:
    HMOs and PPOs, 195–197
    Medicare and Medicaid, 192–195
Pay for performance, 110
Pennsylvania Hospital, 50, 53
Personalized medicine, 152, 155–160
Pfizer, Charles, 34
Pharmaceutical prices, 17
Pharmacies:
    in hospitals, 24–26
    independent, 37
    See also Drugstores
Pharmacists:
    choosing, 191–192
    communication with, 43–44
Pharmacy Checker web site, 206
Pharmacy college graduates, work of, 30
Pharmacy colleges, 28–29, 43
Phoenix Indian Medical Center, 188
Physician assistants, 97
Physicians:
    as care coordinators, 103–104
    choosing, 18–19, 189–190
    Civil War and, 88–89
    education and training of, 86–87, 88, 89–91,
        92–93
    evolution of American, 85–91
    fixed fees for, 122
    incomes of, 114

Physicians *(Continued)*
in managed care, 121
mystique of, 11
nationalized health care and, 113–114
as part of team, 94–98
as primary care doctors, 203
shortage of, 85
successful health care system and, 74–75
variation between, 106
as volunteers at early hospitals, 60
See also Doctor-patient relationship;
Doctor visit
Pinnacle Care, 191
Piston, David, 148
Pittsburgh Regional Healthcare Initiative
(PRHI), 71–73, 74, 79
Porter, Michael, *Redefining Health Care,* 129
Preexisting medical conditions, traveling
with, 209
Preferred provider organization (PPOs) plans,
121, 196–197, 201
Presbyterian Hospital, 144
Prevention, focus on, 127, 133, 200–202
Price ceilings, 128, 130, 175
Primary care doctors, 201
Privacy issues, 159
Private insurance industry, *See* Insurance
industry
Procter, William, Jr., 29, 30, 42
Productivity and consumer-centered system,
146–147
Profit, customer satisfaction and, 115
Prostate cancer, 198
Proteomics, 157
Protocols, national system of, 106–107
Public Citizen Health Research Group web
site, 204–205
Public health, 57
Pure Food and Drug Act, 36

Quality of care:
end results and, 64
improving, 171–173
as low, with high costs, 20–21
Medicare and, 129
non-MD trained specialists and, 97
outcomes and, 69
problems with, 10–12
rating of, 167–168
retail health care clinics and, 45
scorecard for, 165
technology and, 2

Radio-frequency identification (RFID) tags, 14
Raffles Hospital, 79
Ratings web sites, 145
Redefining Health Care (Porter and Teisberg), 129
Regression theory, 163
Regulation, by government, 128
Reimbursement, cost-based, 129–130
RelayHealth web site, 204
Reminders, electronic, 100
Reporting medical errors, 190
Residency programs, 89, 95
Resistance to change, 162–164
Retail drug business, 37
Retail experience, health care as, 20
Retail health care clinics, 44–45, 97, 150–151
Rexall brand, 38
RFID (radio-frequency identification) tags, 14
Rice University, 150
Rite Aid, 44
Riviere, Cameron, 149
Robbins, Daniel, 31
Robotics and consumer-centered system,
149–150
Rockefeller, Doc, 85–86
Rockefeller, John D., 89–90
Rockefeller Institute for Medical Research, 90
Roosevelt, Teddy, 117
Rush, Benjamin, 51, 52, 86, 88

Safety of health care industry, 9–10. *See also*
Medical errors
Salesmen, traveling, 35
Sanitation, 62
Satterlee Hospital, 54–55, 56
Savings from upgrading health care system, 15
S-CHIP (State Children's Health Insurance
Program), 123, 125
Scorecard:
accessibility rating, 167
A+ accessibility, 169–170
A+ efficiency, 173–175
A+ innovation, 175–176
A+ quality, 171–173
applying, 176–179
designing, 164–167
efficiency rating, 168
innovation rating, 169
quality rating, 167–168
Second opinion, era of, 93
Sharing best practices, 147–148
Sinclair, Upton, 36
Six sigma, 41, 70–72

65-year handoff, 131–133
Skin cancer, 198
Skin in the game, definition of, 9
Smith, Joan, 58
Soda fountains, 37–38
Southwest Texas Methodist Hospital, 41
Spartanburg Regional Hospital, 144
Specialized hospitals, 188
Spreading risk, 16
Squibb, Edward R., 33, 34, 36
Squibb Works, 34
St. Luke's Hospital, 74, 78
Standardization of health records, 139
Standards, national system of, 106–107, 130–131
Stanton, Edwin, 54, 89
Staph infection, 62, 71–72
State Children's Health Insurance Program
    (S-CHIP), 123, 125
Stethoscope, 153–154
Supplemental health insurance, 207
Surgery, 63

Target, 44
Tax treatment, equalizing, 181
Teaching hospitals, 92–93
Team-based medicine, 94–98
Technology:
    adoption of, 152–155
    distributing and dispensing medicine and,
        41–45
    incentives for investment in, 138
    nanotechnology, 149–150
    personalized medicine, 152, 155–160
    quality of care and, 2
    stethoscope, 153–154
    See also Information technology
Teisberg, Elizabeth, Redefining Health Care, 129
Telehealth, 151
Television doctors, 83, 93
Thompson Drugs, 37
Thomson, Samuel, 87
Throughput demands on doctors, 93
Training for doctors, 86–87, 88, 89–91, 92–93
Transformation in health care system, 4–5
Transparency:
    consumer-centered system and, 134–135, 145
    costs and, 19–20
    demand for, as growing, 80
    information access and, 18–19
    market-based system and, 79
    quality and, 171–172
    scorecard and, 166

Travel:
    arranging emergency medical treatment
        during, 207–209
    for medical treatment, 79–80
Truman, Harry S, 119–120
Type 2 diabetes, 199

UCompare Healthcare web site, 203
Uninsured population, 16
United Drug Stores, 38
United States Pharmacopoeia, 28
Universal health coverage, 15–16, 126–127, 180
University-affiliated hospitals, 188
University of Chicago, 91

Vaccine business, 17
Vanderbilt Medical School, 91, 96, 158, 159
Venter, Craig, 155
Veterans Administration (VA), 96, 97, 98–99,
    176–177
Vision statement, 179–183

Walgreen, Charles R., Sr., 37–38
Walgreens, 44
Wal-Mart, 44
Warren, John, 51–52, 53
Washington Business Group on Health, 126
Watson, James, 154–155
Web sites:
    Centers for Disease Control, Travelers' Health
        page, 199
    for getting medical care, 205–206
    for health care and medical research,
        203–204
    for health care assistance, 204–205
    Joint Committee, 78
    medical billing, 207–208
    medication, 206–207
    patient advocates, 191
    for reporting medical errors, 190
    for staying organized, 208
    for travel resources, 198–199
Welch, Jack, 70
Welch, William Henry, 89, 90
Wellness, focus on, 127, 133, 200–202
Western Wholesale Druggists' Association, 35
Wholesale drug distribution business, 29–32,
    39–41
Wright Medical Center, 188
Wyeth, John, 34

X-rays, 154